LIFE OF SAINT AUGUSTINE
by John Capgrave

edited by
Cyril Lawrence Smetana, O.S.A.

This edition of Capgrave's *Life of St. Augustine* is found in a unique Middle English manuscript, British Library, Additional MS 36704, written about 1451. To make the text more readable, this diplomatic transcription expands Capgrave's abbreviations and includes modern punctuation, capitalization, word division and paragraph breaks. As well the extensive glossary makes the edition accessible to readers whose knowledge of Middle English may be elementary.

Capgrave's *Life* provides a detailed and very human representation of Augustine, his friends, and his formidable mother, Monica. This volume will also be of interest to those who are studying Capgrave's language, because the manuscript is an autograph and is also corrected with evident care by Capgrave himself. It provides rare evidence for the language of King's Lynn, Norfolk, in an age when the London dialect was becoming the 'received standard'.

The edition's introduction provides basic information about Capgrave's own life and the body of his work; a description of the manuscript and of Capgrave's language; a consideration of his alterations made to his main source–Jordanus of Saxony's *Vita s. Augustini*–evidently in order to make the text more attractive to the 'gentill woman' at whose request he prepared the life.

The volume also includes an edition of Jordanus' autograph copy of the *Vita* (Paris, Bibliothèque de l'Arsenal, MS 251), which allows for a detailed study of Capgrave's methods of translation–at times word-for-word, at others allowing scope for omission, digression, expansion, and the inclusion of local colour and relevant exempla.

The bibliography includes the most recent studies of Capgrave, whose work is enjoying something of a revival because of the unusual number of extant autograph manuscripts in his corpus, and also because of his evident interest in a female readership (reflected not only in this work but in his *Life of St. Katharine*), a manifestation of the rise of literate lay women in the fifteenth century.

Studies and Texts 138

Life of Saint Augustine by John Capgrave

edited from British Library Additional MS 36704
together with
Jordanus of Saxony's *Vita s. Augustine*
from Bibliothèque de l'Arsenal, MS 251

by

Cyril Lawrence Smetana, O.S.A.

Pontifical Institute of Mediaeval Studies

This book has been published with the help of a grant
from the Humanities and Social Sciences Federation of Canada,
using funds provided by the Social Sciences and
Humanities Research Council of Canada
and through funds made available
by the Order of Saint Augustine

CANADIAN CATALOGUING IN PUBLICATION DATA

Capgrave, John, 1393-1464
Life of Saint Augustine

(Studies and texts, ISSN 0082-5328 ; 138)
First text in Middle English; second text in Latin; introduction in English.
Includes bibliographical references.
ISBN 0-88844-138-X

1. Augustine, Saint, Bishop of Hippo. I. Smetana, Cyril Lawrence, 1920- . II. Pontifical Institute of Mediaeval Studies. III. British Library. Manuscript. Additional 36704. IV. Bibliothèque de l'Arsenal. Manuscript. 251. V. Jordan, von Quedlinburg, d. 1380. Vita s. Augustine. VI. Title. VII. Series: Studies and texts (Pontifical Institute of Mediaeval Studies) ; 138.

PR1845.L53 2001 270.2′092 C00-933014-3

Pontifical Institute of Mediaeval Studies
59 Queen's Park Crescent East
Toronto, Ontario, Canada M5S 2C4

www.pims.ca

Manufactured in Canada

To the memory of
Fr. Rudolph Arbesmann, O.S.A., Ph.D.
1895-1982

Contents

Acknowledgements

Shortly after I had completed this edition of Capgrave's *Life of Augustine*, I was informed that my increasingly poor vision was the result of advanced low vision glaucoma. It became virtually impossible for me to do any further work, and I was forced to put the project on hold for several years.

Happily, two of my colleagues at York University offered their help in preparing the edition for publication and securing a publisher. For them, this has involved work over a number of years: updating the introduction and bibliography in light of recent Capgrave scholarship, re-reading the Middle English and the Latin texts against the manuscripts, expanding the notes and re-ordering the glossary in response to the recommendation of outside readers.

I am grateful to Professors Frances Beer and Michael Cummings for their invaluable contributions. Without their encouragement and their help this edition would not have been possible. They in turn have asked that I express their particular thanks to A.G. Rigg, Angie Wong-Hayes, Douglas Hayes, and Ron B. Thomson for their crucial assistance in the preparation of this volume.

Cyril L. Smetana, OSA
Marylake, King City. Ontario
November 2000

Abbreviations

Ad fratres	*Sermones ad fratres in eremo*
BL	British Library (olim British Museum)
CCL	*Corpus Christianorum series Latina*
Conf.	St. Augustine, *Confessions*
CSEL	*Corpus scriptorum ecclesiasticorum Latinorum*
Etym.	Isidore of Seville, *Etymologiorum sive originem*
JEH	*Journal of Ecclesiastical History*
PG	*Patrologia Graeca*
Pisciculi	*Pisciculi Studien zur Religion und Kultur des Altertums*
PL	*Patrologia Latina*
RB	*Revue Bénédictine*
REA	*Revue des études anciennes*
Retract.	St. Augustine, *Retractionum libri duo*

Introduction

A. Life[1]

The name of John Capgrave (1393-1464) does not appear in contemporary catalogues of recognized authors.[2] A century after his death, however, he is listed among eminent British writers, ironically, by the Protestant bibliophiles, Leland and Bale,[3] where he emerges as the most learned of English Augustinian authors. The existence of two Augustinians named Capgrave, however, gave rise to considerable confusion about his identity, his birthplace, and his university, problems resolved only in our own day.[4] He has been denigrated as a 'flunkey',[5] and raised to the status of 'almost a kind of latter-day Church Father'.[6] Capgrave could certainly have de-

1 For biographical and bibliographical data we are indebted to de Meijer, 'John Capgrave OESA (1393-1464),' *Augustiniana* 5 (1955) 400-440 and 7 (1957) 118-148, 531-575; Seymour, 'John Capgrave' (1996); and Lucas, *From Author to Audience* (Dublin, 1997).

2 de Meijer, *Augustiniana* 7 (1957) 118-119 mentions four catalogues, among them two by Augustinians: Ambrogio da Cori (1458) and Giacamo Filippo Foresti da Bergamo (1518).

3 Ibid., 119, 121.

4 The General Archives of the Augustinian Order confirm the existence of two English Augustinians of the same name. A John Capgrave was nominated for studies at Oxford on Oct. 13, 1390. Our author, born in 1393, was approved for studies at Cambridge in 1422 and served as Provincial between 1453 and 1457. Seymour asserts that the first John Capgrave was uncle to ours. De Meijer, *Augustiniana* 5 (1955) 405, 409; Seymour (1996) 204, 208.

5 Furnivall, foreword to Capgrave, *Katharine* (ed. Horstmann [1893]) xv: 'Capgrave, being an Englishman, was of course by race and nature a flunkey, and had an inordinate reverence for kings and rank .... While Henry VI was alive, Capgrave was his profound admirer .... But as soon as York has turned-out Lancaster, and Edward IV is on the throne, Capgrave dedicates his *Chronicle* to him ....'

6 Capgrave, *Abbreuiacion* (ed. Lucas [1983]) xxiv: 'In the Middle Ages the mendicant friars were the "principal exponents of dogmatic, moral and biblical theology" (Roth i, 176) and a number of Augustinian friars were well known as scholars and literary men. Among them Capgrave was pre-eminent .... He was a kind of latter-day Church Father .... [His] collection of works is very similar in

fended his political orientation on the one hand,[7] and would, no doubt, have taken modest exception to alignment with the Church Fathers.[8]

In the Prologue to the *Life of St. Katharine*,[9] Capgrave says that he is a native of Lynn in Norfolk, and in the *Abbreuiacion of Chronicles* that he was born on the 21 of April, 1393.[10] It is not known when he entered the Augustinian Hermits' Order—*Ordo fratrum eremitarum Sancti Augustini*: Seymour (1996) suggests 1404, Lucas (1997) prefers 1410; but it is likely that he was ordained at twenty-four in 1417, after which he would have gone to the *studium generale* in London. The General Archives of the Augustinian Order document his progress from Lector on April 8, 1421 through his appointment as a student at Cambridge on April 13, 1422 to his degree of Bachelor of Divinity on March 20, 1423. They later confirm his election as Provincial of the English Province on July 22, 1453 and his re-election two years later on August 6, 1455.[11] Leland says that he died on August 12, 1464.[12]

Except for his studies in London and Cambridge, Capgrave probably spent most of his life in Lynn, Norfolk. He confirms his own early years in Lynn in asides on portents and events at Lynn which he had witnessed.[13] After 1427 there is no record of an assignment for over ten years. Fredeman conjectures that he may, during these years, have been stationed at the Friary in Northampton.[14] We know that he was at Woodstock on Janu-

---

scope to those produced by some of the early Church Fathers, such as St. Jerome.' (F. Roth, *The English Austin Friars, 1249-1538* [New York, 1961-1966].)

7 Fredeman, *Augustiniana* 29 (1979) 235-36.

8 The number of works attributed to him is phenomenal, but he is essentially a compiler and translator.

9 'My cuntre is Northfolke, of þe town of Lynne.' *Katharine* 16.240.

10 'In þis ȝere, in þe xxi day of April, was þat frere bore whech mad þese annotaciones.' Capgrave, *Abbreuiacion* (ed. Lucas [1983]) 203.12, 13; Seymour (1996) 209; Lucas (1997) 8.

11 de Meijer, *Augustiniana* 5 (1955) 408, 410, 401, 400 quotes the pertinent decrees from the General Archives.

12 Leland ii, 454, quoted by de Meijer, *Augustiniana* 5 (1955) 419.

13 Examples include memories of comets, severe weather, floods, a kidnapping, the departure of Princess Philippa to become queen of King Eric of Denmark.

14 Fredeman, *Augustiniana* 29 (1979) 221-22. Although St. James's Abbey in Northampton was home to Augustinian Canons rather than Hermits, and there was a longstanding dispute between the two, this assignment could explain Capgrave's acquaintance with John Watford, abbot of St. James, to whom he dedicated his *Concordia* (c. 1442); indeed, perhaps the purpose of Capgrave's mission was to make peace (see note 42 under 'Source').

ary 1, 1439, when a copy of his *In Genesim* was presented to Duke Humphrey. Seymour suggests that this presentation, pointing to a 'smouldering quarrel between seculars and friars', was a gesture of gratitude by the Hermits for the duke's support. He further speculates that Capgrave became Prior of Lynn in 1441, at forty seven; certainly, he was at Lynn, and probably as prior, when he entertained Henry VI in 1446. In 1449, Capgrave did journey to Rome, subsequently recording details of his visit in the *Solace of Pilgrims.*[15]

B. WORKS

Early bibliographers credit Capgrave with a large number of biblical commentaries but only three are extant.[16] Peter Lucas has demonstrated that the *Nova legenda Anglie* is not by Capgrave[17] and this also may be the case with other titles attributed to him. His twelve extant works, however, prove considerable competence in exegesis, theology, hagiography, biography, topography and history.[18] Capgrave was a serious scholar with a passion for order and orthodoxy, but also with a penchant for local colour and homely *exempla.*

Two of his saints' lives are written in rhyme royal, competent if not inspired. Except for his *Tretis*, which as Capgrave notes (BL Add. 36704, f. 116r) was based on a sermon preached at Cambridge in 1422, none of his works are original compositions; he translates and compiles. Though not given to radical departures from his sources, he is selective and magisterial in the use of them. He translates in the tradition of King Alfred, *hwilum word be worde, hwilum andgit of andgiete*, but lacks the king's originality and creativity.

Though the envoy of Capgrave's first work, *Life of St. Norbert*, was written in Assumption week, 1440, and dedicated to John Wygenhale Abbot of West Dereham, a reference in his *Tretis* indicates that it was

15 Seymour (1996) 211, 215, 226; Capgrave, *Henricis* (ed. Hingeston [1858]) 137-139.

16 *In Genesim, in Exodum, Super actus.* For particulars on these unpublished manuscripts see the Bibliography, where Capgrave's extant works are listed chronologically.

17 Lucas, *The Library* (1970) 1-10; see also *Nova legenda Angliae*, ed. Manfred Görlach (Heidelberg, 1994).

18 Lucas states that Capgrave 'wrote the lives of saints who inspired the foundations of, or themselves founded, religious orders ... for the heads of religious houses to be read by the inmates of those houses.' For his other works he sought a wider audience ([1997] 17).

completed before 1422 for an earlier, unnamed abbot of Dereham.[19] *Norbert* is a verse translation of a twelfth-century prose *vita* attributed to Hugh of Fosse, Norbert's successor at Premontre. Like much medieval hagiography the Latin text is preoccupied with *mirabilia*. Except for a few flashes of local colour and some contemporary reflections, Caprave adheres to both the substance and the tone of the original.

The Latin commentaries, *in Genesim* and *in Exodum*, dated 1438 and 1440 respectively, are all that remain of the Old Testament exegesis attributed to him by earlier bibliographers. In his dedicatory letter to Duke Humphrey in *Genesis*, Capgrave promised further commentaries on the Pentateuch. Its reception must have been encouraging, for within two weeks of his return from Woodstock, Capgrave began his commentary on Exodus.[20]

Though *The Life of St. Katharine* bears no date, Capgrave's confrere, Osbern Bokenham, recommends it as a 'newly compylyd' work. This would place it before 1445.[21] Unlike the other vernacular *Lives* it does not have a dedicatee, and is not, except for Book V, a translation from Latin. His source, he reports, is in a dialect of the 'west cuntre' which 'maner of spech', 'style', 'straungenesse' and 'derk langage' challenged him 'to translate þis story and set it more pleyn'.[22] St. Katharine's cult was widespread during the Middle Ages, but as patroness of studies in the Augustinian Order, she had special relevance for Bokenham and Capgrave.

De illustribus Henricis, dedicated to Henry VI, is a *tour de force* on the name Henry, twenty-four Henries in all: six emperors, ten kings, two bishops, three noblemen, and three literary men, among them Henry of Friemar, an Augustinian. The last recorded event in the book is the visit of Henry VI to the Lynn Friary in 1446. It was probably written before 1447 for it makes no mention of Duke Humphrey's death.[23]

The *Life of St. Gilbert*, completed in 1451[24] at the request of Nicholas

19 Lucas, *The Library* (1981) 328-330. Dialect evidence also points to the early 15th century (Colledge, Smetana 433); Seymour, however, asserting a debt to Lydgate, argues 1440 as the date of *St. Norbert's* completion ([1996] 221).

20 I.e., on January 17, 1439; de Meijer, *Augustiniana* 7 (1957) 534-535, and Seymour (1996) 216.

21 *Legendys of Hooly Wummen* (1938) 173. Bokenham's *Katharine* follows *Maudelyn* which bears the date 1445.

22 *Katharine*, Prologue 14.225-26; 6.61-62; 16.232-233; see Jane C. Fredeman, *Style and Characterization in John Capgrave's* Life of St. Katharine (Manchester, 1980).

23 de Meijer, *Augustiniana* 7 (1957) 545.

24 Ed. Munro (1910) 142.28: 'Thus endith þe lif of Seint Gilbert ... þe ȝere of þe incarnacion of oure Lord a Mccccli.'

Reysby,[25] is a faithful translation of a Latin life written under the direction of Gilbert's successor at Sempringham. This English version was for the Gilbertine nuns who were unable to read Latin. Of MS Cotton Vitellius D.xv, another copy, only a few fragments survived the Cottonian fire. *Gilbert*, the *Tretis* and *Augustine* were later bound together in British Library Add. MS 36704.

The Solace of Pilgrimes, a guide-book to the monuments of Rome based on the *Mirabilia urbis Rome*, was begun by Capgrave after his visit there in 1449,[26] and completed before 1452.[27] It is an important witness to the topography of mid-fifteenth-century Rome and invaluable for a record of Latin inscriptions no longer legible on several Roman monuments.

The *Abbreuiacion of Cronicles*, dedicated to Edward IV, is a universal history in the tradition of Higden and Trevisa beginning with Creation and ending with the year 1417, though after 1066 it is effectively English history with a strong British bias.[28] Capgrave dedicated his commentary, *Super actus apostolorum*, and *De fidei symbolis*—a collection of eighteen formulations of the Christian creed together with Augustine's *De symbolo*—to William Gray, who had visited him during his illness in Rome. The strong premonition of approaching death in the dedication suggests that *De fidei symbolis* (c. 1462) was his last work.[29]

All of Capgrave's vernacular works have been edited. Lucas's definitive edition of the *Abbreuiacion of Chronicles* (1983) supplants Hingeston's unreliable text (1858). The present edition of *The Life of Saint Augustine*, it is hoped, will offer a more readable text, as well as fuller Notes and Glossary, than the Munro edition (1910). I also include Capgrave's source, the *Vita s. Augustini* which I transcribed from Jordanus of Saxony's autograph manuscript, Paris, Bibliothèque de l'Arsenal, MS 251.

The Life of St. Augustine, though not dated, is mentioned in both *St. Gilbert* and the *Tretis* with which it is bound. This would place it sometime before 1451. It was commissioned by an unnamed benefactress and, like Capgrave's other vernacular lives, is principally a translation of a Latin *vita* by an Augustinian of the fourteenth century, Jordanus of Saxony.

25 Ed. Munro (1910) 61.1 *Nicholas Reysby* appears in Capgrave's hand in the margin.

26 Fredeman, *Augustiniana* 29 (1979) 231-232.

27 de Meijer, *Augustiniana* 5 (1955) 422. In 1452, Cardinal Kemp became Archbishop of Canterbury with the titular Church of St. Rufina; Capgrave notes his church as St. Balbina, his titular as Archbishop of York.

28 *Abbreuiacion* (ed. Lucas [1983]) xciii-xcv.

29 'solum michi superest sepulchrum'; cf. Appendix 2 , *De illustribus Henricis* 213-217.

C. The Manuscript

British Library's Additional 36704 was purchased at the Fountaine Collection Sale, Sotheby's, June 11-14, 1902 (lot no. 167). The name 'Andrew Fountaine' appears on fol. 120 with the date Sept. 25, 1817. A number of other names appear on fol. 121, probably as suffrages for the deceased, and there is no evidence that these or the cryptic 'Sorel Thome' on flyleaf 2 or 'R. Barn', whose name occurs on fol. 122v, signify ownership.

The manuscript consists of four vellum flyleaves excised from a fourteenth-century *Digestae*, liber xlvi, tit.i[30] The unique autograph text is written in Capgrave's cursive script on 119 sheets of paper;[31] the folio size is 206x144 mm, and includes two of his vernacular saints' lives, *St. Augustine* (fol. 5r-45r) and *St. Gilbert* (fol. 46r-116r), along with a *Tretis* (fol. 116v-119r). All three lack his feliciter and monogram, but on fol. 3r there is an inscription *Magister Johannes Capgraue conuentus Linn fecit istum librum ex precepto unius generose*. On fol. 4v a later hand records, 'John Capgraue, a Monke of Bury [sic], translated this booke out of Latin into English. No. 25.'

Arabic numerals begin with the flyleaves and continue to fol. 123. The Prologue begins on fol. 5r; Roman numeration begins on fol. 6r (Chapter 1) and ends with fol. 45r. Written to the left and above the Arabic numerals, all Roman pagination has been crossed through. The sequence is erratic: numbers v, xx, xxvii, xxxi are omitted; fols. 27 and 35 each have two Roman numbers: xxiv, xxv and xxxv, xxxvi respectively; xxxviii appears twice. The sequence at this point is congruent with the Arabic numbers to fol. 45. There is no Roman numeration in the *St. Gilbert* or the *Tretis*. The text of *Augustine* is without signatures or catchwords, while *Gilbert* and the *Tretis* were prepared for binding with catchwords. These discrepancies suggest that Augustine was originally a separate booklet, that the gathering of the two *Lives* and the *Tretis* into one manuscript took place sometime after the composition of the three works.[32] The three-line red capitals at the beginning of each chapter might suggest that they originally were intended as presentation copies, but all three pieces are riddled with excisions, erasures, interlinear and marginal corrections, symptoms of 'negligence and

30 The first part of Justinian's *Codex iuris civilis*.

31 See Lucas (1969) for a description of Capgrave's holograph MSS.

32 See Lucas (1997) 47-48 for further detail as to the later binding of the three works, including the cropping of *St. Augustine* to fit the later two MSS. He postulates the existence of a small Capgrave scriptorium at the Augustinian friary in Lynn, where he had scribes and binders to help produce copies of his works.

rape'. The interlineation of '*conuentus Linn*' in the inscription on fol. 3r suggests more probably inattention rather than an after-thought. On the other hand, Capgrave's exceptional care in correcting his mistakes may indicate that the three were working texts for fair copy.

The binding seems to be original—oak boards covered with calfskin and straps with metal stud-clasps. The front cover was originally inscribed with a coat of arms now faded.[33] Modern, probably nineteenth-century, red leather labels with gilt lettering have been applied.

The text of *St. Augustine* is in block form with 31 to 36 lines per page, though more than half of the 45 folios have 32 or 33 lines. The text on the lower corners of the first three folios has faded. Capgrave's hand is, however, generally legible, and, except for the interpretation of minims, flourishes, and some contractions, poses no major difficulty.[34]

Each of the 45 chapter titles is preceded by a horizontal extender and a vertical descender; a smaller version of the same figure in brown is used to indicate a new division or change of topic. My text reflects the intent of these markers without their duplication. Latin phrases are also underlined and have been reproduced as italics.

The editorial practise has whenever possible been kept consistent with my edition of Capgrave's *The Life of St. Norbert* (1977) 16-17.

Punctuation, capitalization and word division follow modern conventions. Square brackets mark editorial emendations when the addition of letters has been required, with the manuscript reading provided in the textual apparatus. Since the manuscript is an autograph, corrected with evident care by the author, many of what would have been its mistakes were repaired by Capgrave as he went along. Usually these errors simply involved such obvious factors as anticipation, omission, homoeoteleuton and dittography. Some are altered subsequently by excision or interpolation; others are clearly corrected 'en route', as they are part of the regular manuscript line. Both sorts of corrections are noted in the textual apparatus.

The spelling of the manuscript has been preserved. Where it was obviously intended, *þ* is read for a graph that appears as a *y* or *wynn*; *th* and *þ* are used interchangeably; *ȝ* can represent *y* (as *ȝet*), the final *-gh* spirant (as *thouȝ*), or s (as *baptiȝe*).

33 Lucas, *British Museum Quarterly* 36 (1971) 80-83. Following a lead from the Additional Catalogue to statements of Tho. Gibbon in Harley MS 980, fol. 120, Lucas gives convincing proof that the coat of arms is that of Sir Robert Kemp and that the *Gilbert* and *Tretis* manuscripts belonged to him.

34 Lucas has recently identified two distinct scripts used by Capgrave, both of which are found in BL Add. 36704 ([1997] 25 ff.).

Capgrave's abbreviations and contractions have been expanded silently. The curl on final *-r* has been expanded to *-re*, where the forms are regularly spelled out with *-re* elsewhere. The regularly crossed final *-ll* is expanded to *-lle* only when an expanded form is found elsewhere (thus *alle* vs. *gospell, councell*). The suspension over *u* in *ou* is treated as a nasal suspension, and the loop after *-g* as *-is* (as *amongis*). Double *ff* has been reproduced except when it begins a sentence, when it has been treated as a capital *F*. I have let the ampersand symbol stand.

D. Language

The vernacular works of John Capgrave form a unique body of evidence for the language of King's Lynn, Norfolk in the fifteenth century. The volume and variety of the texts—history, legend, biography in both prose and poetry—lend it special value, especially the autograph or holograph texts with corrections by Capgrave himself.

Capgrave claims Norfolk as his country and Lynn as his native town. The brief biography given above suggests that he spent most of his 71 years in Lynn. His studies in London and Cambridge no doubt gave him first-hand familiarity with both dialectical diversity and the beginnings of standardization, but his language manifests marked differences from other dialects, and from London Standard.

One of the earliest studies of Capgrave's language by W. Dibelius was published serially in *Anglia* (1901). It is of limited value depending as it did on Hingeston's unreliable transcription of the *Chronicle*. Meech's study of the language of Margery Kempe was exceptionally well supplied with supplementary material from all Capgrave's vernacular works, except *Norbert*.

In recent years some studies on Capgrave's language based on modern editions and computerized texts have appeared. In 1972, preliminary to my edition of *Norbert*, Edmund Colledge and I published a paper on the diction, dialect and spelling of this the earliest of his works in the vernacular.[35] Prof. Lucas in his monumental edition of Capgrave's *Abbreuiacion of Cronicles* (1983), and in his more recent *From Author to Audience* (1997), produced exhaustive studies of its morphology, phonology and vocabulary.[36] In light of his work, it seems superfluous to marshal a host of forms

35 Colledge, Smetana, *Mediaeval Studies* 34 (1972) 422-434.

36 *Abbreuiacion* (ed. Lucas [1983]) xliii-lxxi. See also Lucas (1997) 203-248 for a detailed account of Capgrave's orthographic usage, and *A Linguistic Atlas of Late Medieval English* (3: 333-4) for the linguistic features of BL Add. 36704.

duplicating the phonological and morphological forms already so competently illustrated and evaluated. I shall limit this section to a few remarks and illustrations.

As Capgrave's *Augustine* was prepared for a literate but not scholarly noble-woman, it called for clarity and simplicity of language. Nonetheless, Capgrave was also at pains over the form of English he wrote, in an age when the London dialect was becoming the 'received standard'. He avoids two features common in Lynn documents: first, nowhere in *Augustine* does he spell 'sc-' as 'x'; second, only once in 288 occurrences of 'whech' is it spelled 'qwech', a singular lapse into the local dialect. On the other hand, he regularly conforms to the local tendency to drop the velar 'h' before 't', e.g., *almity*, *brith*, *brout(e)* (40), *douteres*, *doutir* (2), *myth* (42), *nyth* (9), *nytes*, *parfith* beside *parfite*, *rith* (4), *rithful*, *rithfully*, *rowt*, *sith* (3), *þout(e)* (10) beside *þoutȝ* (2). He drops the final palatal 'h' in *low*, and *ny* (13), but he spells *þou ȝ* (25) beside *þow*. His use of the feminine pronouns *sche* (109) and *hir(e)* (108) conforms with other Lynn documents, as do the third-person plural pronouns (*þei/thei, here, hem*). These pronomial forms originated in the East Midlands and supplanted other dialectical forms in literary records after the middle of the fifteenth century. But the fact that the Glossary shows only three present participle forms in *-and* may also be an indication of Capgrave's efforts to adapt to the London standard.

Also noteworthy is the occasional conservative 'i/y' prefix in the past participle; the presence of 'o' forms in the past tense/participle (*goten*, *ȝouen*); and the penetration of the northern 'g' into words that would eventually keep 'g' (*gyuyst*, *gaf* beside *ȝeueth*, *ȝaue*).

E. Source

In 1943 two scholars simultaneously published articles identifying the *Vita s. Augustini* by Jordanus of Saxony (alias von Quedlinburg) as the source for Capgrave's *Augustine*.[37]

In the Prologue Capgrave says that he translated it 'treuly oute of Latyn'; he does not, however, identify the source. Munro (1910) had concluded that Capgrave 'himself is the original composer, and that his reference to translation from Latin signifies his use of Augustine's books, from which he translates whole passages.'[38]

37 Arbesmann, *Traditio* 1 (1943) 341-355 and Sanderlin, *Speculum* 18 (1943) 358-362.

38 Ibid., 348-350.

The literal translations adduced by Arbesmann in fact demonstrate that Capgrave used Jordanus from Chapters 5-6 through 45. It is possible, however, that he had a *Vita* with several introductory chapters which also included the two later chapters from the *Confessions* (6.9, 9.12).[39] If the added chapters and the other substantive changes are the work of Capgrave, he proved himself much more innovative than in his other translations.

Notes on Capgrave's *Augustine* record sources used for the 39 chapters. 'Capgrave's Debt to Jordanus' (below, p. 119) identifies the lines in the *Vita* which he translated. Additions and omissions are duly recorded. Capgrave regularly omits Jordanus' citations to the *Confessions*, Possidius and the *Legenda famosa* and the tags, *Hec ipse ibi, Et infra*. He rightly divined that such information 'long not to þis maner of wryting þat is cleped narratyf.'[40]

The *Vita s. Augustini*, written in Jordanus' own hand in Paris, Bibliothèque de l'Arsenal, MS 251 (ff. 54rb-70rb), is part of a collection of materials on Augustine, Monica and the origins of the Augustinian Order. The nature of the collection and the numerous fragmentary notes suggest that it was a preliminary collection of materials for Jordanus' *Liber vitasfratrum*,[41] a comprehensive treatise on the religious life illustrated by examples from the lives of Augustinian brethren.

MS 251 is a treasury of scriptural paraphrase, quotations from the Ante and Post Nicene Fathers, with the greater number, understandably, from Augustine. Later medieval writers from Bede to St. Bernard of Clairvaux are represented, along with such ancients as Cicero and Seneca. The sources of the *Vita* are much more modest. For the period prior to Augustine's conversion Jordanus used the *Confessions*; for his life as a priest and bishop he followed Possidius' biography and a *vita* by a Premonstratensian, Phillipus de Harveng; for his writings, the *Retractations*. Augustine's two sermons on the Common Life, eloquent in defining what he considered the heart of religious life, are quoted several times. Beside these *bona fide* sources, Jordanus used five of the forty pseudo-Augustine *Sermones ad fratres in eremo*, a series concocted in the later Middle Ages to prove that Augustine founded three communities. The aim of these apocrypha was to show the primacy of the Hermits over the Canons.[42]

39 Fredeman, *Augustiniana* 28 (1978) 291.

40 Capgrave, *Augustine* 22/23-24. All references to Capgrave's text in this volume are to capitulum and line.

41 Arbesmann and Hümpfner, eds., *Vitasfratrum* (1943) xi-xvi.

42 Arbesmann, *Traditio* 1 (1943) 345. Seymour (1996) 222 comments that 'this dearly held belief [that Augustine personally founded the Hermits] was deeply resented by the Augustine canons, the foundation of whose order pre-dated by al-

In the dedication of this autograph manuscript, which contains the *Vita,* to the *studium generale* in Paris, Jordanus expresses the hope that his confreres would read, be inspired by and copy this work. There are two other copies extant, one at Toulouse, the other in Vienna; in 1686 J. Hommey OESA printed Jordanus' *Vita s. Augustini* together with other selections from the *Collectanea.*[43]

There is no record of a manuscript of Jordanus' *Vita* in England. It is possible, however, that Capgrave on his journey to Rome copied the sixteen folios and brought them back to England.[44] Whether he had his own copy or an enlarged *Vita* before him, his translation bears his own stamp and special charm from the fact that he was adapting it for the 'noble creatur' who, though literate, was neither a theologian nor an Augustinian scholar.

F. Capgrave's Additions

A number of additions distinguish Capgrave's *Life* from Jordanus' *Vita*, and can be attributed to his desire to suit his work to the 'gentill woman' at whose request he prepared it; in large part these additions could be said to have a 'humanizing' effect on the text.

Most notably Capgrave includes more personal information about Augustine. The Prologue and the first five chapters provide an etymology for Augustine's name and tell of his birth, his infancy and boyhood, his parents and relatives. In capitulum vi he inserts the well-known anecdote of the young Augustine's envy of a neighbour's apples. He also adds details concerning the decision of Augustine and his friends to choose wives (11/47), and of Augustine's frugality as a bishop (37/20). Interestingly, he describes Augustine's relationship with his mistress, mother of the beloved Adeodatus (18/3-8), citing Augustine's assertion, from the *Confessions*, of their mutual fidelity.

In the same vein, Capgrave adds personal details about other characters: Ambrose (13/9-12, 19/9-13, 41/6-8), Alipius (12/1ff.) and Vitalis (21/31ff.). Evidently assuming that his female reader would be particularly interested in Monica, he amplifies her role: she comforts the frightened shipmen during a storm (11/7-9), she fasts on Saturdays (11/33-34), she exhibits her particular wisdom (16/36-39).

Through the addition of various minor details the text becomes more

most two hundred years that of the upstart Hermits.'

43 Arbesmann, *Traditio* 1 (1943) 347, notes 32 & 33.

44 Ibid., 352-353.

informative: the 'makyng of schippis' began at Carthage (25/8); '*monos* in þe oþir tonge is as mech to sey as solitari' (41/33); the Rebaptizatores would only admit the newly baptized to their sect (40/21-23).[45]

It will be obvious that these kinds of changes suggest that Capgrave altered his text in ways that he thought would make it more appealing to a lay female reader. In deference to her sensitivity he softens the story of the obdurate rich man to include the possibility of his conversion (27/12ff.); perhaps out of consideration for her (less scholastic) interests, he abbreviates one of Jordanus' catalogues with a tactful 'þis I ley beside' (34/39-40). And he addresses his friend directly in a final affectionate apostrophe (45/41-45): 'Thus I comende ȝou to god, and me to your prayeries; þat we both may com sumtyme where oure fadir is, we schal prey both. Amen.'

45 See the Notes for a more complete description of Capgrave's changes [e.g., 6/19-23 (the story of the apple tree), 22/16-19 (negative details about the Manichees), 29/5-8 (the founding of the order), 42.10-13 (the addition of the names of the Roman gods)].

John Capgrave

Life of Saint Augustine

The Manuscript

London, British Library, Additional MS 36704, fol. 5r-45r.

Textual Apparatus

In the manuscript, letters, words or phrases crossed through are excised; those with subscript periods are deleted. Insertions are indicated by a caret (^) or slanted line (/).

[Prologue]

5r A grete reule to alle lerned men was sette be Seint Paule in þe first capitle *Ad romanos*, where he saide þat he was dettoure onto wise men and onwise. Wise men clepid he men gretly lerned, and onwise, simple ydiotis, to whom longith þe blisse of heuene and of whom oure lord Ihesu spak in þe gospell and seid þat here aungellis see euyr þe face of þe fadir whech is in heuene. To þese both þe holy apostell saide he was dettoure to paye ech of hem aftir þat he sauoured. And þouȝ I þat write now þis be a man sumwhat endewid in lettirure, ȝet dare I not take upon me for to be dettoure onto hem þat be endewid in sciens more þan I. But I dare sauely seye þat I am detoure to oþir simpil creatures þat be not lerned so mech as I. Wherfor my dettis wil I pay, of swech tresoure as I haue in possessioun, with more esy laboure þan euyr I receyued hem.

The cause of þis writyng whech meued me moost now wil I telle. A noble creature, a gentill woman, desired of me with ful grete instauns to write onto hire, þat is to sey to translate hir treuly oute of Latyn, þe lif of Seynt Augustyn, grete doctoure of þe cherch. Sche desired þis þing of me rather þan of anoþir man because þat I am of his profession, for sche supposed veryly þat I wold do it with þe bettir wil. Sche desired eke þis lif of þis seynt more þane of ony oþir for sche was browt forth into þis world in his solempne feste. Than wil I in þe name of oure lord Ihesu beginne þis werk to þe worchip of þis glorious doctoure and to þe plesauns and consolacioun of þis gentil woman þat hath so willed me with sundry retribu-
5v ciones / þat I coude not disobeye hir desire.

20 br *excised before* for 23-24 retribuciones] retribucione *MS*

3 *Ad romanos*] 1.14

6 here aungellis see...] Matt. 8.10

14-15 A noble creature] not identified, but possibly the mother or the wife of Edmund Rede of Borstall, whom Capgrave recognizes as the rightful founder of the Augustinian monastery at Oxford. The letter to John Stockton, prior of the monastery dated 1456, is printed in an Appendix to Capgrave, *Abbreuiacion,* ed. Hingeston (1858), 331-332.

16 treuly oute of Latyn] see Arbesmann, *Traditio* 1 (1943) 348.

21 solepmne feste] August 28, the day of his death. Capgrave mentions the date at Cap. 45/26, "þe v kalende of September."

This glorious name Augustinus is mad comendable amongis oure auctouris for iii þingis. On is for þe excellens of þe man. The secund for þe brennyng loue of charite with whech his hert was fyred. The þird for þe noble ethimilogie whech longeth to þe name. Ethimilogie is cleped in gramer þe trewe exposicioun of a word. As touching þe first, þat is to sey þe excellens of þis seint, it acordith ful wel onto his name, for þis word *augustus* was first ȝoue onto þe emperoure Octauiane as to þe moost honorable and excellent prince þat euyr regned in þe empire. For it soundith in oure langage as a morer of þe lordchip and þis same Octauiane engrosed nere al þe lordchip of þe world onto þe empire of Rome. So sey we of þis glorious doctoure þat he berith þis name for excellens aboue alle oþir. Therfor þe oþir doctouris be likned onto þe sterres and he onto þe sunne, as it is pleynly conteyned in þe epistil red in his feest, where he seith þat lich as þe sunne schynyth in heuene so schynyth he in þe temple of oure lord.

As touching þe secund diuision, þat is to seye his feruent loue whech he had onto oure lord, þis acordith eke onto his name, ffor *Augustus* is þat month in heruest whech is þe hattest month and moost riping of frutes þorwoute alle þe ȝere. So þis man brennyng in charite wrote onto þe Cristen puple swech swete exhortaciones of loue þat he is cause next God, dare I sey, þat many a soule hath ripere frutes of deuocioun because of his
6r labour. Off þis brennyng charite whech þis noble clerk / had, is spoken be his owne mouth in þe ix book of his *Confessiones*, where he seith þus of him & his felawis neuly conuerted onto God. 'Thou lord', he saide, 'hast hitte oure hertis with þe hote arowys of charite and eke we receyued þi wordis into oure hertis as þouȝ þei had be scharp arowys.'

Eke touching þe ethimologie of his name, it berith witnesse of his grete excellens, for þis name as auctouris sey is compownyd of *augeo auges*, þat is as mech to sey as to make þing more þan it was. It is eke compowned of *ana*, þat is as mech to sey as aboue. It is eke compowned of *astim*, whech

35 b *excised before* name 36 kilned *deleted*; likned *in left margin* 50 arowys] harowys *MS*; h *deleted in red*

25 This glorious name] See Arbesmann, *Traditio* 1 (1943) 351. Sanderlin, *Speculum* 18 (1943) 358 attributes the etymology to Jacobus de Voragine, *Acta s. Augustini*.

33 morer] Capgrave's usage is unique; see OED morer [f. more v. + er], 'one who increases.'

37 epistil red in his feest] Sir. 50.7 'quasi sol refulgens, sic ille effulsit in templo Dei'.

48-50 Thou lord...hast hitte oure hertis] *Conf.* 9.2, 'Saggitaveras tu cor nostrum charitate tua et gestabamus verba tua transfixa visceribus....' Augustine is depicted holding a heart aflame, pierced with an arrow.

is as mech to sey as a cite. So for to putte alle þese parties togidir, þe name of þis glorious seynt is þus browt onto þis reson a morer of þe cite aboue, a gret encreser of þe blis of heuene, for he was cause whil he lyued with his tonge, and aftir his deth with his bokis, þat many a soule is ledde þe rith weye to heuene.

Of þe cuntre & þe town where he was bore. Capitulum i.

At oure beginnyng ȝe schul vndirstand þat þis world is departed into iii parties and it was þus departed as oure auctouris seye be oure fader Noe. For in þe flood were saued he and his iii sones, and to þese iii sones was alle þe world departed. Thei þat cam of Sem were sette in þe est side of þe world cleped now Asia. Thei [þat] cam of Iaphet were sette in þat partye of þe world cleped now Europa. And þei þat cam of Cam were sette to dwelle in þat partie whech is clepid Affrica
6v where / þis glorious man was bore.

Asia is in þe est side of þe world and it conteyneth as mech in space as do þe othir too parties. In þis Asia stant Ynde and Pers, Mede, Mesopothamia, Surry, Araby, Capadoce, Comagene, Palestine, Iude, Galile & many mo provynces. Europe conteyneth Scithie, Russie, Hungarye, Achay, Macedony, Dalmacy, Ytaile and alle þe Duche tonge with France, Ynglond, Spayn & many moo. Affrica hath principali þe prouynce of ȝeugis where grete Cartage stant. It hath eke anoþir prouynce clepid Tripolitane, Getuly, Byzance, Numedye, Mauritania. In þis Numedie stant þat cite where Seynt

55 ast *before* þe name *excised*
1 Capitulum i] capitulum i cap i *MS* 4 saued] d *interlineated* 6 Thei þat cam] Thei cam *MS* 11 Ynde] *red mark above* Y 13 Russie] Nussie *MS*

2-3 departed into iii parties] Arbesmann, *Traditio* 1 (1943) 351; 'There is nothing essentially new in this sketch. It is the cosmology which since Orosius, St. Isidore of Seville and the anonymous Ravennese Geographer of the mid-seventh century, had been repeated over and over again throughout the Middle Ages.'

4 For in þe flood were saued] Gen. 10.

12 Surry] Syria.

12 Comagene] district SE of Cappadocia annexed to the Roman Empire by Vespasian in 72 AD.

12 Russie/Nussie] Munro thought it could be either Tuscany or Russia; the context calls for Russia.

15 ȝeugis] modern Tunis.

16 grete Cartage] Isidore, *Etym*, 15.4.8, 'Yeugis ubi Cartago Magna'.

16 Getuly] Varro called the area south of Numidia and Mauretania 'Gentulia.'

Austyn was bischop cleped Ypone, and in þis same Numedie stant þat same cyte cleped Tagatensis where þis doctoure was bore, sumwhat upward more onto Cartage.

Thus haue I schewid ȝou in what partie of þe world he was bore, nowt in þe Greke tonge, ne in þe Latyn tonge, but in the Barbare tonge. Neuyrþelasse we rede of him þat whan he cam to lerne dyuers sciens whech were þan most in Greke tonge, þat he hated þe Greke letteris and loued weel þe Latyn be whech inclynacioun we vndirstand þat þat same langage in whech he was bore was more approximat onto þe Latyn tonge þan onto þe Grek tong. For in very treuth he had so grete knowlech of both tongis þat alle his bokys he mad in Latyn, and oute of þe Greke tonge he himselue translate into Latyn a grete book whech Aristotle mad cleped his *Cathegories*, for I wot who hath þis book of ful eld hand. This is seid to my entent to proue
7r þat he was bore amongis / hem þat speke þe Barbare tonge. The Barbare tonge is euery tonge in þe world whech is fer fro þe iii principall tongis, Hebrew, Grek & Latyn.

Off þe progenitouris and þe kynrod of þis man. Capitulum ii.

Off his progenitoures þus we rede þat þei were not of þe despect laboureres in þe puple, but born of good and rich kynrod aftir þe fame of þe world; for þis man aftir here deth had sufficient possessioun for to lyue by. And he himself seith in his *Confessiones* þat whan he was sent to skole to Cartage, because þei herd sey þat here child had a grete corage to lernyng, þat he was founde as wel and with as grete cost as ony lordis son þat went to skole. This myth not be do withouten þat þei had substauns of possessioun.

The name of his fader was clepid Patrik, whech was a hethen man onto þe tyme þat he schuld deye, for þan be laboure of his modir he was mad Cristen man and so deyed newly baptiȝed. His modir hith Monica. Sche was a Cristen woman fro hir childhold, and norchid in þe best condiciones

26 he was bore *in right margin* 28 g *before* þe Greke *excised*
7 þei *before* founde *excised*; he was *in right margin* 8 n *before* lordis *excised*

27 so grete knowlech of both tongis] Augustine confesses that he could not read the Greek Fathers with much comprehension. See B. Altaner, *Pisciculi*, 19-40 and RB 62 (1952) 201-221.

28-29 he himselue translate into Latyn] See note below at Cap. 8/4.

3 rich kynrod] It is clear from *Conf.* 2.3 that Augustine's family was not affluent. Romanianus, to whom he dedicated his *Contra academicos*, CCL 29.5.1, was probably his sponsor.

and moost plesaunt to God and to man. Sche had moo childyrn þan him as it semeth be his writing in his *Confessiones*. And þouȝ þat he telle not here names þere, we haue sout hem oute of oþir of his bokis. For in þat book whech is cleped *De beata vita* þere tellith he of his broþir whech at þat festfull day was with him and with his modir in an hothous, whech þei clepe a stewe, þe day of his birth. For he was bore on Seynt Brices day as þat / 7v same book makith mencion, and custumablely he used whil he was paynem to make a gret fest on þat day. But aftir he was mad bischop he turned þis bodely fest into spiritual talkyng and, as I suppose, þis bok was mad þat first day þat he mad þis chaunge or he was bischop. For his moder was at þis fest and sche deyid before þat he was preest. This mannes name of whom we talk of here, whech as we saide was his broþir, was cleped Nauigius. He spekith here eke in þis same book of too cosynes of his, on of hem hith Latridianus, þe othir hith Rusticus. Thei both were at þis feest of whom he seith þat þei were trewe Cristen but not lettered. He had a sistir but I haue not herd hir name, and to hir he wrote a book whech he cleped *Þe book of Cristen mannes lyf*. It begynnyth þus: *Et ego peccator*. The rubrich before þe bok is writyn þus: The book of Seynt Augustin þe bischop onto his sistir, a widow. Eke he had anoþir cosyn þat hith Patricius as his fader hith, and þis man was on of þe chanones þat lyued with him in þe þird monasterie aftir he was bischop. In þe þird monasterye seid I, for because þat he mad iii; on or he was preest, anoþir whil he was preest vndir bischop Valerie. And who long he dwelt þere and who dwelt þere with him schal be touchid aftir whan it comth in his place.

22 fest] festyn *MS*; yn *deleted*

19 he was bore on Seynt Brices day] November 13, 354. See *De beata vita,* CCL 29.68, 'Idibus Novembris mihi natalis'.

25-26 his broþir was cleped Nauigius] mentioned in *De beata vita* 2.6, CCL 29.68 and *De ordine* 1.2.5, CCL 29.91.

27 Latridianus...Rusticus] *De beata vita* 2.6, CCL 29.68.

28 a sistir] Possidius 26, PL 32.55.

30 *Of Cristen mannes lyf*] a spurious work, written by Fastidius Britto, PL 40. 1031. It is laced with texts from *De gestis Pelagii* which had been vigorously repudiated by Augustine.

32 anoþir cosyn] *Sermo* 356, PL 39.1575, 'Patricium meum nepotem, tales inueni quales desideraui'.

33-34 þe þird monasterie] See Arbesmann, *Augustiniana* 6 (1956) 37-145. Henry of Friemar's *Treatise* precipitated a long and bitter controversy between the Hermits and Canons of St. Augustine. It was finally ended by Pope Sixtus IV who branded it as 'quaedam minus necessaria minusque laudabilis controversia', Arbesmann, *op. cit.*. 59, n. 58.

8r

Of þe condiciones of his fadere and / his modir. Capitulum tercium

Off þis mater spekith þis glorious man in þe ix book of his *Confessiones*, where he seith of his fader þat he was of nature ful frendly and goodly and redy eke onto ire as many men be, kynde and fre of hert and sone meued to malencolie. This holi woman weddid onto him, whan sche had aspied his hasti condicioun, sche had swech gouernauns in hir dedis and swech moderacion in hir wordes þat he coude neuyr cacch no hold to be wroth with hir in alle his lyf. Sche wold if he excedid, as Augustinus tellith, abide til his ire were goo; þan wold sche reherse onto him þe euel avised wordes whech he had spoke or þe onresonable werkis whech he had do. Sumtyme it happed þat sche sat among oþir matrones of hir knowlech, of whech women summe had merkys in her face whech here husbandis had mad only for þei wold speke ageyn whan here husbandis were wroth. And þan wold þese women say onto Monicha, 'We haue grete wondir of þe and þin husband þat þou bringgist neuyr no merk of his strokys, ne non of us haue herd þat euyr þere was ony strif betwix ʒou too, notwithstand þat he is an irous man and hasty as ony dwellith amongis us.' Sche wold answere onto hem on þis manere: 'Iff ʒe haue mynde of ʒoure tables matrimonial þat were mad betwix ʒou and
8v ʒoure husbandis at ʒoure weddyng, / ʒe wold not þan haue meruayle whi þat I suffir my husband þouʒ þat I haue wrong. For þere is it writyn þat þouʒ wyuys and husbandis be o flesch and o blood, ʒet ar wyuys put in swech manere of subieccioun þat þei be bounde to do dew seruyse onto men; wherfor as me þinkith þe best seruyse þat þei may doo is to kepe pes in houshold and suffir wrong rather þan pes schuld be broke.' For hir wordis many of þese women were stered to more paciens and leued in more rest þan þei dede before.

There was with hir þe modir of hir husband dwellyng in houshold, and as often is sene þei make sumtyme debate betwyx wif and husband, namely where ʒong damesellis be with clateryng tongis. Swech seruantis were in Patrik hous; but for no tales of hem ne no suspicioun of þe elde moder Monicha was neuyr put in no blame, so redy was hir paciens, so besi was hir

20 mynde *interlineated before* of 23 wyuys[1,2] *in left margin*; wifis *and* wifys *deleted; double strokes over words in text and margins*

36 Valerie] Valerius, bishop of Hippo (d. 396).

20 tables matrimonial] wedding contract written on wax tablets with an iron stylus.

32 elde moder] mother-in-law; *Conf.* 9.9.

plesauns. The elde moder seing þe good disposicioun of hir doutir was compelled be consciens to compleyne of hir servauntis onto hir son, desiryng of him þat he schuld snybbe þe maydenes þat þei schuld not be redy to telle swech tales with whech pes myth be broke in Patrik hous.

Many mo noble condiciones rehersith þis man of his modir whech as now schul not be touched, for in the orisoun or ellis þe compleynt whech he mad aftir hir deth it schal be talked more largely aftir þe forme of his
9r *Confessiones*. / O þing he touchith here gretly longing to hire comendacioun in norching of hir childyrn; he seith þat sche trauayled for hem neuly ageyn as often as sche say hem do ony þing whech was ageyn þe plesauns of oure lord, þat is to sey it greued hir as mech whan sche say hir childyrn trespas onto oure lord as euyr it greued whan sche bare hem bodyly.

Of þe age of Seint Augustin whech is clepid Infancia. iiii

Infancia is on of þe vii ages as oure auctores say whech lestith fro þe birth onto þe tyme þat þe child is come to þe age of vii ȝere, and þouȝ it be soo þat we sey comounly þat childyrn synne not in þis age, þat is to sey dedly, ȝet in sum on or to haue be seyn þe reuers as Seint Gregorie telletȝ in his *Dialoges* li, 4 þat a child of þis age was sodeynly be þe deuele rawt from his faderes armes. Notwithstanding þis or oþir whech myth be rehersed as we said, comounly childyrn of þis age be clepid innocentis, for þei lak vse of resoun for to discerne vice fro vertu. But of þis age and of synnes do in þis age Seynt Augustyn makitȝ open confession in þe first book of þat matere, where he seith þat sum childyr þat can not speke þei can loke angrily on hem þat greue hem, and with handes and teth proferen in manere of a veniauns. Nowt had þis doctour mynde þat he ded soo, but for he say oþir childyrn do þus; þerfor supposed he þat he ded
9v soo. / Mech more þing he rehersith of þis matere in his first book of his *Confessiones* whech is now not gretly nedful to be writyn.

42 sche *interlineated* trauayled] trauayle *MS* 45 oure *interlineated before* lord *with* ^

3 n *deleted before* is come 6 g *excised before* Gregorie 12 hem[2] *interlineated before* and *with* ^

1 Infancia] 'Ages of Man' was a commonplace medieval topos with usually seven stages: *infancia*, *puericia*, *adolescentia*, *iuventus*, *gravitas*, *senectus*. Cf. Isidore, *Etym*. 11.2 and Jones, *Archaeologia* 35 (1853) 167-189.

6 *Dialoges* li.4] PL 77.148. Exact citation of sources is uncommon among medieval writers. Trapp, *Augustiniana* 25 (1975) 282-292, claims that 14th-century Augustinian theologians initiated the practice.

15 Mech more þing he rehersith of þis matere] *Conf*. 1.7.

Of þat age of him whech þei clepe Puericia. v

Puericia also is þe secund age, and þat lestith fro seuene ȝere to xiiii ȝere. It is as mech to sey in Englisch as þe age of clennesse, for þis age is not mech defiled with dedis of leccherie or onclennesse. What defautes þat be in þis age of whech oure maystir had ful grete consciens, is writin in þe same book. At þis age he seith he was put to skole, and whane he schuld be bete he prayed God þat he myth skape it; but oure lord herd him nowt and þat displesed him, for he knew not þat tyme who profitable it was to his soule to be bete for lernyng. With sad men and eld men whech mad a game whan he was laschid, he was in partie wroth. He lerned lesse þa[n] he schuld or myth a lerne. He loved bettir veyn games þan skole. The smale elementis of lernyng receyued he first in þe same cite where he was bore. His gramer lerned he in a cite beside, whech is cleped Maudauris. He loued bettir as we sayde before þe Latyn letteris þan þe Grek, notwithstand þat he lerned first þe Grek letteres.

In þis age he had grete sekenesse in his stomake, and euyr was his modir bisi þat he schuld be baptized; but þe fader wold not suffir it. And
10r þis was þe cause as men / suppose whi oure lord wold not suffir him to be baptized, for it was lesse greuauns to his soule þat þe filth of heresie schuld be in him rather before his baptem þan aftir his baptem. Thus lerned he þe smale scienses as spellyng, reding and constrewyng in his ȝong age.

Who he was sent to Cartage to lerne grettir sciens. vi

Whanne he was fully xvi ȝere old his frendis sent him to Cartage, a grete cite whech held batayle with Rome & alle Itaile many ȝeres. There lerned he rethorik and eloquens oute of Tullius

11 þan] þat *MS* 16 sike *excised before* sekenesse 19 soule *in right margin*

1 Parts of v and vi are from Jordanus; from vii on Capgrave follows Jordanus closely, although he includes interpolations from the *Confessions*, and numerous additions of his own.

1 Puericia] Isidore, *Etym*. 11.1.10: 'Puer a puritate vocatus, quia purus est'.

11-14 He loued bettir...þe Latyn] *Conf*. 1.13.

21 spellyng] speaking, elocution.

21 constrewyng] composition.

2 his frendis sent him to Cartage] cf. Cap. 2/3 above.

3 held batayle with Rome] the Punic wars, 264-241, 218-201, 149-146 BC.

4-5 Tullius bokes] Marcus Tullius Cicero 106-43 BC. *De oratore, De claris oratoribus* and *Orator* formed a complete course in rhetorical training.

bokes, and oþir rethoricianes whech were before him. But in þis first ȝere þat he cam to Cartage he abod litil at his study but rood to and fro, now to his fader now to Cartage; for what for euel felauchip þat he was falle in, what for insolens of his wauntown age, he used tauernes and stewis and swech sory gouernauns as þei vse whech haue no men to vndirtake here defautes. For his fadere low at his gouernauns & rebuked him of no defaute. But his modere with ful sad cuntenauns forbade him alle suspecious cumpany, and he took ful litil heed at hire wordis.

In þis same tyme was his fadere conuerted onto þe feith and mad a cathecume. A cathecume is as mech to seye as a newe receyuour of þe feith, for in elde tyme men had certeyn dayes assined betwix here conuercion and here baptem þat þei myth lerne wel þe articules of oure feith or þei were bounde þerto. And so schuld men do now as I suppose if
10v þei schuld be bap/tized at þat age. He schryuyth him also þat in þis age he ded many insolens more for vanite þan for nede, and in special of an appil tre þat stood fast by his faderes vyne on anoþir mannes lond. Of whech he makith grete consciens because þat he myth haue had bettir appillis in his faderes possession, and eke for whan he had þese appelles he ete hem nawt but þrew hem onto hoggis.

In alle þis vanyte of his lif he happed to fynde a book þat Tullius Cicero mad, þe grete rethorician of Rome, whech book þe maker clepid *Hortencius*, because it exhorted men gretly to fle þe vanite of þe world and to folow þe noble study of philosophie. This book chaunged his hert gretly, & mad him þat he had not so grete ioye in þoo vanites as he had before. But for al þat þe book plesed him not fully, for he fond not þe name of Crist in al þis book. This name was couchid in his hert fro his moder tete, þat what book he red were it neuyr so wys ne so wel ispoke, were it neuyr so trew, he was not fully plesed with it but if Cristis name were þere.

11 him *interlineated in red before* alle 13 tyme *interlineated in red; red* ^ *before* was 17 do *interlineated in red before* now 18 him *interlineated in red before* also 20 tre *in right margin;* ^ ^ *in text and margin* 26 h *deleted before* exhorted 31 it[1] *added in right margin after* were

5-12 Capgrave expands upon Augustine's wild ways, which were encouraged by his father, and mourned by his mother.

8 stewis] here 'brothel', but cf. *stewe* (Cap. 2/19), 'garden house'.

14-17 A cathecume...bounde þerto] the explanation is Capgrave's.

19-23 The story of the apple tree, from *Conf.* 2.4, is added by Capgrave; the 'forbidden tree' was, however, a pear tree: 'Arbor erat pirus in vicina nostrae vineae...'.

25 *Hortencius*] a lost work by Cicero. See Taylor (1968) 487-498 and Testard, *Saint Augustin et Ciceron*.

Than purposed he for to rede holy scripture, but because þat as Seint Paule seith, cunnyng withoute charite makith a man proude, and þis sciens requirith meke disciples, þerfor þe eye of his mynde was iqwenchid with þe grete lith of sotil vndyrstanding whech is conteyned in scripture, and þus left he þis holy study. Tho felle he into þe grete erroure of þe Maniches; for
11r þei saide þat Goddis son of heuene was not bore of a may/de, ne he had not very flesch and blood as oþir men haue, but rather a fantastical body mad of þe eyr in whech he semed for [to] deye, but deth was þere non, for very body was þere non. In þis fals heresie whech avoideth þe most substauns of oure feith fell he. Many mo heresies held þei whech were ful perilous to be rehersed specialy in oure tonge. In þis heresie abood Augustin ny ix ȝere, inqwiring and sekyng groundes and treuthis or ellis resones for to defende þis heresie, but he fond non.

Of þe sorow þat his modir had for his erroure. Capitulum vii

His modir whan sche herd þat he was falle onto þis heresie sche wept and sorowid more hertly þan women do þat folow here childyrn to þe graue and witȝ many menes and many exhortaciones was bisi nyth and day to bryng him fro þis mischef. In alle þis tribulacioun and weping oure lord wold not suffir hir to go fully desolat but schewid hir a consolacioun be an aungel in hir sleep. Sche þoutȝ þat sche stood on a faire tre planed al rith lich a reule, and a faire ȝong man stood beside hire with rich cloþis and a mery chere, whech inqwired of hire what was þe cause of hir weping. Sche answered onto him with ful heuy cher. 'The losse of my son Augustin I wepe.' Tho þe ȝong man bad hir be of good counfort and loke wel aboute hir for þere þat sche was hir son schuld be as he seide. Tho loked sche and say Augustin hir son stand in þe same reule
11v / where as sche stood. The wise woman and vsed to swech reuelaciones

35 þ *excised before* eye 40 for to deye] for deye *MS* 42 fell he *in left margin; red ^ ^ in text and margin*

1 ca *excised before* erroure 6 lord *in right margin after* oure 10 cher] c *added with two //*

34 cunnyng withoute charite] Jordanus: 'scientia sine caritate non edificet sed inflat'. The ascription to Paul (1 Cor. 8.1) is by Capgrave.

37 erroure of þe Maniches] Manichaeism, a radically dualistic system opposed to Christian theology. The stress on certain Pauline statements gave it a Christian tinge. See Frend, JEH (1953) 13-26 and Decret, *Afrique Manicheenne.*

42 Many mo heresies] the caveat is by Capgrave.

took of þis a gret counfort, vndirstanding herby þat sumtyme sche schuld se him standing in þe same feith where þat sche stood.

Aftir þis not longe she comound þis visioun with hir son, and seyd onto him þat sche hoped for to se him a trewe Cristen man or sche deyid, for þis consolacion had sche fro heuene and þis voys proporcioned to hir ioye: 'Wher þat þou art þere schal he be.' 'Nay', quod Augustin to his modir, 'ȝe vndyrstand þe wordis amys; he seide, "Þere þat I am þere schulde ȝe be."' 'Nay son, nay', quod sche, 'I vndirstod ful and noted his wordes. He seid not, "Þere þat he is þere schal þou be," but "Þere þat thou art, þere schal he be."' Thus was þe woman in hir consolacioun stabil and coude not be led oute fro hir trewe beleue with no sophisticacioun þat hir son coude make.

Sche receyued anoþir consolacioun be an holy bischop þat was gretly lerned in holy scripture and gretly excersised to lede men fro erroure. To þis man went sche oft, desiring of him þat he wold speke with hir son and comoun with him in þat heresie, and schew þe fals and þe onresonable doctrine whech þat heresie susteyned. The bischop answerd to hir ageyn and seide, 'Forsoth þi son as ȝet is not disposed for to be led ony bettir weye, for he is neuly come onto þis doctrine and mech redyer for to purpos ques-
12r tiones þane to receuye ony doctrine. Wher/fore be my councel suffir him for a tyme, & pray to God for him withoute ony letting; and þou schal se þat he in his redyng and in his stodie schal aspie ful wel in what erroure he is falle, and who many horible þingis þat it techith. For I was sumtyme deceyued with þe same doctrine and had ful grete corage to lerne þe noueltes þerof, but þorw þe mercy of oure lord with long redyng of her bokes I aspied þat it was a secte rather to be fled þa[n] folowid.' This answere myth not suffise to þe woman, so grete desire was in hir hert þat he schuld speke with hir son; so þat þe bischop was compelled to voyde hir with swech wordys: 'Go fro me woman, go fro me with þis sikyrnesse. It is impossible þat a child whech hath so many teres wept for him schuld perisch.' This wordis of þe bischop imprended sche in hir mynde as þouȝ an aungell had spoke hem fro heuene.

17 ont *before* onto *excised* 21 ȝe be *in right margin after* schulde 24 stabil *in right margin after* consolacioun 30 schew] schewid *MS*; id *excised and deleted in red* fals] falshed *MS*; hed *excised and deleted in red* 36 schal] a *interlineated over blotted* a 40 þan] þat *MS* 45 wordis] is *added in red*

14 vsed to swech reuelaciones] Capgrave expands upon Jordanus' "magne fidei."

27 an holy bischop] *Conf.* 3.12.

What þat he ded fro þe tyme þat he was xx ȝere onto xxix. Capitulum viii

At þe age of xx ȝere he dwelt stille at Cartage and þe maystires þat were, redde him þe book of Aristotle cleped his *Cathegories*. We clepe hem at þese dayes þe *Predicamentis*. Augustinus gat þis book of his maystir and hom to his chambir he went, red it, vndirstood it withoute ony techere. For in þe iiii book of his *Confessiones* he is aknowe þat alle þe bokes of philosophie or gemetrie or arsmetrik or ony of þe vii sciens whech he myth haue at leysere, he vndirstood hem withouten
12v maystir / or withoute ony techere.

Aftir he was þus lerned in philosophie and oþir dyuers sciens, he cam first hom into þe cite where he was bore and þere taute he gramere, meruelyng alle þe cuntre of þe noble reules þat he had founde to redinesse of childirn þat schuld lerne. Whan he had kept þis exersise longe in his owne cite, tho he resorted ageyn onto Cartage and þere taute he retorik on þe moost excellent wise. In þe xxvi ȝere of his age he wrote iii bokes onto a rethorician of Rome. Þei cleped him Hermes. Þese bokes be intituled *De pulcro & apto*, þat is to sey in Englisch 'Of þing whech is fayre and able'. Þei ar not in hand now; I coude neuyr speke with man þat sey hem. For his bokes whech he mad aftir he was Cristen be more in deynte þan þoo whech he mad before.

In þe xxix ȝere of his age spak he with Faustus, a grete snare of the deuele, for þis man was þe moost famous heretik of alle þe Manicheis. But he was ful famous in fayre endytyng, ffor he mad a ful cursed book ageyn

13 he *interlineated in red* 15 *erasure before* onto gramer *deleted in text*; retorik *in right margin* 17 Hermes *in left margin; red // in margin and text*

4 *Cathegories*] translation attributed to Augustine by Alcuin, but it is probably by Boethius. See Minio-Paluello, *Opuscula* 1-27.

14 Whan he...longe] probably a misreading of Jordanus: 'in sua ciuitate Thagatensi scholas regens...regressus Carthaginem pluribus annis in ibi docuit rethoricam'. From *Conf.* 4.4 it appears that Augustine taught one year in Thagaste.

16 In þe xxvi ȝere of his age] detail by Capgrave.

17 Hermes] Jordanus recte, Hyerius; a Syrian who mastered Greek and Latin eloquence.

18-19 Þei ar not in hand now] They had been lost in Augustine's time. Cf. *Conf.* 4.13: 'Non enim habemus eos, sed aberraverunt a nobis, nescio quo modo'.

22-23 a grete snare of the deuele] *Conf.* 5.3; Augustine admits (*Conf.* 5.6) that despite personal charm, and a penchant for the right word, Faustus's inability to deal with his doubts weakened his adherence to Manichaeism.

oure feith, to qwech book þis same Augustin mad notable answeres in a grete volume whech conteynyth xxxiii bokes. The cause whi Faustus was desired for to cum speke with Augustin is þis: Augustin had many questiones with þe Manicheis of her feith and of here lawe, and aspied so many notable errouris in here bokes, þat he ne non of hem coude make no answere to his resones. Tho seid þei whan þei were concluded with argu-
13r mentis on alle sides þat Faustus schuld come and he schuld make / answere onto alle þese motyues. For Faustus was in swech opinion amongis hem þat whos[o]ever folowid him and was conuersaunt with him, þei saide þat he folowid no man but rather þe Holy Goost.

So Faustus is come to Cartage anon. As he was come, Augustin with certeyn of his felawchip went onto him. There had þei too grete communicacioun of þoo questiones for whech þei were in trouble before. And withinne fewe dayes Augustin aspied wel [þ]at Faustus was a mery man and a iocunde, a fayre spoke man eke, but not gretly grounded in sciens. Tho began Augustin to reherse onto him þe doutes and þe articules compound afore & writyn in billis ageyn Manicheis lawe. Faustus, whan he had aspied þe grete cunnyng of Augustin and þe sotil inuectiones whech he mad, he durst not dispute with him; but before hem alle he was fayn to sey þat he coude not answere to þo motiues. Fro þis day forward had Augustin no deynte in here bokes whan þat he say here grete maystir and here prince coude not satisfie his resones. Thus lyued he with suspense mynde in grete doute what secte he schuld hold or what wey he schuld take. Al þis is touchid in þe v book of his *Confessiones*.

Who Augustin aftir this went to Rome. Capitulum ix

Certeyn frendis þat he had at þat tyme, seing þe grete desire of lernyng in him, ȝoue him councel þat he schuld go to Rome, and þis was here cause: ffor at Cartage both he and his disciples were lettid gretly with felauchip and reuel. And as þei herd sey and
v summe / of hem knew it by experiens, at Rome was more liberte ȝoue onto

25 in *interlineated before* a grete 26 xxxiii] iii *interlineated* 28 lawe *interlineated with red* ^ 33 whosoeuer] whoseeuer *MS* 38 þat] what *MS* 39 grounded] groundes *MS; excised and deleted in red* 46 not *interlineated* he *in right margin in red*

26 grete volume] *Contra Faustum libri 33*, CSEL 25.251-797. Jordanus does not mention this work.

5 lettid gretly with felauchip and reuel] Augustine, *Conf.* 5.8, admits that the desire for money and fame were factors, but not motivating reasons.

skoleres, and more quiete þan was at Cartage. This same desire þat was in his hert was þe dispensacion of oure lord. For oure lord knew ful wel where he schuld be conuerted, and what tyme, and had ordeyned before þe menes and the minstres and þe places as he wold dispose.

Thus he disposed him fully for to saile to Rome. His modir folowid him to þe seside, for sikirly sche wil go with him, and he disseyued hir in þis manere. He feyned first þat þei had no wynd, ne likly non for to haue many day. Wherfore he desired þat sche schuld goo to hir in ageyn, and whan tyme cam he wold clepe hir. To þis wold not sche consent, for fro his presens wold sche not. Tho with grete bisinesse he councelled hire for to abide as for þat nyth in a oratorie þat was consecrat in þe name of Seint Cipriane, for it was ny þe schip. And sikirly he told hire þat þe next day þei wold saile. Thus deceyued he his modir, for þat same nyth þei pulled up sail & stale þe schip from hir.

Al þat nyth lay sche praying and sobbing, desiring of oure lord þat þei schuld no wynd haue til þat sche cam. In þe morow whan sche cam to þe brynk and say þe schip goo, þan wept sche intollerablely and filt þe eres of God with grete compleintis; and ȝet wist sche not what ioye God wold cause hire of his absens. Thus went sche hom ageyn and prayed for him deuly, and he went forth to Rome.

14r When he was com þidir he felle / in greuous seknesse, & his moder knew not þat; but þouȝ he were absent sche prayed for him deuly, þat oure lord schuld send hir ioye of hir son. For in þis mater sche had more sorow for him þan euyr sche had to bryng him forth onto þe world. Euery day sche offered for him at þe auter; euery day sche gaf elmesse. Twyes on þe day went sche to cherch, not for to telle veyn tales, but for to here tydyngis of oure lord of heuene in deuoute sermones, or elles for here diu[in]e seruyse, þat God schuld accept hir prayeres whech were principali for þe goostly helth of hir son Augustin. Be hir prayeres Austyn is now rered fro his seknesse and hath begunne for to do þing for whech he was come, þat is to seye to tech rethorik. Many disciples he gadered onto his skole and his fame began fast to springe.

8 lord^2 *in left margin in red;* ^ ^ *in text and in margin* wl *before* wel *excised and deleted* 21 lord *in right margin in red* 23 intollerablely] r *interlineated* 28 þouȝ *extended into right margin* 33 diuine] diue *MS*

8 For oure lord knew] this aside on Providence is by Capgrave.

11-38 Capgrave expands the episode of Augustine's desertion of Monica and her subsequent prayers on his behalf.

Who Austin eke was sent to Melan to lerne hem rethorik. x

At þis tyme þe cyte of Melan wher Seynt Ambrose was bischop sent onto þe meyre of Rome, whech hith Symachus, praying him þat he wold sende onto hem a weel lerned man for to teche here iuuent rethorik. And he with ful good avise sent hem Austyn, a proued maystir, as he wrote, and a man of grete cunnyng. Thus be þe prouidens of God cam Austyn to Melan, and þere felle in knowlech of Seynt Ambrose þe bischop, a noble man and a holy, knowyn þorw alle þe world.

Ambrose receyued Augustin ful faderly and cherischid him in þe best manere. Augustin went oft onto cherch for to here Ambrose preche, not for 14v [to] lerne / treuthes of oure feith ne nowt to amende þe erroures of his soule, but only to aspie wheithir his fame and his speche acorded. For he was noted þorwoute Itaile a fayre spoke man and gretly roted in rethorik. Thus went oure Augustin day be day only to reporte þe wordis; for þe sentens had he smal delite, and ȝet as he is aknow in his *Confessiones*, þe wordes of Seynt Ambrose abiden in his soule magre his hed, and were dayly grucching ageyn swech lif as he had. Happed on a day oure fadere Ambrose prechid of þe incarnacioun of oure lord Ihesu Crist, who þat for þe special loue whech he had to mankynde he disdeyned not to take þe flesch and blood of man with alle þe infirmites saue synne. Augustin stood in þe puple and sodeyn fere felle upon him, so þat þe þoutes whech were pryuy withinne him mad his face pale and his body for to tremel þat alle þe puple myth aspie it. Aftir þe sermon was ended he went onto Ambrose and told him of his new chaunge and who longe he had ben in þe Manicheis heresie, and who sith þat tyme þat he spak with Faustus þat secte was ferre fro his plesauns. Whan Ambrose herd þat he had no trost ne no confidens in þe heresie of þese Manicheis, he þankid God heyly, and because he knew wel be inspiracioun of þe Holy Gost what Augustin schuld be, he treted him ful fadirly with swete exhortaciones, þinking with swech menes to brynge

8 a noble] and noble *MS*; nd *excised and deleted* 10-11 for to lerne] for lerne *MS* 27 in *interlineated before* þe heresie 28 God *deleted in text*; Gost *in right margin in red*

2 Seynt Ambrose] while governor of Milan and still a catechumen, Ambrose (c. 339-397) was chosen bishop by popular acclamation. His preaching and eloquence were important in the conversion of Augustine, *Conf.* 5.13, 14.

3 Symachus] Quintus Aurelius Symmachus, a pagan patrician, prefect until 385.

18 prechid of þe incarnacion] this detail is not in the *Confessions*; Jordanus took it from Dacius. See note to Cap. 17/48-49, below.

15r him to þe trew beleue. Tho Augustin cast in his hert fully to / despise þe Manicheis heresi foreuyr; þe feith of Crist he purposed for to take, but baptized wold he not be onto þe tyme þat he myth know þe treuthis of Cristis feith.

In what maner his moder sowt him. Capitulum xi

In þis same tyme, Monicha, his modir, took þe se and put hirselue to grete perel for to se hir son. Hir grete feith and hope þat sche had in God, hire grete charite þat sche had to conuercioun of hir son, mad þe womannes hert bold and in maner turned it to a mannes hert, þat not only sche wanted feer or dred in þe se, but þe schipmen whech were aferd sche counforted in þe best maner, saying onto hem in þis manere: 'Beth of good counfort seres, for treuly I had a visioun fro heuene þat we schul skape þis iornay ful weel.'

Sche is come to lond and to þe speche of hir son, and aftir longe daliauns he told hire pleynly þat oute of Manicheis skole was he go foreuyr, but onto Cristis skole whech sche desired him to come was he not parfithly entred. ȝet whan sche herd him sey þis sche hopped with ful mery chere þat sche had o part of hire desire, for too þingis desired sche: on þat he were delyuered fro þat fals heresie of þe Manichees, and þat was fulfilt; þe oþir þat sche schuld se him a trew Cristen man, and þis sche hoped. With a grete spirith and a merie chere sche cried and seide, 'Now beleue I in my lord God þat or my soule passe out of þis world I schal se him a trew Cristen man.' Than sent sche praieres onto heuene with grettir bisinesse þan
15v euyr sche ded, þat oure lord schuld hast þis matere / & make brith þe þirknesse of Augustines soule. Sche loued Ambrose as an aungel of God, for be him sche wist weel þat hir son was brout þus to swech fluctuacioun. Fluctuacioun calle we here whan a man is broute fro an euel entent, and ȝet þe same man stand in study wheithir he schal to þe good wey or nowt. In þis plith stood oure Austyn.

1 In what...sowt him *in right margin* 6 fer *excised before* feer 13 chere *interlineated in red* 14 o part of] o part of part *MS; latter* part *excised* 19 heuene] ne *interlineated in red with red* ^ bisinesse] *medial* e *interlineated over blotted* e

3-9 The description of Monica's heart as being like that of a man, and her exhortation to the sailors are by Capgrave; Jordanus following *Conf.* 6.1, reads 'pollicens eis peruencionem cum salute'.

23-25 Fluctuacion...Austyn] the gloss is Capgrave's.

The custom of his moder and eke of þe cuntre whill sche dwelt in Affrik was to offer bred and potage and wyn at þe aucteris where martires were byried. And þis custom was forbode hire be þe kepere of þe cherch at Melane, seying onto hir þat it was þe bischoppis wil, Ambrose, þat swech mete and drynk sche schuld ȝeue to pore men, and to þe memories of þe martires sche schuld brynge, he seid, a deuoute soule ful of holy prayeres. Whan sche herd þis, deuoutely sche chaunged hir vse aftir þat informacioun. Seynt Augustin hir son tellith of hire þat sche used to fast þe Satirday as deuoute folk ded þan at Rome. And þo persones þat ete and dronk with hire continuely at Melane saide þat it was not þe vsage þere at Melane, wherfor hir dyuersite was in maner of a slaundir to þe cumpany. In þis matere sche took councell of Seyn Ambrose, and he sette hir þis reule, þat wheresoeuyr sche cam sche schuld do aftir þe custom of þe felauchip whech sche dwelt in.

In þis same tyme come too of Augustin grete frendis onto hi[m], Alipius and Nebridius. This Alipius was bore in þe same town where Augustin
16r was bore, and Nebridius bore fast be Cartage, / where he had faire possession. But it likid him bettir to forsake alle þat he had and come to dwelle with Augustin. These iii men togidir at Melane had grete councell and grete stody what maner secte þei schuld chese and what lyf þei schuld hald. At þese dayes was Augustin xxx ȝere of age. So alle iii were acorded first to chese hem wyues and alle sex dwelle in on hous, and þei for to stody swech bokes as þei wold haue and do non oþir bisinesse. Than was alleggid amongis hem what sorow þere schuld be if þei acorded not, & specialy for her wyuys who þe[i] schuld lyue if distauns fel betwix. God oure lord had ordeyned anoþir wey, and for þat cause he put a delay in þat matere, for he suffered þe hert of Augustin to be sette on swech a mayde and of so ȝong age þat he must nede abyde tyl sche were able.

27 was *in right margin in red with red* ^ 37 hir] his *MS*; s *excised in red*; r *interlineated in red* 40 him] hinn *MS* 49-50 & specialy... betwix *in right margin with endings cropped* 50 þei] þe *MS*

26-33 The custom of his moder...] *Conf.* 6.2.

33-39 sche used to fast þe Satirday...] not in Jordanus; from Augustine's letters, 34 and 56, CSEL 34.62 and 160.

40-41 Alipius and Nebridius] life-long friends of Augustine. Alipius, a native of Tagaste and later its bishop; Nebridius, well-to-do Carthaginian with a philosophical bent. Correspondence between him and Augustine (*Epistolae*, 3-14, CSEL 34.4-35) gives evidence of his depth.

46-47 So alle iii...chese him wyues] Capgrave's addition from *Conf.* 6.14., but there were 5, not 3 couples: 'videremur nobis esse posse decem ferme homines'.

On what maner oure lord suffered Alipius to be appechid of theft. xii

This processe tellȝ Augustin in þe vi book of his *Confessiones* in þis maner. Alipius, he seith, was at Cartage stodying in rethorik. It was þe vsage at þoo dayes þa[t] þe rethoricianes schuld pleten in court for euery cause whech was litigious. This Alipius, a litil before þe court schuld be hold, walkyd alone with his reporting tables in his hand stodying ful bysily, for it was his cours þat day for to plete. Beneth þat hous where he walked was housyng be þe ground in whech dwelt coynoures of siluyr and wroute þere ful bisily. Owt of þe strete comth a ȝong child, a theef, with an ex in his hand, and went on to a certeyn roof whech was cured with leed, and euene ouyr þe coynouris hous he began for to
16v hewe. / The coynouris herd þe noyse and sent up too or thre of here felauchip to loke what theef was so bold þat tyme of þe day and so ny þe dome place to stele þe metall of þe houses. The boy herd men com with grete noyse; he left his exe þere and ran hom in grete hast. Thus com þe men and se no persone þere but Alipius alone. Þei se þe led broke, þei fynde þe ex by, and on him þei go alle and areste him for þis dede. Alipius, þat was innocent and because of his study took non hed at þe boy, neythir whan he cam ne whan he went, is þus led forth as a theef onto þe iuge.

Happed a man þat knew him, and knew what vertue he was of, for to mete him with þese tormentouris. He pulled him o side and inqwired of him who þis myth be, a man & of swech birth and swech kunnyng þat he schuld be take in swech defaute. He seid it was grete merueile. Alipius answerd onto him and told him þat he was ongilty in þis matere, but he had mynde þat he say a boy renne fro þe place and leue þere his ex. The man caused þat þei turned alle ageyn into þe same strete, and as it happed þe same boy stood in þe dore þat had doo þe dede. This man whech ȝaue so grete fauoure onto Alipius took þe ex in hand. Rith þus he seide onto þe boy: 'Here haue we founde an exe. Knowest þou owt to whom it schuld longe?' 'Ȝa, forsoth sere', seide he, 'þat same ex is oure.'

Thus was Allipius wrongfully attached and meruelously delyuered. God
17r almyty suffered þis, as Augustin writith / in his *Confessiones*, for to lerne him whech schuld be aftirward a iuge of mennes soules in þe cherch, þat he schuld not deme ouyr sone of signes owtward.

5 þat] þa *MS* 17 Þei[1]] i *added in red* 27 caused] cause *MS*; d *interlineated* 29 to *before* so grete *excised*

1-35 Not in Jordanus; the entire Cap. 12 is from *Conf.* 6.9.

Who he went to Simpliciane. xiii

Now is Augustin dryuyn so ferre þat he is fully consentid to go be þe wey of Crist, but because of þe hardnesse of it, he was ful loth þerto. But oure merciable lord putte a new counfort in his hert þat he schuld go to an hermyte in þe desert fast by Melan, whech hermyte hith Simpliciane. Augustin had herd mech þing of him þat he had serued God in ful vertuous lyf, and þe fame was trewe in dede. This man Simpliciane lyued in a monastery fast by Melan with othir heremites of holy lyf at þe costis & expens of Seynt Ambrose. For Seint Ambrose had Simpliciane in so grete reuerens þat he worchipid him as his fader and aftir his deth asined onto his clerkis and his puple to be chose bischop successoure onto him and so it was in dede. To þis Simpliciane teld Augustin þe besinesse of his hert, in who many errouris he had falle an[d] what dowte he stood in to what lyf he schuld drawe. The good fader Simpliciane gaf him exhortacioun to folow þe meknesse of oure lord Ihesu and despise þe fals delectacionis of þis world. He rehersed onto him eke a grete exaumple of þe conuercion of on Victorine, a worthi man, a grete rethorician, a famous philisophre whech man for grete sciens had a statua rered to his liknesse in the markette at Rome. This same man cam to Simpliciane often tyme and
17v inqwired of him many þingis, and oft tyme wold say / onto Simpliciane: 'Knowe now wel þat I wil be a Cristen man.' Simplician wold say agayn onto him: 'I wil not beleue it til þat I se þe withinne þe kirk.' And Victorine wold þanne in scorne conclude be maner of an argument: 'Ergo þe wallis of þe cherch make a Cristen man.' This iteration of wordis was oft tyme vsed betwix þese too men, but at þe last oure lord enspired soo Victorines hert þat sodeynly he seid to Simpliciane: 'Go we to þe cherch, for in very treuth I wil be a Cristen man.' Thus was þis worthi man conuerted to þe feith; and al þis told Simpliciane to Augustin þat he schulde folow his steppis. Be þis holy fader Simpliciane was Augustin brovt onto þis desire þat al maner worldly delectacioun displesed him, for þe loue of his hert is now only sette to serue God. He say many men in þe cherch lyuyng in sundry manere, summe þus & summe þus. Wherfore he hatȝ not chose as ȝet þe lyf whech he wil lede.

13 and] an *MS* 16 of[2] *interlineated in red before* þe conuersion

1 Simpliciane] succeeded Ambrose as bishop of Milan in 397.

9 at þe costis & expens of Seynt Ambrose] a detail not in Jordanus.

17 Victorine] Marius Victorinus, born c. 300, was forced to resign from a prestigious professorship in Rome during the reign of Julian the Apostate. His works have recently been published: CCL 83. I Exegetical (1971), II Theological (1981).

19-33 The details of Victorine's conversion are provided by Capgrave.

Off þe comyng of Poncian onto Augustin and of what þingis þei talked of. Capitulum xiiii

In þis tyme was Augustin & Alipius dwellyng togidyr, for Nebridius was not with hem at þat tyme. So happed it þat a man of court whech was dwellyng in þe paleys at Rome whos name was Ponciane, because he was bore in Affrica rith as þei were, cam onto hem to se her welfare as þe maner of men is whech be bore in straunge cuntre & dwelle fer fro hom. He fonde hem sittyng in a hous and befor hem a bord on
18r whech þei vsed to pleye certeyn games / to refresch with þe sadnesse of her study. Vpon þis bord lay a book, whech book Ponciane supposed had be of sum seculere sciens whech as þei vsed. Poncian vnsperd þe bok and say wel þat it was a bok longing to Cristen feith, whech bok we clepe þe epistoles of Seynt Paule. This Ponciane with myry chere mad in manere of a þankyng to God þat Augustin his cuntreman was falle into studye of swech holy bokes, for þis same Ponciane had neuly take cristendham and was a stedfast and a trewe Cristen man. Augustin sayde onto him þan þat al þe felicite of his study was only ȝoue to rede swech bokes.

Tho begunne þei to speke of þe dyuers cumpanyes of holy heremites whech dwelled in wildyrnesse both in Itale and in Egipt, and in special of grete Antonie whos name was ful famous to alle þe seruauntes of God; but to Augustin and his felawes it was onknowyn onto þat houre, ffor whech cause he satte ful stille and herd Ponciane with grete silens. Ponciane told him who he & oþir thre felawis þat dwelt with þe emperoure went on a day into the wodis to her disport, and happed Ponciane and his felaw to walk in þe o side of þe wode and þe oþir too felawes in þe othir side. On of þese too with whech Poncian was not, cam into a caue where a heremyte dwelled, whech heremite was uphap into þe cite for to fecch him mete, and fond þere a book with Seynt Antonies lyf. He sat down and red it, and in þe redyng was sodeynly compunct to forsake þe world. Thus saide he þan
18v / onto his felaw: 'Here in þis same place I purpose me foreuyr to serue God and þis same houre I wil begynne. If þou list not to do as I wil, I pray þe grucch not my dede.' His felaw answered agayn on þis manere þat he wold not part cumpany, but swech lif as he hath chose he wil folow: to forsake al þis world and leue þere in solitarie lif. Ponciane and his felaw sey þe

1 g *with / added to* comyn

5 Ponciane] Jordanus, 'Poncianus'; cf. *Conf.* 8.6. 'Ponticianus'.

20 grete Antonie] St. Athanasius wrote his life (PG 26.835-978); Evagrius translated it into Latin (PL 73.1225-170).

27 whech heremite was unhap into þe cite] the hermit's absence is Capgrave's addition.

sunne draw fast to inclinacioun, sout þese oþir too felawis, fonde hem and hasted hem homward, for þe day was ny at a ende as þei saide. Tho told þei her holy purpose onto hem, what avow þei had mad whech þei wold not breke. Ponciane and his felaw praised here entent, and þankyng God of her holy conuercion went ageyn onto þe paleys. Thus dwelt þese men stille þere in þat caue perseuering in holy lif. And to ȝong women whech schuld be weddid onto hem, be here exhortacion avowid here maydenhed to God.

What sorow Augustin mad aftir þis exhortacioun. xv

Grete sorow and horribil ran in Augustin mynde þanne, whan he had herd þese holy exaumples of þe seruauntis of God, whech seruauntis oure lord God had brout fro þe grete blaknesse of synne onto þe faire white vertuous lyuyng. For alle þese exaumples had Augustin gadered into þe bosom of his hert, whech brent him ful sore and mad him aschamed þat he was not þus disposed. And whan Ponciane had take his leue & was go, thoo Augustine with a troubled mynde
19r began / to loke upon his felaw Alipius, and with a sobir voys he cried: 'What suffir we? What are þese þingis þat we here? These onlerned men rise and sodeynly wynne heuene and we with alle oure doctryne are drenchid euene in helle. Because þei went before us, þerfor schul we be aschamed to folow hem?' Whil Augustin saide þese wordes Alipius bisily loked upon him for he pronounsed not his wordis as he was wone to doo. For nowt only were þese wordes expressed with laboure of his tunge, but his forhed, chekis, his eyne and alle his membres in maner laboured in pronounsyng of þese wordes.

Sodeynly þanne he stirt fro þat hous in whech he had herd þese þingis and into a gardeyn whech was annexid to þat hous he stert. Alipius folowid him foot be foot, merueling sore of þe sodeyn compunccion þus neuly com. Thus þei sat in þe gardeyn as fer fro þe hous as þei myth sitte, and Augustin began to accuse himself sore in þe sith of oure lord of the slauth of his returne to God; and þe grete hepes of synne whech he had vsed he gadered onto mynde whech mad him for to wepe plenteuously. And þat he schul haue þe more leysere to wepe, he roos fro his felaw Alipius and went onto a figge tre. There he þrew himselue down vndyr þe tre and swech lament-

4 brout] broun brout *MS*; broun *excised* 15 of his tunge *in right margin in red with red* ^ *in text*

12 Capgrave substitutes 'helle' for Jordanus' 'carne et sanguine'.

able voyses he þrew onto heuene: ‘O blissed lord, who longe, who longe, who longe wilt þou suffir, lord, þat I go so ferre fro þi seruyse and differre my conuercion fro day to day? Tomorow schal it be, tomorow? Why not
19v now, lord? Whi schal not þis same houre / make an ende of alle my filth?’

Whil he lay þus with grete contricion of hert and with ful sobbyng voys uttirryng alle þese wordes, al sodeynly he herd a voys as þouȝ it had ben at þe next hous soundyng þese same wordes: ‘Tak and rede, take and rede.’ Tho began he forþink withinne himselue if childyrn with ony game þat þei vse had ony swech wordes in her playing, and he coude not þink þat he had herd ony swech. He þout þan þat þis voys cam fro heuene, ȝeuyng him a warnyng þat he schuld ope þe bok whech he brout with him fro þe hous onto þe gardeyn, and þe first letter þat his eye felle upon he schuld rede. Thus ded he and þese same wordis red he: *Non in com[m]essacionibus & ebrietatibus, non in cubilibus & impudiciciis, non in contencione & emulacione, sed induimini dominum Ihesum Christum et carnis curam ne feceritis in desideriis.* The sentens of þis texte may be englischid in þis wise: Not in grete festis, ne in dronknesse, not in soft couchis and in scha[m]ful dedis, not in strif a[n]d envye but be clad with oure lord Ihesu & fulfille not þe bisinesse of þe flesch in his desires. He sperd þe bok whan he had red þis, and leyd at þe same reson a merk be whech he myth rydily turne þertoo, for þis same texte put in his hert a lite of swech a grace þat alle þe derk errouris whech he had hold were passed awey fro him.

Tho toke he þe book onto his felaw Alipius and with his fynger or sum othir tokne schewid him þe clause before red. Alipius red ferþer whech Augustin had not red and schewid to Augustin what it was þat folowid. Thus folowith in þe texte: That man þat is feynt in þe feith loke ȝe be /
20r redy for to receyue. Into þe hous þei go both. Þere þei fynde þe blessed woman Monicha, þe modir of Augustin. Þei told hir al þis processe, þat sche whech had be in so mech sorow for hir son schuld haue part of his new ioye. Sche þankid God with ful humbil hert þat oure lord had graunted hir hir long desire & mech more þat sche desired. For not only he had brout him to purpos to be a Cristen man, but he had stered his hert to despise al þis worldly plesauns.

39 Ad romanos 13 *in left margin beside the quotation* commessacionibus] comessacionibus *MS* 43 schamful] schalful *MS* 44 and] ad *MS* 47 his] s *interlineated* 51 þat *interlineated in red with red* ^ 58 him *interlineated in red*

39 red he] Capgrave omits Jordanus’ reference to reading ‘in silencio’.

39-42 Romans 13:13-4; the English translation is of course provided by Capgrave.

45 He sperd the bok] the detail is Capgrave’s.

Who he left his skole of rethorik only to haue his hert fre to God. xvi

Now began his hert to be sette stedfastly in oure lord, for þoo vanytees and þoo opinyones in whech he had before ful grete ioye now are þei falle clene fro him, and þat skole whech was a peyne to him þat he schuld leue it, now for to leue it, it is to him ioye. But ȝet him þout for to leue his skole sodeynly and his skoleres desolat þat it was not best, ffor þe heruest dayes were ny whan skole is wone to cese. So longe he þout for to suffir hem þat þei schuld solemply goo fro him. Whan xx dayes were go for, þan entred þe cessacion whech dayes were onto him longe, for þe grete desire þat he had to serue God with more solitarie lif; than was he dysmittid of his grete laboure whech he had in teching of rethorik.

And because þat al his desire was for to prey and study solitarily, he left þe cite of Melan and forth into þe cuntre he went into a feld þei cleped Cassiate, to a place longing to a worchipful man cleped Verecundus. This
20v Verecundus graunted him to dwelle þere / onto þe tyme þat he schuld be baptized. So in þis same place abood he and Alipius and oþir frendis of his with his modir, alle in o desire to forsake þe delectable onstabilnesse of þis world.

And in þis same place mad Augustin dyuers bokes, þat is to sey a book *De achademicis* whech soundeth in oure tonge of oncerteyn opiniones. For Achademia was a town where Plato tawt, and alle þoo disciples of þat skole

3 lord *interlineated in red with red* ^ 9 hem] h *traced over* ?s 15 þei] þe *MS*; i *added in red*

16 Cassiate] Jordanus, 'Cassiaco'; *Conf.* 9.3, 'Cassiciaco'. Two locations have been suggested: present day Cassago de Bianza, 35 kilometres, and Casciago, 55 kilometres from Milan. Perler, *Les voyages*, 179-196, on the basis of linguistic, archaeological and geographic factors, holds that Cassago de Bianza is the most likely site of ancient Cassiciacum.

16 Verecundus] a pagan married to a Christian hoped to join the projected philosophical community (cf. Cap. 11/40-45 above). Augustine, *Conf.* 9.3, pays tribute to this generous and devoted friend.

22 *De achademicis*] Jordanus mentions the title only; Capgrave's confused explanation, which posits two books, stems, perhaps, from Augustine's ambivalence in *Retract.* 1.1, CCL 47.7. 'Nondum baptizatus *Contra achademicos* uel *De achademicis* primum conscripsi'.

22-26 For Achademia was a town where Plato tawt] in the suburbs of Athens where Plato had acquired property. The term Academy may have derived from a gymasium built there to honour a certain Hecademus.

held þis opinion þat no þing is sette in certeyn. This book of Augustin serueth not mech, for he was fayn aftir to make a book ageyn þis secte, and þat is cleped *Contra achademicos*. Aftir þis he mad anoþir book in þat same place whech he clepith *De ordine*, in whech book as me semyth he tretith be what order or what forme a man schuld studie. The þird book mad he in þat same place whech he clepith *De beata uita*, þat is to sey Of þe blessed lyf. The cause whi he mad þis book is þis. Many men in þis world, specialy þe hethen men, mad a gret feest þat day þat þei were bore. Augustin had vsed þis al his lyf onto þat tyme. So happed þat day to falle þe same tyme þat he dwelt in þat possession of þe forsaid man Verecundus. And because he wold chaunge þat fleschly fedyng into goostly talkyng, þerfor with his moder and certeyn of his frendis he mad þat day þat book where he disputeth what we schuld calle þe blissed lyf. Alle þe cumpany saue his moder saide it is a blessed lyf a man for to haue alle þat he desireth. His
21r modir put moo wordis onto þis diffinicioun. Sche saide / he hath a blessed lif whech hath al þat he desirith, and eke þat he desire noþing but good þing. Mech more þing is touchid in þis book, speciali of þe knowlech of God, whech þing as now we may not declare.

Who bisily he red holy scripture and speciali þe psalmes of Dauid & of his baptem. xvii

Now is þe delectacioun of Augustyn only sette in redyng of holy scripture. Grete swetnesse hath he now in þoo lessones whech kyndeled þe fyre of his hert and mad him to encrese sore in þe loue of God. He mad ful grete sorow þat he had be so bold to berke ageyn þese holy letteris whech be swete as hony to þoo soules þat desire heuene. For þei were dewid fro heuene be þe holy vesseles of þe prophetis, and most specialy be oure lord Ihesu and his aposteles. Tho cam Augustin onto þe psalmis of Dauid whech he red with ful ryp deuocyoun. And specialy in iiii psalme þere mad he grete taryng, redyng euery vers by and by with gret sobbyng of hert, with wepyng and lamentable voys. And

2 & of his baptem *extended into margin* 9 lord *interlineated in red*

27 *De ordine*] the description of the book's subject is Capgrave's, but he is far from the mark; Augustine gives a gist of the work (*Retract*. 1.1, CCL 47.7-11) 'utrum omnia bona et mala diuine prouidentiae ordo contineat'.

28 The þird book] Capgrave omits Jordanus' reference to the 'librum Soliloquiorum'.

37-40 His modir...] Capgrave adds Monica's intervention, but omits Jordanus' reference to his letters to Nebridius.

whan he cam to þat vers: *In pace in idipsum dormiam & requiescam*, þan wold he crye: 'A þou pes, a lord, þou art þe very pes in whech we schal both slepe and rest.'

Amongis alle þese swete consolaciones oure lord sent him sum bittirnesse, þat he schuld tast þe loue of oure lord both in bittyr and in swete. For þat same tyme in whech he was come to þis grete deuocioun, he fel in grevous seknesse of þe heed, most special of þe teth, whech peyne encresed so þat he myth not speke. Tho ran it in his mynde for to pray þo men
21v whech were about him to make a / supplicacioun onto oure lord þat he schuld of his mercy relese sum of þis peyne. And because he myth not speke þis for peyne, þerfor he took a peyre tables and wroot in þe wax al his desire þat þei of pite schuld pray for him. And sodeynly, as þei alle sette hem down on knees to pray for him, þe peyne went awey. Of whech chaunge he was gretly astoyned for he had neuyr non experiens of so sodeyn helth in al his lyf.

Tho sent he letteris to Seynt Ambrose, in whech letteris he renounsid foreuyr alle his elde erroures, and in the same letteris he desired of Ambrose þat he schuld assigne him what book of holy scripture was most necessarie for him to rede, be whech redyng he myth be more able and more redy to receyue þe Cristen feith. Ambrose wrote onto him ageyn þat he þout best he schuld rede þe book of Ysaie þe prophete because þat þis book tretith most openly of callyng of hethen men to þe feith. Augustin red þis book and þe beginnyng was passyng straunge onto him, for he had not mech vsed þat maner stile. Wherfor he leyd þis book aside as for a tyme tyll he were more vsed in study of scripture.

Sone aftir þis he went to Melan agay[n] only for he cast him þere to be baptized. And ȝet or he was baptized he mad þere a book whech is intituled *De immortalitate anime*. This book tretith who þat a mannes soule is not dedly but hath lyf foreuer. Aftir þe makyng of þis book he was baptized
22r of Seynt Ambrose þe ȝere of his age xxxiii, in þe pase tyme, in / þe baptisterie whech is halowid to þe name of Seynt Ion Baptist, alle þe cite of Melan standyng aboute meruelyng and praysing God. And þese too men in þe

20 pray] r *with long descender added in darker ink* 26 so *interlineated before* sodeyn 33 þat] þe *MS*; at *interlineated over deleted* e 38 agayn] agay *MS*

40 *De immortalitate anime*] PL 32.1021-34; Augustine in *Retract*. 1.5 (CCL 47.15-7), admits that upon re-reading it, he found it almost unintelligible: 'sic obscurus est ut fatiget cum legitur, etiam intentionem vixque intelligatur me ipso'.

42-43 þe baptisterie] built by Ambrose in 378, it was discovered under the piazza of the Milan Duomo in 1960. Cf. articles by Paredi and by Mirabella Roberti, in *Il Battistero Ambrosiano*.

tyme of baptising, whan þe principal sacramental wordes were said, mad þis ympne whech þe cherch vsith now cleped *Te Deum*. Ambrose began þe first vers and Augustin þe secund, and þus þei said it to an ende. This witnesseth a seynt clepid Dacius, bischop aftir of þe same cherch of Melan, in his *Cronycle* whech he mad, þe x book, þe first capitule.

Of his son Adeodate whech was baptized with hym and of oþir alsoo. Capitulum xviii

Augustin had a son be a sengil woman whech folowid upon him where he went as longe as he was hethen, onto þat tyme þat he and his felawis were sette in þat purpos for to wedde wyues of good birth. For aftir þat tyme þe woman sewid him no more. These be his wordis in his *Confessiones* where he seith eke þat he had neuer no woman but hire, ne sche no man but him. O child was bore betwix hem too, whom þei cleped Adeodatus, þat is to seye ȝoue of God, a mal child, a child ful of witte and of vertu. But oure lord took hym sone oute of þis world aftir he was cristened with his fadere. His witte was so gret and so sotill as Augustin tellit þat it passed in conyng many men of grete age and grete experiens. Augustin his fader had gret meruyl of him þat a ȝong þing of xvi ȝere age schuld so meruelously asken questionis, so sotilly argew.
22v His fader had more bisinesse for to / take heed at his questiones þanne at þe answeris whech schuld be ȝoue þertoo. This child with ful grete bisynesse laboured to knowe þe trewe wey of God both in study of sotill sciens and eke folowing with vertuous lyf. But sone aftir his baptem, oure lord took him oute of erde & sette him in swech place where he is sikir of euyrlasting ioye. This same Adeodatus caused his fadere to write þat book

4 tyme þat *in right margin* 6 For *interlineated in red* 7 *long descender excised after* where 12 o *excised before* men 14 ag *excised before* argew

46 *Te Deum*] the earliest reference is in the Rule of St. Benedict, Chapter 11; attribution to Ambrose and Augustine only in the 8th c. See Kaehler, *Studium zum Te Deum*. Capgrave adds the fact that Ambrose and Augustine alternate verses.

48-49 Dacius...in his *Cronycle*] the Chronicle was incorporated by Landulfus Senior in his *Historia Mediolanensis*. See Arbesmann, *Traditio* 1 (1943) 346-347.

3-8 Augustin had a son...no man but him] Capgrave adds comments on Augustine's mistress from *Conf*. 6.15.

9 Adeodatus] Augustine's natural son appears in *De beata vita* 6.12. *De magistro* grew out of discussions with him. See *Retract*. 1.12, CCL 47.36.

whech tretith of þe quantite of þe soule, for it is a dialoge betwix to, where on makith interogaciones and þe oþir ȝeueth þe answeres. Thus aftir her baptem Augustinus with his felauchip leued in ful grete ioye þat þei had receyued so clene a lif, whech lyf was more dere onto hem þan gold or precious stones.

Who Augustin had grete delite in þe song and ympnis songen in þe cherch of Melan. Capitulum xix

Thus whan he was confermed in þe feith of holy kirk, al þe ioye and þe hope whech he had in þis world he forsok. And in þis tyme myth neuyr his soule be saciat or fulfillid of good desires, most special consideryng who þat oure lord of his hie councell had refreschid mankynde with his presens. He began at þese dayes for to vse þe cherch mech where he herd redyng and synging of delectable materes and swete melodies, whech melody was onto him a ful grete solace. Ambrose had þat tyme mad neuly many ympnys, for alle þe temporal ympnys ar ny of his making, as *Primo dierum omnium* & þoo þat folow. And þis same bisschop Ambrose mad hem to be sunge delectabily with consent of dyuers
23r tewnys whech / had not be used þere before.

The cause whi þat þese newe songis were begunne þus in Ambroses tyme is þis. The emperesse cleped Iustina was infect with þe venemhous heresie of þe Arianes, whech held þat þe Fadere and þe Son and þe Holy Gost be not of o substauns. For þe Son calle þei a creature mad of þe Fadere, and þe Holy Gost clepe þei a creature mad of a creature, þat is to sey, of þe Son. Thei sey ferþermore þat Crist took flesch and blod withouten ony soule. This woman, þus infecte at instauns of certeyn prestis

22 a *excised before* þe oþir 23 felauchip] felauch *in text*, ip *in right margin with* ^ ^

6 who *excised before* consideryng 7 ba *excised before* began 11 omnium *in left margin*; conditor *deleted in text*

21-22 of þe quantite of þe soule] *De quantitate animae*, PL 32.1035-108 written in Rome in the form of a dialogue with Evodius, a member of his circle. See also Cap. 22/21-22.

22-23 aftir her baptem] Capgrave fails to mention that this information is from Dacius. See note to Cap. 17/48-49 above.

9-13 Ambrose had...mad neuly many ympnis...] this digression, from *Conf.* 9.7, is not in Jordanus. Of the 18 hymns attributed to Ambrose, 14 are authentic. See Walpole, *Early Latin Hymns*, 260-264.

16-20 heresie of þe Arianes] explanation by Capgrave.

whech taute hir þat heresie, hated Ambrose for he prechid mech ageyn hem. This persecucion was so gret þat Ambrose was constreyned to kepe þe cherch both nyth and day, and mech of his puple abod stille with him in tuycioun of his person, redy for to deye with her fadere. So for to make hem more lith in here wecch, þis same bischop ded ordeyn swete songis and delectable aftir þe vse of þe cherchis in þe est side of þe world, þat þe puple þus occupied with swech swete songis schuld forgete þe heuynesse and þe perel in whech þei stood.

Eke whan þis persecucioun was ended ȝet þe good custom of þese songis abood stille. For onto þis day þe vse of þe cherch is for to singe his ympnis with mery notes, whech is plesauns to God and a grete encres of mannes deuocyoun, specialy whan þei be songe deuoutly. For in þese songis had Augustin so grete delite þat he herd hem with ful bisy eres, for þei mad him to þink on þo songis whech aungell[is] syng in heuene. And
23v in þis same deuocion be alle / his felawes now whech ar newly baptized. Thus can oure lord make dyuers bodies lyue in on hous, with o soule and on entent in þe seruyse of God.

Who Augustyn aftir þis took an habite of Sympliciane whech his hermytes used. xx

Because þat Simpliciane with his holy exhortaciones had brout Augustin onto þe feith, þerfor had Augustin grete recors onto him, most special aftir his baptem. For of þis same Simpliciane took he þe forme of an habite whech his heremytes vsed aftirward, and he eke. And nowt only þe habite, but þe manere of holy conuersacioun lerned he of þe same Simpliciane, rith as he sey with his eyne. The forme of þis habite is touched in his bokes, where is seid þat þe habite was schape lich a crosse and girt aboue with a girdil whech had no barres. And alle was of blak coloure, þat he schuld neuyr forgete who þat he was hethen sumtyme and lyued in þe blaknesse of synne. Off þis informacioun whech he recey-

34 aungellis] aungell *MS*

5-14 took he þe forme of an habite...] Capgrave misunderstood Jordanus' 'habitum formamque viuendi' and interjects a description of the monastic habit which is anachronous.

9 in his bokes] i.e., the pseudo-Augustinian *Sermones ad fratres in eremo*, PL 40.1235-1358; the quotation here is from *Ad fratres* 5, PL 40.1246. Later he contrasts the garb of the Canons and Hermits (see Cap. 29/19) but omits reference to symbolism.

ued of Sympliciane spekith himselue in a sermone þat he mad and it begynnyth, *In omnibus operibus vestris &c.*

Thus he wrytith þere onto þe prestis whech were gadered be him in þe monasterye at Ypone, he dwellyng in desert as for a tyme with his hermytes. 'What is þe cause þat ȝe grucch for I abood stille with myn heremites alle þese estern halidayes? It plesed me as for þis tyme to departe fro ȝou and dwelle with hem whom, as I haue said often, I haue founden swech as I desire. Whi are ȝe troubled? Be not þei very pore men in Crist
24r and for his loue haue for / sakyn al þis world? Be not þei very buxum onto alle my comaundmentis? And in þe forme of good lyf þei ar fer befor ȝow, ffor be her good exaumples was I turned onto þe rith feith. Euyr haue I loued hem and euyr haue I desired for to folow here holy conuersacioun. Be þat good man Simplician, whech is amongis hem as a foundour, was I broute onto cristendam and lerned in þe feith. Wherfor be ȝe not heuy of myn absens. Do thoo þingis whech are plesaunt onto me and I schal be with ȝou alle dayes onto þe worldes ende.'

Who Augustin went onto Simpliciane and Simpliciane graunted him xii heremites whech went with him to Affrik. xxi

Afftir þis his moder Monicha desired þat he and sche schuld go hom ageyn onto here owne cuntre and leue Melan and alle Itale, for sche had alle hir desire whech sche desired in this world whan sche wist þat he was a trewe Cristen man. Tho went he to Simpliciane and prayed him in most special manere to graunt certeyn persones of his felauchip, whech he wold lede onto his cuntre, as he saide, and leue þere with hem in holy conuersacioun. Simpliciane was ful glad of his desire and graunted him xii þe moost proued men in perfithnesse of alle þat college. So he and his moder and þese xii, with foure of his frendis, Nebridius, Euodius, Alipius & Poncianus, mad hem redy to go to þe see where þei schuld schippe.

Off þis matere spekith þis same glorious doctoure in a sermon whech he mad of iii gendres of munkys. Þus begynnyth þe sermone, *Vt nobis per litteras*, and þus writith he þere: 'These be þe parfite men to whom I drow
24v mech in tyme of myn errour, / be whom eke I receyued þe lith of my feith; & for þe fame of her holinesse was I baptized in Crist. For at þe comaundment of my modere and desire of my frendis, I went onto þat god fadere

3 Monicha desired] Jordanus' 'instigante eius pia matre' is from *Ad fratres*, Sermo 21, PL 40.1268.

Simpliciane and desired of him certeyn persones of his felauchip þat we schuld leue togidyr in þe boundes of charite at hom in my cuntre. And he ful faderly, whan he sey me wepe for swem þat I had whan I schuld depart fro him, graunted me þe same men whech I desired. But whi hope ȝe þat he graunted onto me þis felauchip so redyly? For he knew wel þat my desire was to edifie a monasterie in Affrik in whech we schuld dwelle, folowyng þe steppis of þe apostoles, specialy in forsakyng of worldly richesse and in chois of wilful pouerte. Of þe men whech I led with me fro Simpliciane into Affrik þese be þe names: Anastasius, Fabianus, Seuerus, Nicholaus, Dorotheus, Ysaac, Nicostratus, Paulus, Cirillus, Stephanus, Iacobus & Vitalis.

Off þis Vitalis speketh he specialy in a book cleped *De uerbis domini & apostoli*, in þe sermone lxxxiiii whech beginnyth þus: *Beati apostoli epistola*, where he tellith þat þis Vitalis was a huscher of gramer in Melan or þat tyme whech he cam to þe skole of Simpliciane. So happed him to fynde a grete bagge of gold þat a marchaunt had lost. And anon as he had found it, he sette up scrowes on certeyn gates in Melan, þat what man cowde telle very toknes schuld haue his gold ageyn. The man cam þat had rith þertoo and told him þe very toknes, & he delyuered him his gold with[oute] ony
25r delay. Tho þat / man þat had lost þis mony sey þe treuth of þe fynder, profered him for his laboure xx s. Vitalis wold non receyue. He profered him x s, and þane v s & euyr he refused it. He þat had lost þe mony was in partye wroth with þe fynder for he wold not take for his laboure, þrew down þe bagge saying on þis manere, 'I lost nowt; take þou al.' So was þis Vitalis compelled in partie to receyue þis v s as for his laboure, and he anon gaue it to pore men, kepand to himselue no part. For þis good dede praiseth Seint Augustin þis man, and for þis dede writith he here a comoun proposicion mech used in þe decrees: *Quicquid inuenisti & non reddisti rapuisti*. This is to sey in oure tonge: Whatsoeuyr þou fyndist and gyuyst not ageyn, þou stelist.

35 bagge] ge *interpolated* 36 scl *excised before* scrowes 38 withoute] with *MS* 40 Vitalis] Vitalus *MS*; *one minum of* u *deleted*

28 þese be þe names] the list is originally from *Ad fratres*, Sermo 21, PL 40.1268.

31-49 Off þis Vitalis speketh he...] Capgrave's addition. Augustine tells the story but does not name Vitalis (PL 38.964).

40 xx s] 20 solidi. The solidus was 4th-century Roman currency, but the term was still used in ME to designate a gold coin.

47-48 The Latin maxim and its translation are added by Capgrave; *reddisti* is his form.

Who Augustin with alle þis meny went to Rome to take þe se in Hostia fast by Rome & whi he taried þere. xxii

To alle þis felauchip þus gadered in fere was Monicha a very moder, as goodly and as frendly to hem alle as þouȝ sche had be modere to hem alle, and eke as seruyseable onto hem as þouȝ sche had be doutir onto hem. Fro Melan he went to Rome be Tussie, where he fond many heremites dwellyng in wodes and in feldis, euene sette in þe same purpos in whech he was sette. Alle þese men for þe moost partie he visite with swete exhortacioun of oure lord, with whech both he and þei were ful vertuously refreschid.

Than cam he to Rome and þere herd he mech noyse of þe Manichees, whech were in Rome at þat tyme teching here errouris ful pryuyly be nyth,
25v specialy / for aspying. There, at þe prayere of Cristen men, he mad too bokys: on hith *De moribus Manicheorum*, þe oþir hith *De moribus ecclesie catholice*. This is to sey in Englisch: Of þe maneris of Manicheis, and Of þe maneris of hem þat be in þe Cristen feith. In on of þese bokes tellith he þat þe Manicheis held here skoles be nyth and þedir cam both men and women. And alle sodeynly aftir þe lesson þe lith schuld be blow owt; and þan schuld þei pley, as Wiclif disciples played, 'Sistir me nedith.'

In þis cyte eke, or he went ouyr þe se, mad he þe book of whech we spoke before. It is cleped þe book Of þe quantite of þe soule, whech is mad be maner of a dialoge betwix him and his son Adeodatus, in whech book many sotil þinggis ar touchid whech long not to þis manere of wryting þat is cleped narratyf. In þis same cite and þis same tyme eke mad he a notable

22 be mad *excised before* be maner

6-10 to Rome be Tussie...] the Tuscan trip is apocryphal, part of the legend of Augustine's preference for the Hermits over the Canons. See Arbesmann, *Augustiniana* 6 (1956) 37-145.

13 specialy for aspying] Capgrave's addition.

15-16 This is to sey in Englisch...] Capgrave's addition.

19 'Sistir me nedith'] neither the Wycliffites nor the Manichees were known for sexual excesses; Augustine admits later that the accusation was based on hearsay (Coyle, *De moribus*, 78). However, the use of this catch-phrase to accuse the Wycliffites of such practices is not unique to Capgrave: cf. 'Friar Daw's Reply' (c. 1419-20) to Jack Upland's attack, "who marriþ more matrimonie, ȝe or þe freris? / Wiþ wrenchis & wiles wynnen mennes wyves /...And call on hem for her lessouns with 'Sister me nediþ!' " (in *Jack Upland*, ed. P.L. Heyworth [Oxford, 1968] 99-104).

20-21 þe book of whech we spoke before] see Cap. 18/21-22 above.

22 Adeodatus] see note to Cap. 18/9.

book þat is cleped *De libero arbitrio*, þat is to sey Of þe fre choys þat a man hath to good or to euele. This book was mad in maner ageyn þe Manicheis, for here he determineth agayn hem þat alle euele spryngith of þis fre choys. For þei seid þat euele was coeterne with God. So þei put to þingis coeterne, on called þei good, þe oþir euele. Alle þis þing witnesseth himselue in his first book of his *Retractaciones*.

Who þei went alle in fere fro Rome into Hostie. Capitulum xxiii

Thus alle þing sped at Rome for whech Cristen men had reqwired 26r him in defens of oure feith. With alle his felauchip / he went forth to Hostie. Hostie is a fayre town xvi myle fro Rome, where þat Tibir rennyth into þe se, for *hostium* in þe Latyn tonge is a dore and þat is clepid so as a dore of þe se. There þei abood þe wynd and mad hem redy for to sayle. So upon a day as his moder and he stood lenyng out at a wyndowu and lokyng into a gardeyn whech longid onto her in fer fro pres of puple, þus alone þei too talked ful sobirly of þe euyrlestyn lif whech is ordeyned for blessid soules. Thei talked so long þerof, and lyft up her hertis in contemplacion of þat holy place, þat þei had forgete in maner þis world and alle erdly þing, so were þei rauyschid with her holy wordis. Thei stood stille both a grete while and þout swech þingis as þei coude not vttyr, and eke ageyn in her holy comunicacion þei felle.

Tho saide sche onto hir son swech maner wordis: 'Son, as to my part, I telle I haue no delectacion in no manere þing þat is in þis world. What I schal do in þis world, or why þat I am here so longe, I wote not veryly. Sumtyme I desired to abyde þat I schuld se þe a trew Cristen man or I deyid. God hath graunted me þat and mech more, for I se þe now nowt only a Cristen man, but I se þe a special seruaunt of God, for þou hast despised alle worldly felicite.' This saide sche to hir son with ful sobir chere, and withinne v dayes aftir sche fel in a feuer; whech feuer encresed so sore upon hir þat in maner as for a tyme it had awey hir wittis. And whan sche

11 lyft] left *MS*; y *interlineated over deleted* e 13 with] *bis; first deleted in red* 15 heli *deleted before* her 21 þe *interlineated in red before* a special

25 *De libero arbitrio*] a record of a conversation with Evodius.

28-29 For þei seid þat euele...] Capgave's explanation.

30 *Retractaciones*] *Retractationum libri duo,* CCL 47.1.9.

5 xvi myle fro Rome] accurate according to the English mile then measuring 5000 feet.

6 for *hostium* in þe Latyn tonge...] Capgrave provides the gloss.

was restored ageyn to hir wittis, sche lokid on hir son and þus sayd onto
26v him: 'Wher was I'? Thei þat / stood about were al astoyned and answered not. Than spak sche agayn in þis maner: 'Ley þis body whan I am ded in what place ȝe wil; haue no besynesse in no maner where it schal be byryed. O þing I pray ȝou of specialte: where euyr ȝe be at ony auctere where ȝe schal minstir þe holy sacrament, in þat place haue of me sum special mynd.' Sche had forgetyn, as Augustin tellith, al hir cuntre and þe byrying of hir husbond whech was mad ful costly, and a space left for hir where sche schuld ly. For a litil befor hir seknesse þei þat were aboute hire aftir grete communicacioun of þe contempte of þe world and of desire of good deth, þei inqwyrid of hir if sche was not aferd for to deye so fer fro hir cuntre. Sche answered to hem rith þus: 'No þing is fer fro God. I am noþing aferd þat God schuld not knowe fro whens he schuld reise me.' So þe ix day aftir þe seknesse took hire, þat religious soule, þat meke soule was losed fro þe body þe ȝere of hir age lvi þe ȝere of Augustyn age xxxiii. And many noble men and religious women cam to hir exequies as hir son tellith [in] þe ix book of his *Confessiones*. Thus was sche biried at Hostie and lay þere a thousand ȝere and more or sche was translate to Rome.

The comendacioun & þe orison of Augustin for his moder. xxiiii

In þe nynth book of his *Confessiones* in þe last ende, þere touchith he þe deth of his modir, and þe grete compleynt mad for hire both be oþir men and be him. Thus aftir oþir þingis he seith of hir: 'Thi ser-
27r vaunt, lord, whom / þou hast now take onto þi mercy, as þou knowist & as I beleue, aftir þat tyme þat sche had take þi feith and þi baptem, sche defouled neuyr hir lippis with no vnclennesse whech schuld be offense onto þi lordchip; no lesingis were founde in hir tonge, no slaunder, no vice

34 and] *bis; first* and *deleted in red* 40-41 tellith in þe] tellith þe *MS*

29-30 where ȝe schal minstir þe holy sacrament] an anachronism. Augustine was ordained four years after Monica's death. Jordanus is faithful to *Conf.* 9.11: 'tantum illud vos rogo, ut ad domini altare memineritis mei'.

41-42 lay þere a thousand ȝere and more] Jordanus does not mention this fact although his *Collectanea*, l'Arsenal 251, includes a treatise, *De translatione sanctae Monicae*. It is printed in *Acta sanctorum* Mai 4, 486-493. See Arbesmann, *Traditio* 1 (1943) 344. In *Solace*, 93, Capgrave notes that Pope Martin V had Monica's body brought to Rome in 1420.

1-24 Capitulum 24 is from *Conf.* 9.12.

whech longith onto þat membir. Thou saide, lord, þat what man with angri hert said onto his broþir euele, or cleped him fool, was gilty onto þe peyne of helle. Here me, lord, now clepyng onto þi grace for my moder whech stant in þi grace. Here me for þe medycyne of þoo woundis whech þi son souered in his body for þe helth of oure soules. Forgif hir alle þe trespas with whech sche offendid þe in þout, word or werk. Entyr not with hir into þi dom. Lete þi mercy flete aboue þi dom. I hope veryly þat þou hast doo now al þat I pray þe, but ʒet alowe my good wil whech I offer onto þe for hir as a deute of hir child. Sche bond hir soule onto þe prys of thi blod whil sche lyued, for þere was no day left but sche wold be present where þe sacrifise and þe memory of þi holy blod schuld be had in mynde. Inspire, lord, alle þe rederes of þis book þat in presens of þe sacrament of þe aucter þei may haue of þe soules of Patrik my fader and Monicha my moder deuoute mynde, be whos flesch I was brout forth on to þis wor[l]d.' Many oþir holy conceytes hath Augustin here if we had tyme to reherse hem.

Aftir deth of his moder who he went into Cartage with his felauchip. Capitulum xxv

Whanne his moder was ded and byried at Hostie, as we seid before, with þe next wynd he and his felauchip sailed streit /
27v onto Cartage, whech was a grete cite and strong, and mech named in the world specialy amongis marchaundis. I haue mynd þat I haue red in Augustin bokes, I wot not now where, þat alle marchaundise and al manere makyng of schippis began þere. There were þei herborowid in a worthi mannes hous; þei cleped him Innocent.

This same Innocent swech tyme as Augustin was þere had a greuous sore, whech sore myth not be hol, as þe lech said, withouten þat it were slitte. The man was weyk and dred mech þe knyf. So Augustin meued of very compassion prayed deuoutly to God for helth of his hoost, and sodeynly he was hool. There was gret merueyle of hem þat dwelt aboute.

23 world] word *MS*

11 cleped him fool] Matt. 5.22

15 Entyr not with hir] Ps. 142.2. Used previously in the Funeral Liturgy: 'Absolutio super tumulum' (Roman Missal).

5-8 a grete cite...schippis began þere] not in Jordanus. In his commentary on Ps. 47 Augustine says: 'manifestum est autem, quod primordia regni Carthaginis navibus floruerunt, ut inter ceteras gentes excellerent negotiationibus et navigationibus...et ipsae naves condita Carthagine ad negotiandum non defecerunt'.

14 sodeynly he was hool] *De civitate Dei* 22.8, CCL 48.816-817.

But þei alle with grete deuocion þankid God of his werkis. Of þis same myracle don at Cartage spekith Augustin in þe xxii book Of þe cite of God, so fer as þouȝ anoþir man had do þe same.

Fro Cartage went þei hom to þe houses and feldis þat longid onto Augustin of herytage. Thus leued þei alle of þe godis whech were left him be his frendis, not vsyng husbondry, but seld now o part now an oþir, for þei leued alle be þat possession ny iii ȝere. Augustin had take ȝet non ordres but brout with him certeyn prestis amongis þoo heremites whech he had of Simpliciane. And þei alle, folowyng þe steppes of þe apostoles, dwelt
28r togidir in on hous with o soule in prayere and fasting. / And he himselue, swech þingis as God had schewid to him, vttered it to oþir men in writyng and teching to her gret lernyng.

What bokes he mad whil he leued þus in his owne possession in þe town of Tagatensis. Capitulum xxvi

Dwellyng þus in his owne possession, he wrot too bokes ageyn þe Manicheis, & þese cleped he *De genesi*, for þere tretith he mech of þe werkis of oure lord whech he wrout in þe begynnyng of þe world. There also mad he an ende of vi bokes of musik whech he began at Melan. The first v bokes ar not redyly founde; þe sexte is had, where he tretith who we may ascende in owre vndirstanding fro bodely and chaungable noumbres onto goostly and permanent, whech permanent noumbres be in þat treuth whech is God. So he concludeth þat þoo inuisibil þingis whech be in heuene ar vndirstand þe bettir for knowlech of bodely þingis whech God mad in erde. He seith ferþermore, þat þouȝ þer be cer-

15 God *preceded by* o *and long descender excised* 17 so fer *in left margin, carets in text and margin* 18 and *in margin*; ad *in text with two marks above* 21 Thus *preceding* Augustin *deleted*

11 be *interlineated in red*

17 as þouȝ anoþir man had do þe same] 'as though another man had done it' (cf. Cap. 38/8-9).

22-23 certeyn prestis...whech he had of Simpliciane] legendary. See Cap. 21.

4-6 *De genesi...*]: *De genesi contra Manichaeos*, PL 34.173-194. Augustine set out to challenge the Manichaean criticism of the Old Testament. Jordanus merely mentions the work.

6 vi bokes of musik] *De musica libri sex*, PL 32.1081-1194. The first 5 books contain a pedestrian treatment of prosody (probably written in Milan); the 6th book is a psychological analysis of poetic rhythms–Capgrave's 'noumbres' (line 9).

teyn men here in erde þat haue so dul wit þat þei cannot vndirstand þis matere, ȝet if þei kepe treuly þe Cristen feith þei schul sumtyme se alle þese þingis, & fele hem in swech sikirnesse þat þei may not fayle. He seith eke þat summe men þat haue sotil wittis and vndirstand þis wel inow, if it be so þat þei despise Crist, for al her sotil kunning þei schal be da[m]pned in helle.

In þat same tyme eke mad he anoþir book þat is entitled þe bok Of þe
28v maistir. Þis bok is / in maner of a dialoge betwix him and his son, for sone aftir þe bok was mad his son deyid. In þis book he seith þat þere is no very maystir to tech men þe treuth but God alone. That same tyme eke he mad anoþir book whech he nameth *De uera religione*, where he tretith þat þere is no trewe ne very religion in al þe world but in þe Cristen feith.

What was þe cause whi he went first to Ypone. xxvii

Thus lyued oure maystir in holy study and contemplacioun so þat his fame began to sprede. What lyf he held and what doctrine, he comuned to hem þat cam onto hym, so þat þe lith of his doctrine myth not be hid, but raþer spred himselue þorw þe cuntre. Of him herd a certeyn rych man þat dwelt þat tyme at Ypone swech meruelous tydyngis þat þe man was gretly stered to se him a[n]d speke with him. For whech cause he sent messageris and letteris onto Augustin, in whech letteris he comendid gretly his cunnyng and special his deuocioun; þat he was only ȝoue to lernyng and good lyf, for whech exercise he had despised al þis worldly felicite. This man wrote ferþermore þat if he wold com to Ypone he was redy to forsake al þe couetyse of worldly possession, and folow his steppes in the wey of God. For þis cause Augustyn consented onto þe man, hauyng a grete desire to wynne swech a soule to Goddis seruyse whech was so defouled in worldly vanyte. Anoþir cause was þere eke, for Augustyn þoutȝ he schuld lyue þere in more quiete contemplacion þan at
29r hom amongis his kynrod and aqueyntauns. / For he is in very purpos to edifie a monastery and to lyue þerin with his brether aftir þe forme and þe ordinauns of þe aposteles.

17 her] r *interlineated over an erasure* dampned] dapned *MS* 19 þe bok m *excised before* bok 20 is] *bis; no deletion*

4 hym] hem *MS*; y *interlineated over* e 6 swech *preceded by* sw *excised* 7 and] ad *MS* 14 hauyng] haue *MS*; e *deleted*, yng *interlineated in red*

19-20 Of þe maistir] *De magistro*, CCL 29.157-203.

23 *De uera religione*] CCL 32.187-260.

4-5 lith...myth not be hid] Matt. 4.14.

Thus is he come to Ypone and þe man þat sent aftir him receyued him ful worchipfully. But þe principal cause whech Augustin supposed to spede þat failed, ffor þe man herd deuoutly alle hise wordes but to þe very contempt of richesse coude he not bring him as ȝet. Summe men suppose þat he cam to þat ende aftirward, for as þei sey, it myth not renne in veyn þe laboure þat oure lord purueyid in so swete a vessel.

That þese to þingis were þe cause why þat Augustin went onto Ypone he witnessith himselue in a sermone intitled Of þe comoun lif of clerkis, where he seith þus: 'I þat with þe grete mercy of God ȝe se now ȝoure bischop, I cam ȝong onto þis cite and, many of ȝow knowe, I soute þat tyme a conuenient place where I schuld make a monasterie to lyue þere with my bretherin. I cam eke onto þis cite for to wynne my frend onto God, þat he schuld lyue with us eke in þe monasterie. Me þout at þat tyme a sikir comyng onto þis cite because þei had a bischop, ffor þat place whech had non I refused as suspecte, þat I schuld not be chose.'

Who he edified a monastery in desert for him and certeyn heremites. xxviii

He had not longe dwelt at Ypone or he fel in aqweyntauns of Valery, bischop þan of þat cite. This Valerie was a ful goodly man, fre hertet and namely onto straungeris. Augustin, not fer fro þe
29v cite, þorw his fauoure edified a monasterie in desert / and sowt alle þe wodes aboute for alle þe heremites whech he myth fynde; he gadered into o congregacion, as he witnessith in a sermon writyn onto þe prestes of Ypone and alleggid before, where he seith þus: 'As ȝe know I cam onto þis cyte with my welbeloued frendis Euodio, Simplicio, Alipio, Nebridio & Anastasio. I cam hidir with a maner of a sikirnesse, for I wist wel þat þe good fadere Valerius was bischop here. I cam hidyr not for to haue powere ouyr ȝou in dignite, but for to dwelle as an outcast in þe hous of oure lord alle þe dayes of my lyf. I cam hidir not for to receyue seruyse

3 q *excised before* aqweyntauns

23-25 Summe men suppose...] speculation by Capgrave.

27 Of the comoun lif of clerkis] *De vita et moribus clericorum*, Sermo 355, PL 39.1568-1574.

8-9 a sermon writyn onto þe prestes] *Ad fratres* 5, PL 40.1243-1244.

10-11 Euodio, Simplicio...Anastasio] Capgrave retains the Latin ablative case forms.

13 dwelle as an outcast] Ps. 84.11.

of oþir men but for to lyue pesibily in desert with my breþerin. I brout no richesse with me, but fauoured with þe grace of oure lord and with þe good help of þe old man Valerie, I mad a monasterie here in desert with grete laboure and bisinesse, whech monasterie stant alone fer fro þe puple. And with grete þout I haue gadered þere seruauntes of God, whech dwelt alone disparplied be þe wodes, and þere begunne we for to lyue aftir þe maner and þe forme of þe aposteles lif, þat alle oure godis schul go in comoun and no man haue no maner þing propir to himselue.'

Thus lyue þei in prayer and wecch and fasting & many oþir vertues more þan we may now expresse. That þis good old bischop gaue fauour and god onto edifiyng of þis first monasterie witnessith Augustin eke in þe forsaid sermone, *Vt nobis per litteras*, where he seith þus onto þo same heremites: 'ȝe be my vyne chosen of me, sette in þe myddis of þe cherch as
30r þouȝ it / were in þe myddis of paradys. This vyne haue I in þe vertu of God gadered togydyr and werk men haue I sette þere, þat þei schuld trauayle and bryng forth frute in here tyme. To þis vyne I haue chose ȝou, to þis heritage I haue gadered ȝou with þe fauour of þe holy man Valery, whech of þe cherch godis ȝaue me grete plente to þe edificacion of my monastery, for my patrimonie myth not suffise to þe grete expense and he had not holpe me.'

Of þe noumbyr of þo heremytes whech he gadered and of her holy conuersacioun. Capitulum xxix

In þis same monastery Augustin or he were prest gadered a grete noumbyr of heremites, whech lyued as we sayde before aftir þe forme and þe ordinauns of þe apostoles. And he her began þat ordre whech we clepe at þis day, and þe cherch of Rome clepith hem þe same in alle þe bullis of here priuylegis, Þe Ordre of þe Heremites of Seynt Augustyn. First dwelt þei in dyuers wodes here on and þere anoþir, and euerych of hem lyued as hym lyked tyl þat oure auctoure gadered hem togidyr & mad of anachorites cenobites. He spekith himselue of hem in þe

15 lyue] loue *MS*; y *interlineated in red* 23 þei *in right margin in red* 25 edifiyng] edifieng *MS*; y *interlineated over* e 29 þere *preceded by* þidir *excised* 33 þe *in right margin in red*

5 her *in right margin in red* 10 of hem *interlineated*

26 *Vt nobis per litteras*] *Ad fratres*, Sermo 21, PL 40.1268-1271.

5-8 her began þat ordre...Seynt Augustyn] not in Jordanus.

10-11 þe sermone often rehersid] *Ad fratres*, Sermo 21, PL 40.1268-1271 is quoted five times by Jordanus.

sermone often rehersid þus: 'I cam into Affrik, my good modyr ded, & edified as ȝe se a monastery in desert ferre fro dwellyng of men. And blessed be God I haue gadered þere a noumbir of breþerin whos hertis are so inspired with gostly lith þat not only þei be foloweres of holy faderis whech lyued in solitarie lif, but now þei folow þe noble steppes of þe aposteles, for al þing is comoun onto hem. Many faderis were before me whom for to folow is ful profitable, but non of hem went nyher þe apostoles
0v lif þan I. Therefore / may I sey þat I am fader and hed of ȝou alle.'

The habite of þis ordre was a blak cope girt with a girdil of ledir withouten ony barre, as he witnessith in þe forsaid sermone, hauyng þese wordes onto þe prestis þat dwelt in þe monasterie: 'Go to myn heremites and lerne of hem to be meke of hert, pore of spirit and childyrn of obediens. Loke if ȝe be swech as þei be. Wold God ȝe were swech as I fynde hem. 3e be renneres aboute þe cyte, and þei fle þe sith of men. 3e be arayed with dyuers coloures and dyuers furris; þei are content with a blak cloth. 3e haue girdilis lich knytys and þei with þongis of chamel skynnys as Hely and Ion go girt in here lendes.' To þese same heremites mad he a book of certeyn reules who þei schuld lyue, whech reules he cleped þe Margarites of paradise; and þei be comprehendid in þe first sermone þat he mad to hem, whech sermone beginnyth, *Fratres mei & leticia cordis mei.* Many of þo same put he aftirward in his reule whech he called a merour, as a man may sone perseyue.

19 girt *preceded by* l *deleted* 30 to hem] *bis; first excised and deleted* 32 as *interlineated*; and *deleted in red*

20 þe forsaid sermone] *Ad fratres*, Sermo 5, PL 40.1244-1246. Capgrave omits Jordanus' polemic: 'Ubi comparacionem faciens inter ipsos presbyteros canonicos suos et fratres istos in heremo'.

27 Hely and Ion] the prophet Elias (Vulgate 1 Kings 17 ff.) and John the Baptist: 'Ipse autem Iohannes habebat vestimentum de pilis camelorum et zonam pelliceam circa lumbos suos' (Matt. 3.4).

28-29 whech reules he cleped þe Margarites of paradise] Jordanus, 'tradiciones...quas margaritas paradysi appelat in sermone primo ad fratres eosdem. Deinde regulam scripsit...' (*Ad fratres*, Sermo 1, PL 40.1235-1237).

30 *Fratres mei & leticia cordis mei*] *Ad fratres*, Sermo 1, PL 40.1235-1237.

31 his reule whech he called a merour] Jordanus included a 'Regula sancti Augustini quam speculum appelat' in the *Collectanea* with two other Rules ascribed to Augustine. Augustine's *Praeceptum*, the eight chapters, generally known as he *Rule of St. Augustine*, refers to a mirror in the final chapter: 'Ut autem in hoc libello tamquam in speculo possitis inspicere'.

Who Augustin was chose prest of þe monasterie vndir Valery þe bischop to haue þe reule of þe cherch. xxx

In þis same tyme þe prest of þe cherch at Ypone was ded, and þis Valerius gadered þe puple and þe clergie to ordeyn a new successoure whech schuld bere al þe charge of þe cherch, for þe bischop was old and myth not laboure. He was also a Grek of birth and coude not parfithly þe langage of þat cuntre. Amongis alle oþir Valery sent for Au-
31r gustin, and before alle þe puple sayde it was þe custom / þat þei schuld haue þe chois; but neuerþelasse þe puple knew wel be certeyn toknes þat he wold preferre Augustin to þis dignite. Augustin because he had take ȝet non ordres stood amongis þe puple in a maner of a sikyrnesse, as he þout þat no man schuld chese him because he was not in ordre. Thus as he stood, sodeynly alle þe puple chase him with o voys, leyd handis upon hym and, as þe maner was, presented him onto þe bischop. He wepte and withdrow him, merueyling sore þat þei were þus set on him, allegging þe perel of þat dignite to haue gouernauns of so grete a puple; but þe more he refused it þe more þei desired him and cryed for þat Augustin schuld be her prest. Thus was he brout onto þe bischop, and he with ful grete reuerens and deuocioun gaf him his ordres.

Afftir he was þus mad prest of þe cherch he dwelled stille with his heremites, whos felauchip he had euyr desired, but þe bischop say wel þat it was ouyr ferre fro þe cite euyr for to go to and fro and þe occupacioun of þe cherch was grete. Þe desire eke of Augustin euyr for to be with his heremites of grete discrecioun ordeyned þis mene whech fulfillid both þingis: þat is to seye þat þe cherch schuld be wel seruyd with þe presens of Augustin, and eke he schuld not be fer fro his welbeloued heremites. The mene was þis: þat a fayre place schuld be mad fast be þe monasterie, and certeyn heremites schuld be chose fro þe first place and dwelle in þe secund with whech oure Augustin myth speke whan he list. This was fulfillid in dede and summe of þe best of þis first monasterie were drawe to þis secund. And
31v Augustin gadered to here noumbir mo owt of / þe world, not lewid men,

6 also] alsoo *MS* birth] h *added in red with red /* 9 neuerþelasse] þelasse *interlineated in red with red* ^ 24 fulfillid] fulfill *in text*; id *in left margin in red; two marks over* ll *in text* 25 þat[2]] at *added in red* 28 heremites *added after deleted* hee 30 first *in right margin in red* were *preceded by* wat *deleted*

3-10 In þis same tyme...] details added by Capgrave.

7 þe langage of þat cuntre] i.e., Latin, but Punic was the language of the unlettered.

11 a sikyrnesse] Augustine's Sermo 355, PL 39.1569: 'quasi securus, quia locus habebat episcopum'.

but clerkys and lerned men, and þere sette he hem in þe same reule þat þe first monastery had: þat þei schuld lyue in comoun and no man to haue no þing propir to himself. This same processe writith þis doctour ful pleynly in a sermone: *De communi vita clericorum* allegged before, and in anoþir sermon to þe prestis of Ypone begynnyng: *In omnibus operibus uestris*.

Who Augustin lerned þese men of þe secund monasterie & who he prechid eke in presens of his bischop. Capitulum xxxi

These men þus chosen to þe secund monasterye studied in dy[ui]nyte and in morall bokes at þe comaundment of her maystir, for he lerned hem so þat þei schuld come to þe cite to preche þe puple and edifye hem with Goddis word. The bischop Valery, sey[i]ng þe grete cunnyng of Augustin and eke þe grete desire þat he had to preche þe word of God, þankid God often sithe þat he had sent him in his age so good a vikere. For as he seid to þe puple, his prayer was herd whech he had long prayed: þat God schuld send him swech a man þat myth edifie his puple both with exaumple and doctryne. For he himself was not rith redy to swech þingis, for he was not gretly letteryd and eke born he was of þe Grek tonge and coude not mech skil on Latyn bokes whech were vsed most in þe prouynce of Cartage.

Wherfore he graunted Augustin leue ageyn þe custom of þe cherchis of Affrik to prech in þe cherch in his presens, ffor whech þing many oþir bischoppis grucchid ageyn þis new custom. Be he rowt not ne sette no pryse be swech grucching tongis, þe whilis þat Augustin supplied swech
32r good / werkis whech he coude not do himselue. For be þe prechyng of Augustin many soules were goten to God. He ferd lich a gret lith sette alle on hy, þat alle men in þe grete hous of oure lord had direccion in her werkys be his schynyng. This ensaumple ran oute þorw þe lond of Affrik,

5 dyuinyte] dynyte *MS* 8 seying] seyng *MS* 19 swech *preceded by* g *excised* 22 lord *in right margin red with / before* had

35 *De communi vita clericorum*] Sermo 355, PL 39.1568-1574.

36 *In omnibus operibus uestris*] *Ad fratres*, Sermo 5, PL 40.1244 (the title here is 'De communi vita et moribus clericorum'). Capgrave omits Valerius' visit to the hermitage.

16 graunted Augustin leue ageyn þe custom] Jordanus mentions a precedent for this practice in the Eastern Church.

21 lich a gret lith] Matt. 5.15.

þat þo prestis whech were wel lerned men had leue to preche in presens of her bischoppis.

And as we saide before, Augustin gat leue of Valery þat þese heremites whech dwelt in þe secund monastery were admitted to preche and schryue, not alle but þoo whech were lerned in diuinite and custumablely vsed in good lyf. This witnessith he in þat sermone often alleggid: *Vt bene nostis*, where he seith þus: 'Tho bretherin sette in þe monasterie whech oure good fader Valery endewid, þouȝ it be so þat þei dwelle not in þe cite, because here fame was mech bore amongis þe puple, þerfor haue I ordeyned þat þei schul preche þe word of lif onto þe puple and bryng trew soules be here gode ensaumples to him þat mad al of nowt. Behold who þai deme þe erde and bynde it & lose swech as þei wil euyr with þe fauoure of God.'

Who he disputed with a grete heretik clepid Fortunatus and conuicte him of heresie. xxxii

In þat same tyme þe heresie of þe Manicheis encresid in þe cite of Ypone þorw laboure and doctrine of a grete capteyn of hem cleped Fortunate, whech had peruerted many soules fro þe trewe feith. For whech cause þe best citeceynes requyred here prest Augustin to speke with þis Fortunat & refelle if he myth þe heresie with whech he had de-
32v seyued many soules. Augustyn, whech was redy / to answere euery man,
and for to talk of þe feith, hope and charite whech were plenteuously withinne him, forsok not þis conflicte but obeied rydily here peticioun, inqwiring of hem if Fortunate wold consente to þis dede. Tho went þei to Fortunate and reqwyrid him with swech instauns þat he myth not denye here desire.

Thus is þe day come of þis comunicacioun. Grete puple is gadered and notaries sette on both sides whech schuld report treuly þe wordis þat were

26 þ *and / excised before* þese 31 þouȝ] ȝ *added in lighter ink* 32 mech *preceded by* w *excised* þei *interlineated in red* 33 soules] *final* s *interlineated*

9 charite *preceded by* w *excised*

29 *Vt bene nostis*] *Ad fratres*, Sermo 14, PL 40.1257.

34 deme þe erde] conflation of Matt. 19.28 and 16.19.

5 Fortunate] Augustine debated with him on August 28 and 29, 392. It is recorded in the *Disputatio contra Fortunatum*, CSEL 25.83-112. Details are from Possidius 6, PL 32.38.

6 þe best citeceynes] Jordanus, 'tam Christiani quam Donatisti heretici'.

9 feith, hope and charite] cf. Jordanus' 'de fide et spe'.

saide. For þis was euyr þe practik of Augustin whan he schuld dispute with ony heretik, to write here wordes þat þei schuld not denye o tyme whech þei graunted anoþir tyme. Too dayes lestid þis disceptacioun. The question disputed amongis hem was þis: Fro whens þat euel comth. Augustin held þis opinion þat euel begynnyth in a man rith of his fre choys, for þere schuld no euel be in him but he wold. Fortunate held that euel was a nature coeterne with God, þat is to sey euene as God hath be euyr, so hath þat nature euele euyr be. In þis disputacioun þis Fortunat coude not hurt Augustin with non argument, ne his owne opinione coude he not defende; so faylyng in his answeres & foule aschamed he fled oute of þe cuntre, and þat heresie whech he held fel fro euery mannes hert. This act sette Seynt Augustin in a book, þat men aftirward schuld knowe þe conflict betwix hem.

In þis same tyme mad he anoþir book whech he clepith Of þe sermoun of Crist saide in þe hill where he hath a notable exposicion upon þe *Pater*
33r *noster*; / for þat same is a grete part of þat sermon whech Crist sayde in þe hill. Thus prechid þat nobil prest Augustin; with grete auctorite distroyed heresie & planted new religioun, so þat his name was spred þorw þe lond.

Who Augustyn was chose bischop, Vale[r]y lyuyng in þat see. Capitulum xxxiii

Amongis alle þe ioye þat þis bischop Valery had for oure lord had sent him swech a preest, he caute with þat a gret fere and in partye a gelosie þat Augustyn schuld not go fro hym and be chose a bischop in anoþir cyte. For þat same had be do or þis tyme, had not Valery sent him owt of þe weye, wenyng to many men þat he schuld not sone come ageyn. For þis cause he sent priuy letterys to þe bischop of

23 euyr *preceded by* u *excised* 24 non *preceded by* o *excised* 26 he held *in right margin with red* ^ 29 sermoun *preceded by* cr *excised* 33 name *interlineated in red with red* ^

1 Valery] Valey *MS*

22-23 þat is to sey...euele evyr be] Capgrave's explanation.

29-30 Of þe sermon...in þe hill] *De sermone domini in monte libros duos*, CCL 35.1-188.

33 his name was spred þorw þe lond] Jordanus is more expansive: 'Cuius famam nominis non solum ecclesia Affricana, verum eciam et transmarina iam nouerat'.

4-5 gret fere and in partye a gelosie] Jordanus, 'habet humana fragilitas'.

8-9 bischop of Cartage, primate of þat lond] i.e., of Carthago Proconsularis.

Cartage, primate of þat lond, þat Augustyn schuld be promoted to þis dignite. In whech letteres he alleggid his age, his febilnesse, and eke who he was not redy in langage to erudicioun of þe puple and destruccion of heresie as Augustin was. The bischop of Cartage þat knew Augustin wel sent down letteris of confirmacion, þat alle þat Valery had reqwyrid him he held ferme and stable. This bischop of Cartage was primate þorw alle Affrik. Þan was þere anoþir bischop, primate of al Numidie, and for him sent Valery; and eke for anoþir worthi man, þei clepid him Megasie, bischop of a cite clepid Orilamense. Mo bischoppis sent he fore and clerkys to Ypone, and whan þei were gadered togidyr before þe puple, sodeynly he vttir his desire þat Augustin schuld be & þei both schuld lyue togidyr in
33v comoun of þe / cherchis good. The puple whane þei herd þis þei þankid God heyly and with o uoys þei cryed þat Augustyn schuld be bischop. He mad grete allegaunce ageyn þis eleccion, and seide it was not conuenient þat þei schuld chese a new, þe old lyuyng. But for alle þat he coude say, Valerie is desire was fulfillid, and Augustyn consecrate and þe cure leyd only in him.

And ageyn þis manere of eleccion wrot Seynt Augustyn aftirward to þe court of Rome, þat he schuld be excused of his erroure, for þere was mad a statute of holy cherch in þe councell at Antioche þat þere schuld no bischop make anoþir whil he lyued, as it is pleynly conteyned in þe decres, *Capitulum viii, Questione i, Episcopo non licet*. So Seynt Augustin wold not þat þing do in him not rithfully schuld be drawe to oþir men in ensaumple. Thus whan he was bischop, with grettere auctorite and more feruent loue he prechid þe word of God, nowt only in his owne diosise but where euyr he was reqwyred; most specialy where heresie regned, þidir went he to defende þe feith.

13 þat[2] *added* 16 Megasie] *recte Megalius* 17 Orilamense] *recte Calamense* 20 cherchis *preceded by* chersi *excised* 30 Capitulum viii *preceded by* þe secunde *excised* 31 schuld] schuld not *MS* 33 in *interlineated*

14-15 primate þorw alle Affrik] the bishop of Carthage, the most prominent see, had precedence over other ecclesiastical jurisdictions such as Numidia. Cf. Mansi 4.233.

28 þe councell at Antioche] held in 341, this council had declared, 'nec alicui pro se successorem constituere etiam sit in finem vitae'. The title and quote are correct, though Capgrave's citation, *Capitulum viii, Questione i* does not agree with Mansi 3.880. The Council of Carthage in 398 admonishes bishops to familiarise themselves with conciliar decrees, a point which probably shows Augustine's concern. Augustine himself mentions the Council of Nicaea: 'quod Concilio Nicaeno prohibitum fuisse nesciebam nec ipse sciebat' (Epistola 213.4, CSEL 57.376).

Off þe þird monasterie whech he gadered of chanones withinne þe paleys. Capitulum xxxiiii

Whanne he was mad bischop he say weel þat, for þe grete
multitude of causes & þe grete prees of straungeris þat dayly
cam onto him, he must hold a houshold; and he myth not go
to his refeccioun euery day to neþir of þese to monasteries of
whech we spoke. Therfor he chase certeyn prestis of good lyf and gret letti-
34r rure to leue with him in þat college, and / þo same men bonde to leue
vndir obediens, chastite and fro propirte of temporal richesse as þo here-
mites lyued in þe to monasteries saide before. And owt of þis colege cam
þese chanones þat ar called at þis day of Ordre of Seint Augustin, þouȝ it
be so þat þei be distincte in oþir habite þan þei þat were with Seint Augu-
stin, for þei went in dyuers colouris a[n]d furres as chanones do now in
cathedral cherchis. But because þat þese chanones in blak habite kepe more
streytly þe reule of Seynt Augustin as touching þat poynt to lyue in com-
oun, þerfor I suppose þat þei be nyher Seynt Augustin þan þe othir; and
þerfor is þere meued a question in þe lawe, wheþir þe chanones of
cathedral cherchis be bounde þorwoute þe world for to kepe þe reule of þis
doctour whech he mad onto hem, & it is clepid *De vita clericorum*, or nowt.
And þei sey nay þerto, for because he myth bynde no cherch but his owne.
Wherfor me semeth þat þo chanones whech be clepid regulere ar more ny
Seint Augustin þan þoo þat be cleped seculere.

This same glorious doctoure in a famous sermone whech he mad Of þe
comoun lif of clerkys, and it beginnyth: *Propter quod uolui & rogaui*,
makyth mynde of þis þirde monasterie in swech manere wordes: 'It plesid
God for to sey onto me þat I schuld ascende to hier degre, for aftir þe tyme
þat my fame was bore in þe puple, I began to drawe me fro euery place
whech wantid a bischop; but a seruaunt may not sey nay to his lord.
Wherfor whan I was mad bischop I aspied wel þat I must chere men þat
34v cam onto me with mete and drynk, for if I ded not I schuld / be hald on-
gentil; and if I led my gestis onto þo monasteries whech I haue mad, þe
custom schuld not be good, for þe most part of þo heremites desire not

12 þan] n *interlineated over excision* 13 and] ad *MS* 16 and *preceded by* þere *excised* 19 he *interlineated* 20 bynde *interlineated*

1 Off þe þird monasterie] Jordanus' solution to the controversy between the Hermits and Canons, though he gives pride of place and preference to the Hermits.

10-22 owt of þis colege cam þese chanones...] the term 'Canon' and the excursus on whether all Canons are bound to follow Augustine's *Rule* are by Capgrave.

23-24 Of þe comoun lif of clerkys] see above, note to Cap. 27/27.

mech to haue grete conuersacioun with þe puple. This was þe cause whi þat I gadered þese clerkis in o colege withinne þe hous or þe place whech longith principaly to þe bischoprich.' These same wordes hath he in a sermone to þe same prestis of Ypone whech begynnyth, *In omnibus operibus vestris*. Many þingis myth we plant in here, who þat he loued bettyr þe felauchip of þe heremites þan of þe prestis in þe cathedral cherch, and what grucching þe same prestis made ageyn þis affeccioun; but alle þis I ley beside and wil procede to þe oþir part of his lif.

Who þese heremites were founde be þe possession of þe cherch and what worthy men grew of þis college. xxxv

Nowt only þe prestis of þe colege were founde and fedde with þe possession of þe cherch, but eke þe heremites had part, þouȝ here part were not so plenteuous as was þe oþir. In a sermone þat he mad onto þe same heremites entitled Of prayere, he makith mynde of þis matere and þus he seith: 'Be not wery of ȝoure prayere, for ȝe haue bettir leysere to pray þan summe oþir haue. Ȝe be not ordeyned for to gouerne oþir men, but for to leue in solitary lyf and deuoute prayere to God. And þat ȝe schuld pray þe more hertly and not be lettyd with no cold whech schuld withdrawe ȝoure deuocioun, ffor þis cause of swech godes
35r as longe to þe cherch of Ypone I haue / do mad ȝou clothis & hosyn and schon þerto an hundred and xl, whech I wil þat þei be kept in a comoun vestiary, þat euery man may haue part as him nedith.' Thus norchid þis noble man þese pore creatures. And on þe othir side, þoo persones þat dwelt with him in þe cherch he lerned hem dyuynyte, for at euery mel had þei notable communicacioun of holy scripture, and euyr alle þe answeres must fynaly come fro Augustin.

38 of *before* what *excised in red*
5 so *interlineated in red* 9 but *interlineated in red* 16 mel *in right margin in red with red caret*

36-37 *In omnibus operibus vestris*] see above, note to Cap. 30/36.

39-40 þis I ley beside] Capgrave omits five additional quotations found in Jordanus: *Ad fratres*, Sermo 14, 'Ut bene nostis'; Sermo 21, 'Ut nobis per litteras'; Sermo 5, 'In omnibus operibus' (2 quotations); Sermo 4 'De prudencia'.

6 Of prayere] 'De oracione', *Ad fratres,*, Sermo 22, PL 40.1273. The quotation is from Jordanus, who does not in this instance give the *initium* ('Fratres mei et leticia cordis mei') which is identical with *Ad fratres* 1. Capgrave omits the ending, 'cum omni diligencia et caritate, scientes quod vera caritas non querit que sua sunt sed que dei'.

14-15 Thus norchid...pore creatures] Capgrave's addition.

Owt of his hous, as we rede, him lyuyng, were chose x bischoppes, men of gret lettirure and of parfith lyf. For many famous men at þoo dayes, seing þe grete perfeccioun and holy conuersacioun of þat felauchip whech Augustyn had drawe onto him, forsok alle þe pomp of þe world, com and lyued with him in ful gret perfeccioun, summe amongis þe heremites, summe amongis þe prestis, euery man aftir þat he sauored. And many of hem, whane þei had be with him ȝeres and were roted in religioun, with his leue went fro him into oþir cuntres, mad monasteries, gadered felauchip and so encresid his ordre not only in Ypone but þorw þe lond, him lyuyng.

Of þe maneres and þe habite of Seynt Augustin aftir he was bischop. xxxvi

This same glorious doctoure, fader and norcher of clerkys, in his habite in goyng, in sittyng, in his wordes, cuntenauns and maneres, was of swech sadnesse þat euery man whech cam to his presens was edified be him. To religious men and women he was in his exhortaciones sad and sobir, ȝeuyng hem grete ensaumple who þei
35v schuld do. To othir / seculere men þat were occupied in þe world he was familiare, and in his talkyng had onto hem in manere of mery langage with stedfast chere of sadnesse. The o puple counforted he with sad talkyng to conferme hem in here holinesse; the oþir puple gadered he onto a perfeccioun with goostly myrth & deuoute iocundnesse. Transgressiones ageyn Cristis law or his holy preceptis he correctid not boystously, but fadirly and in fayre manere, þat many euele men seing his swete correccion were þe rather turned fro synne.

His cloþis whech he wered dayly & his cloþis þat serued to his bed þei were not ouyr costful ne ouyr wrecched, but in þe most mesurable maner he ordeyned þei schuld be. In summe men we lakkyn þe grete cost of aray, and with summe ar we wroth with here sluttynesse; þerfor went þis man þe myd weye, þat he schuld ȝeue ensaumple in cloþing to hem þat were his foloweris, and oþir men whech were not of his skole schuld haue no matere of detraccioun. Thus spekith he in a famous sermon þat begynnyth, *Caritati vestre*: 'I wil þat no man ȝyue to me so precious clothis whech þat I, as of a specialte aboue oþir, schuld were.' Ensaumple he puttith, 'I sette case þat

19 bischoppes] *final* s *interlineated in red*
17 wrecched] *final* d *interlineated* 20 her *before* his foloweris *excised*

18-22 In summe...detraccioun] Capgrave amplifies his source.
22 a famous sermon] Jordanus gives the title, 'De communi vita et moribus clericorum'; Sermo 356, PL 39.1580.

sum man gyue me an amyse, more precious þan I am wone to were, þat I schuld haue swech a singuler þing passyng alle my breþerin. Vphap it semeth a bischop for to were swech on, þouȝ it semeth not Augustyn, a pore man born of mene men; for if I receyued swech a þing and wered it, 36r / men schuld sey þat I haue founde more precious garmentis in þe cherch þan I myth haue had in my faderes hous. Lete men gyue me swech cloþis þat in nede my breþerin, be þei prestis, dekenes or subdeknes, may were þe same. I am aknowe befor God and ȝou þat of a precious cloth I am aschamed, for it is no[t] pertinent to oure profession, ne conuenient to my white herys.'

Of his diete and seruyse at his table. Capitulum xxxvii

Lytil mete for þe most partye vsed he at his table, for he had more delectacioun in þe heryng of holy lessones, and talkyng aftir upon þe same, þane in bodely mete. Flesch ete he but seldom, and þat was whane he had gestis; wortes and letuse and swech herbis ete he most. I trowe þat he had þe vse of Itaile whill he studied þere, and coude not litly out of þe same vse, for þei ete not mech at onys. Wyn drank he euyr ful mesurablely, and þat medeled with watyr, for þe wyn of þat cuntre is hoot. Swech mete and drynk as he had in vse was not warned to no man þat wold ask it, were þei dwelleris of þe cite, were þei straungeris.

Amongis alle oþir vices he hatyd gretly detraccion, specialy at mel. For ageyn þat vis had he writyn at his table þese too vers: *Quisquis amat dictis absentem rodere uitam, Hanc mensam vetitam nouerit esse sibi.* This is to sey in Englisch: What man with wordis absent bitith his broþeris name, This bord fro him forbodyn it is with blame. Sumtyme þei þat sat þere wold 36v speke largely of hem þat were absent, & þanne / wold Augustyn say onto hem þat but þei wold leue her detraccioun he must rase oute þo vers. Eke

29 p *before* more *excised* 33 not] non *MS*
9 drynk *interlineated with red caret*

4-7 Flesch ete he...not mech at onys] Capgrave's addition.
7-8 Wyn drank he] Capgrave omits the scriptural justification from Tim. 5.23.
8-9 medeled with watyr...is hoot] Capgrave's addition.
13 *absentem*] as in Jordanus; Possidius has 'absentum'.
13 *Hanc mensam vetitam nouerit esse sibi*] Jordanus, 'Hanc mensam indignam nouerit esse sibi'. Manuscripts of Possidius show both readings. Cf. Possidius, PL 32.51, 52, n.3.
13-15 This is to sey...with blame] Capgrave's gloss.
16 speke largely of hem] Jordanus, 'ad detractionem linguam laxassent'.

sumtyme whan þei wold not leue lithly he wold rise and go fro hem fastyng.

Grete wast was not in his hous of sotil metes. For on a tyme certeyn gestis schuld dyne with him, and a licorous felaw amongis hem stert into þe kechyn to loke what mete was þere in araying, and fond þe hous cold. Tho cam he onto þe bischop and inqwyrid of him what mete he had ordeyned for his gestis, and Augustin answered him þat he knew no more þan he. Deuoute puple cam more to him for goostly communicacioun þan bodely mete.

Vpon pore men had he grete compassion and gaf hem largely of þe cherchis good. For sumtyme made [he] þe vesseles of syluyr whech longed onto þe cherch to be molten, and þe weggis þerof be sold and departed to pore men. And whane he was in grete nede þat he myth not gyue hem whech were in myschef, þane wold he openly denouns þis to þe puple and þei wold brynge him sufficiens to his entent. To his kynrod also he wold gyue part of þat same cherchis good, but in no grete plente, for he wold help hem with þat good but not make hem rich.

Thus spekith he in þis matere in þat same sermon þat beginnith *Vt nobis per litteras*, 'We bischoppis may not haue þese temporal godes of þe cherch as oure possessioun; ne I þat am a bischop haue not þese godes to non oþir entent but for to dispense & departe hem onto pore men, for þe
37r godes of þe cherch / þei be þe patrimonie of pore men. And þerfor I must be ful war þat I take not þe godes of my cherch fro pore men and gyue it rich men. And God be þankid I haue in þis matere do wel onto þis tyme, ffor I haue mech folk of my kynrod and summe of hem rich and wel at ese; and summetyme come þai to me with þretis, sumtyme with fayre wordis, and þus þei sey: "Fader, we be þi flesch & þi blood. Gyue us sum of þat good þat þou hast in dispensacioun". And for alle here crying, þankid be God and ȝoure gode prayeres, I haue no mynde þat euyr I mad with þe cherchis godes ony of my kynrod rych. Pore men be more ny myn hert þan rych men, for we þat be cleped into þe parfite lif in the cherch, if we haue cloth and mete, we schuld be content with al. And in tokne þerof be oure hedes schaue al bare, þat euene as þe her is bare þere, so schuld oure hertis be voyd fro couetise.'

28 made he] made *MS* 30 not *interlineated in red with red* ^ 32 þei *before* wold *interlineated in red with red* ^ 43 to me] tome *MS*; *words divided by red* / 48 we[1] *interlineated in red*

20 Grete wast...of sotil metes] Capgrave's addition.
25 Deuoute puple] Capgrave substitutes this for Jordanus' description of the household utensils.
35-36 *Vt nobis per litteras*] *Ad fratres*, Sermo 21, PL 40.1269.

Off his conuersacion and oþir blessid condiciones whech he had and vsed. Capitulum xxxviii

Faderles childyrn and widowes whane þei were in ony tribulacioun he wold visite, and seke men eke with his owne handis wold he lefte and counfort, and sumtyme þo whech he visite were made hool and sound. There were certeyn men whech were vexid with wikkid spiritis, and he prayed for hem and þei were hool. In þe xxii book Of þe Cyte of God he tellith too myracules of himselue in swech maner as þow anoþir man had do hem: 'I knew', he seith, 'a virgine at Ypone, whech virgine receyued oyle of a prest; and whech tyme sche had anoynted hir
37v with þe same oyle, and þe prest with bittir teris prayed / for hir, sche was hol.' Anoþir tale he tellith þere: he seyth he knew a bischop þat prayed for a ȝong man in whom þe deuele had entered, and anon aftir his prayere þe ȝong man was hool.

To elde men was þis fader a very noryce and supported hem with ful grete reuerens, as men may rede in a sermon whech he mad ageyn ydilnesse, and it beginnyth *Apostolus Petrus*, where he seith þus: 'If it be so þat þere be amongis ȝou in ȝoure monasterie eld men þat passe iiii score ȝere, whech haue lyued in clennesse of body and soule many ȝeres and endewred in holy exercise, þat is to seyn fastyng, wakyng and oþir bodyly penauns, these men fro þat age forward schul bere non office ne no charge of þe monastery, for þei ded whil þei myth. Grucch ȝe not þat be ȝonger þouȝ þei do not now as þei ded sumtyme, for þei may not. If þei rest whan ȝe laboure, merueyle not; if þei be worchippid of me as elde faderes schuld be, lete no heuynesse take ȝou, for þei be wel worthi to receyue swech worchip. Therfor we wil, and in þe name of Crist here we ordeyn þat þei þat drawe to þe age of a hundred ȝere, þei schal sitte stille in her beddis and sey her *Pater noster*, and ȝe withouten grucching schul serue hem. This seruyse schul ȝe do with þe bettir wil, for I wil þat ȝe knowe who þe conuersacioun of hem is now in heuene, and ȝe schal þe sonnere com þidir because of here prayer.'

3 þ *before* whane *excised* 10 receyued] d *interlineated* tyme *interlineated in red* 23 þei[3] *interlineated in red*

5-6 made hool and sound] Jordanus has a quotation from Matt. 16, 18: *Super egenos manus imponent et bene habebant.*

8 Of þe Cyte of God] *De civitate Dei*, CCL 48, 821.

16-17 ageyn ydilnesse] *Ad fratres,* Sermo 17, PL 40.1264.

Anoþir condicioun had þis glorious seynt: þat he wold neuyr occupie
38r himselue with non / worldly occupacioun, for hous ne feld wold he neuyr bye, and many heritages þat men wold leue onto him he forsook hem. He seid it was more conuenient þat her childyrn schuld haue hem þan þe cherch. The charge of his houshold both in receyuyng and in paying he committed onto þe best avised clerkis whech dwellid with him: on had þe gouernauns o ʒere, anoþir, anoþir ʒere, and at þe ʒeris ende he þat went fro þe office ʒaue clere acountis both of þe receytis and eke of þe expenses. He himselue wold neuyr ber keye of non office ne no tresore, but euyr was he ʒoue to study and goostly occupacioun. To þese swete occupaciones inclined he his entent, labourand in þe law of God day and nyth. Newe werkis whan þei schuld be mad he comitted to oþir men, for he wold not haue his soule implicat with swech bysynesse, but kept it fre to holy meditacioun and deuoute lesson. He despised not hem þat wold haue þis occupacion, ne seid not ageyn hem, lesse þan þe werkis were ouyr costful, þane wold he grucch.

There dwelt no woman withinne his hous, nout his owne sistir ne þe douteres of his broþir, and ʒet were þei weddid to God in holy religioun. He wold sey þus: 'With my sistir or my necys is þere no suspecioun, but þere schuld come many women to hem. And eke þouʒ I be of her kyn, al myn houshold is not so.' He wold neuyr speke with no woman alone, þouʒ it were rith grete councell. If he schuld speke with hem, clerkys and seruauntis schuld stande aboute, and þouʒ þei herd not what was sayd þei
38v myth se what was doo. This cautele of so wyis / a man schuld be to us alle a grete lernyng. We rede þat he wold sey sumtyme to hem þat were aboute him, 'Leue me, in þat I wil sey as a man þat hath in þis matere gret experiens; before God, þat I sey I lye not. The grete cedre trees of Lyban, þe grete lederes of þe Cristen flok, haue I knowe þat þei haue falle be þe pestilens of lecherye, of whos fal I had no more suspecioun þan I had of Ambrose or Ierom.'

40 ber] r *added in red*; ber *also in left margin in red* 55 us alle *interlineated over* a man *excised*

48 There dwelt no woman withinne his hous] see van Bavel, *Augustiniana* 39 (1989) 5-53.

57 Leue me] Jordanus, 'Ipse enim dixisse legitur in libro De cohabitacione clericorum et mulierum: Experto crede, episcopus loquor...'. (For 'episcopus' in Jordanus, read 'expertus' in PL 49.1147B [notes].) Neither title nor quotation appear among the bona fide or apocryphal works of St. Augustine. See Warnock and Zumkeller, *Heinrichs von Friemar*, 195 and note where the same title and quote appear in his German Tract on the discernment of spirits.

Of oþir meruelous condicionis of þis man. xxxix

The monasteries where nunnes dwelled wold he neuyr entyr withoute a grete and a notable cause. Thre þinggis he seyde he lerned of Seynt Ambrose: The first þat he schuld neuyr procure no wyf to no man; þe secund þat he schuld neuyr councell man to go to werre; þe þird þat he schuld go to no feest. The cause of þe first is þat if þe husbond and þe wyf acorde not weel þei schuld curs hym þat mad þe mariage; and also it is not semly þat he whech is a religious man and boundyn to chastite schuld excite oþir folk to fleschly lykyng. The cause of þe secund is if it be soo þat he whech schal fytyn make ony fals chalange, þan schul men wite it on him þat ȝaue him councell. The cause of þe þird is if a man go often to festis, he schal ete or drynk sum tyme oute of mesure, and speke sumtyme þat myth be left.

Othis hated he gretly and most special in religious men, for at his bord was mad þis statute þat what man rehersid ony oth þere, he schuld lese o
39r disch of his seruyse. / For it was assigned of grete discrecioun who mech mete a man schuld haue at his bord, and eke who mech drynk, and alle were þei serued equaly vndir a proporcioun.

He praised mech þoo men þat haue desire to deye, and to þis conclusion he wold often reherse exaumples of thre bischoppis. Seynt Ambrose, whan he lay at his last ende and schuld deye, his disciples þere prayed him þat he schuld ask of oure lord lenger lyf. And he answered þus to hem, 'I haue not lyued so amongis ȝou þat I am aschamed for to lyue lenger, ne eke I am non aferd to deye, for we haue a good lord.' This answere of Ambrose Augustin praised mech. Anoþir bischop, he seid, lay on deying, and þei þat were aboute him desired gretly his lyf, for he was as þei said ful necesarie to þe cherch. He answered þus ageyn in schort sentens, 'Neuyr wel, but if euyr schal it be wel, why not now?' He ment as long as a man lyueth he is neuyr in parfith goodnesse; and if euyr schuld he com to rest and parfith pes, it schal be at his deth, specialy if he deye weel. Of þe þird bischop seith he þat Seynt Cypriane told þat whan þis bischop cam to his last ende and schuld deye, at instauns of hem þat were aboute him he prayed God to make him hool agayn. And þan, as he tellith, a fayre ȝong man stood be his bed side and loked angryly vpon him for þat desire, and rith þus he saide onto him, 'To suffir tribulacioun and miseries of þis world

31 þat[2]] t *added in red* 35 world *preceded by excised* wol

14-16 Capgrave omits the specific oaths cited by Jordanus, perhaps out of consideration for his female reader.

28-30 He ment...deye weel] Capgrave's gloss.

35-37 To suffir...no will] Capgrave expands upon the angel's rebuke.

ȝe be euyr aferd, and for to go oute of þese tribulaciones whan messageris
39v com for ȝou, ȝe haue no will. What schal I / do onto ȝou?'

Seldom wold he write for ony causes to lordes or astates withouten grete informacion of treuth; and whane he wrote he tempered so his wordes þat he schuld haue þe grete part of his peticioun. He was more redy to make acord betwix hem þat were not gretly of his aqweyntauns þane betwix his frendis; for he wold sey if he mad acord betwix to þat were not of his knowlech he myth perauenture fauoure þe o partye whech had more treuth, and þanne schuld he wynne on of hem to his frenchip. And betwyx his frendis it myth falle þe reuers; for þat man þat had not his desire wold þe rather falle fro his frenchip.

Who he hatid heretikes and pursewed hem. Capitulum xl

Heretikes hated þis man with an holy angir: as þe psalme seith, Beth angry and synne not. He was an hard hambyr, euyr knokkyng upon hem. And þei were so aferd of his argumentes þat þei desired his deth in so mech þat þei prechid amongis hem, to hem þat were of here secte, þat for to kylle Augustyn it was no synne but an holy dede and a meritory; and what man þat durst do þis dede þei durst vndirtake alle his synnes schuld be forȝoue of God. For þat dede doyngis thei layde grete wayte upon him oftintyme, but oure lord euyr defended his knyth whech was ful necesarie onto þe cherch. For whan he was oute in þe cuntre sumtyme to preche þe word of God and to lerne Cristen soules þe trewe byleue, leyd men of armes prýuyly in þe weye to kille him homward.
40r But / by þe grace of God he was stered to take anothir weye, and so was he saf fro his enmyes. And whan he knew what perel he was in and who meruelously God had delyuered him, him onweting, þanne þankid he God with ful deuoute hert. But for alle þese perell[es] he cesed neuyr fro edificacion of þe puple and destruccioun of þoo enmyes whech berk ageyn þe feith.

2 Heretikes hated þis man] Jordanus, 'Hereticos vir iste sanctus validissime confutabat.'

2-3 Beth angry...] Ps. 4.5.

3 He was an hard hambyr] Jordan does not have this metaphor. Sanderlin, *Speculum* 18 (1943) 362 attributed it to Capgrave; Arbesmann, (*Traditio* 3 [1945] 389-391) showed that it appeared in Bartholomew of Urbino's *Elogia* included in Jordanus' *Collectanea*.

9-10 defended his knyth] Jordanus, 'pugilem suum preseruauit'.

Many heresies were in his cuntre at þat tyme, both of þe Donatistes and eke of þe Manicheis; and both, with þe myty grace of God whech was plenteuously withinne him, he conuicte and ny distroyed. The Donatistes were þei þat be cleped *Rebaptizatores*, for þei wold admitte no man to here secte but if he were baptized newly with here baptem. Thei lyued in continent lif, þat is to seyn in chastite as ferre as myth be aspied. Þei had eke a secte withinne hem whech þei clepid *Circumcelliones*. Þis meny runne aboute on nytes with wepun and armure, and compelled men with strokis to her heresie. The Manycheis had many oþir fals opiniones, for þei said þat Crist was no very man but lich a man, and þat he took no flesch ne blood of þe mayde as we beleue; but he took, I wot not veryly what þei mene, a body þei sey of þe eyr, in whech he ded alle þoo myracles and in whech he suffered passioun. These folk with sly termes deceyued many men. There were also in his tyme oþir heretikes cleped *Pelagianes*. And þei held þis opynyoun þat a child begoten of a Cristen man and a Cristen woman schuld not be baptized ne nedith nowt. And alle þis secte oure Augustin distroyed.

These be þe names of heretikes whech wrote ageyn hym and to whom he gaf answere ful substancial: Felix, Maximinius, Felicianus, Faustus,
40v Pascenous, Secun/dinus, Petilianus, Parmenianus, Fortunatus, Cresconius,
Gaudencius, Iulianus and many oþir. Ageyn alle þese þis souereyn maystir of þe cherch stood as a strong geaunt, wrestiling with argumentis for þe

24 aspied *in right margin red with // text and margin* 26 compelled] compleled *MS*; *first* l *deleted* 27 / *divides* oþir *and* fals 34 not be] be not be *MS*; *first* be *excised*

19 Many heresies were in his cuntre] Jordanus, 'multe et quasi infinite hereses in Affrica pullulabant'. Augustine in *De haeresibus*, CCL 46.286-345, enumerates 87 heresies in the Church from Simon Magus (Acts 8.9-24) to Pelagius.

22-24 *Rebaptizatores*...] the term and the explanation are by Capgrave.

27-31 The Manycheis...suffered passioun] Capgrave's explanation.

32-34 And þei...nedith nowt] Capgrave's explanation.

35-38 These be þe names...] The first seven are from Jordanus; the last five were added by Capgrave. Augustine wrote the following works against them: (1) Felix: *Contra Felicem libri duo*, CSEL 25.801-852. (2) Maximinius: *Contra Maximinium hereticum libri duo,* PL 42.743-814. (3) Felicianus: *Contra Felicianum de unitate trinitatis*, PL 42.1158-1172. (4) Faustus: *Contra Faustum*, CSEL 25.251-797. (5) Pascenous (*recte* Pascencius): *Altercatio cum Pascentio Ariano*, CSEL 57.533-562. (6) Secundinus: *Contra Secundinum liber*, CSEL 25.905-947. (7) Petilianus: *Contra litteras Petiliani*, CSEL 52.3-227. (8) Parmenianus: Contra epistulam Parmeniani, CSEL 51.19-141. (9) Fortunatus: *Disputatio contra Fortunatum*, CSEL 25.83-112. (10) Cresconius: *Contra Cresconium Donatistarum episcopum*, CSEL 52.325-582. (11) Gaudencius: *Contra Gaudentium Donatistarum episcopum*, CSEL 53.201-274. (12) Iulianus: *Contra Julianum Pelagianae defensorem*, PL 44.641-874.

clennesse of þe feith and enforsyng of þe cherch and confirmacioun of parfite soules. Many a man eke þat was in erroure, þorw his preching and disputyng was brout to þe trew wey of oure lord and onto Cristen feith. Sumtyme in his prechyng wold he make a grete digression fro þe matere þat he spak of, onto anoþir desperat matere, and þane wold he sey þat þis was þe dispensacioun of oure lord, for þere was sum man in þe audiens þat had nede to here þat matere. On a tyme he happid in a sermone to go fro his matere and speke ageyn þe errour of þese Manicheis and a rich marchaunt þat was of þat heresie was sodeynly conuerted þerby. Whanne he was cleped to ony councell of bischoppis or of princes, he wold gladly go to hem. And euyr in þoo councell peysed he more þe causes þat long onto God þan þoo þat long onto men.

Of many bokes þat he mad aftir he was bischop. Capitulum xli

Al þat tyme whil he was bischop, he was gretly occupied in studying and wryting and makyng of bokis. On of þe first booke he mad is entitled To Sympli[ci]an. This Simplician aftir Seynt Ambrose was ded was chose archbischop of Melan. For whan Ambrose lay in deying, þe clerkis of þe cherch comound amongis hem who schuld be bischop aftir, and he assigned hem þat þei schuld chese Simpli[ci]ane. This
41r same was þe man we / saide before þat with holy lif and deuoute exhortaciones brout Augustin to þe feith. And whanne he herd sey þat Augustin was bischop at Ypone–and famed þorw þe world as for þe grettest laburere in study and þe grettest enmye to heretikes, eke þe grettest dissoluere of qwestiones þat was leuand–heryng al þis he sent to him certeyn questiones, praying him to dissolue hem and declare onto him þe doutis þat þei conteyned. And Augustyn wrote onto him ageyn with ful grete reuerens to notable bokes, in whech he declareth his questiones with swech wordes þat þei be ful delectable to studious men. This book beginnyth *Gratissimam plane*.

49 gladly] galdly *MS*; gladly *in left margin*
5 Symplician[1]] Symplian *MS* 6 chose *preceded by* chop *excised* 8 Simpliciane] Simpliane *MS* 17 This book *preceded by* In þis same tyme *excised* 18 plane *preceded by* sane *excised*

5 To Symplician] *Ad Simplicianum de diversis quaestionibus septem,* CCL 44.7-91.
6-7 Ambrose ley in deying] Capgrave's addition.
17-18 Capgrave adds the *initium*, *Gratissimam* '*sane*', then substitutes '*plane*'. *Retractationes*, CCL 44.7, has '*Gratissimam sane*', but notes that '*plane*' is found in some manuscripts.

In þis same tyme wrote he xiii bokes of his *Confessiones*, in whech bokes he schryuyth him ful deuoutly of his euel dedis, and of his good dedis he praysith oure lord both mercyful and rithful. Be þese bokes he his selue was excited to ful holy lif, & þe makyng of hem inflawmed his hert to gret loue of oure lord. I dar sauely sey þere is not so hard hertid man in þe world þat redith þese bokes and vndirstand hem, but þei wil stere his hert to swech deuocioun þat perauenture he hath not had experiens of swech deuocioun before. For alle þe processe of þese bokes and alle þe wordes are steryng onto þe loue of God and þo ar spoken with so swete langage þat þei sounde noþing but deuocioun.

He mad þat tyme eke a book whech he clepith Of þe werkis of munkis, for in his cuntre at þoo dayes were encresed many monasteries of munkis and mech noumbir of religious men, for alle þoo heremites whech lyued in desert to whom he was first fadere and norcher were cleped at þat tyme
41v munkis. For *monos* in þe oþir tonge is as mech to say as solitari. / And so *monachus*, þat i[s] to sey a munk, is swech a man þat lyueth in solitary lyf. But whan Seint Benet cam, þane mad he þe ordre of þo men whech be clepid now munkys propirly. For oþir orderes ar now distincte in her propir names, and at þat tyme þat Augustin was, þis *monachus* was a comoun name to alle religious. For not only Seint Benet mad þese cenobites, whech is as mech to sey as many men lyuyng togidir in on hous and vndir o reule, but Seynt Augustin mad swech eke. For his principall laboure, as we rede, was þis whanne he cam first to Affrik: to gadere swech solitari men and bryng hem to o lyf and o reule. For Augustyn was before Benet as ferforth as I haue red vpon a hundred ȝere and fifty.

So þis book *De opere monachorum*, Of munkys werkys, mad he to þis entent: summe of þese religious men saide þat it was not nedful onto hem to praye, but þei were bounde to laboure with here handes. Thei were

27 þei] i *in red added to* þe 34 is[1]] it *MS* sey] y *inserted* 36 oþir *preceded by* or *excised* 41 gadere] gadered *MS*; *final* d *deleted* 45 nedful] ledful *MS*; le *excised*, ne *interlineated* 46 to praye] *bis in right margin*; *second* to praye *excised*; *red / / text and margin* to laboure *preceded by* þerto *excised and deleted*

23 þere is not so hard hertid man] Jordanus, 'non est aliquis ita durus et indeuotus'.

29 Of þe werkis of munkis] *De opere monachorum*, CSEL 41.531-596.

33-43 *monos*...ȝere and fifty] Capgrave's explains and expands. Jordanus does not mention Benedict of Nursia, who is generally recognized as the Father of Western monasticism. Modern studies confirm Capgrave's view. Cf. Zumkeller, *Augustine's Ideal*, 429-433.

meuyd to þis opynyoun be a texte of Seint Poule, whech seith þat he whech wil not laboure schal not ete. And in anoþir place he seith þus: Be nyth and eke be day haue we laboured, þat we schuld greue non of ȝou alle. Summe held þe reuers opynyoun and enforsed hem with þe gospell where he seith: Take hed at þe birdis of þe eyr; þei sowe neythir ne repe, and ȝet ȝoure fadere of heuene fedith hem. And in þat same place he seith: Take hed at þe lylyis of þe feld; þei spynne not ne carde, and ȝet Salamon was not clad so freschly in al his ioye. This contencioun roos onto so grete partye þat alle þe cherch was set o rore with þis mater, so ferforth þat þe bischop of
42r Cartage, whech hith Aurelius at þat tyme, wrote down onto / Augustyn letteris in whech he prayed him and reqwyrid him in Cristis name þat he schuld ordeyn sum remedye in þis matere. And for þis cause oure fadere Augustin wrot þis book in whech he schewith þat certeyn houres it is most conuenient to religious men to synge, rede or pray. And whan þo orisones are do whech are ordeyned be constituciones of þe cherch, þane is it ful necessarie to do sum laboure with hand, þat ydilnesse whech is stepmodir of alle vertu schul non entre haue in hem.

Of oþir bokes whech he wrote at þat same tyme. Capitulum xlii

In þo same dayes he wrote eke þe bokes Of þe trynyte xv, of grete and hy sentens, oute of whech bokes alle þe dyuynes þat haue writyn sithe, specialy in skole matere, haue þe reulys of alle dyuynyte. For Hugo de Sacramentis and þe maistir of sentens, Seynt Thomas Alqwyn, and alle oþir haue here special groundes þere. He mad eke anoþir

59 is *interlineated in red* 62 stepmodir *preceded by* stp *excised*

47-48 he whech wil not laboure] Thess. 3.10.

48-49 Be nyth and eke be day] Thess. 3.8.

51-52 Take hed at þe birdis...] Matt. 6.28. Capgrave provides the full verse in place of Jordanus' abbreviated version.

52-54 Take hed at þe lylyis...] Matt. 6.26. Capgrave provides the full verse in place of Jordanus' abbreviated version.

62 ydilnesse whech is stepmodir] Capgrave's metaphor.

3 Of þe trynyte xv] *De trinitate libri quindecim*, CCL 50 & 50A.

4-7 Remarks on the indebtedness of later theologians to *De trinitate* are by Capgrave; he omits Jordanus' 'quem iuuenis incepit et senex edidit'.

6 Hugo de Sacramentis] Hugo of St. Victor; the sobriquet derives from his *De sacramentis christianae fidei.*

6 maistir of sentens] Peter Lombard (d. 1160).

solempne werk clepid Of þe cyte, and þe cause why he mad þis book is þis. Whech tyme þat Rome was take of hethen men, þe same hethen men scorned Cristen men and blasphemed Crist in þis maner: Thei saide as long as Rome seruyd his goddis–Iubiter, Iuno, Appollo, Minerue and swech othir –so long was it kept be prouision of þoo immortal goddis þat þere myth non of her enmyes ouyrcom hem. But aftyr þat tyme þat Petir and Paule had brout in þe feith of Crist, anon alle her enmyes had þe bettyr of hem. Of whech ymaginacioun þei added to her blaspheme þat Crist had neuyr so mech powere to defende his puple as had Iubiter whech stood in here capitoll.

Ageyn þese grete blasphemes Seynt Augustin answered in þese xxii
42v bokes. In þe first v bokes he repreuyth þe errour of hem / þat seyde alle þe richesse of þis world and alle þe prosperite is ȝouen onto men be þoo immortall goddis; for he schewith here pleynly þat þoo ydoles whech þei clepe goddis ar dampned spirites, and þoo men þat ded worchip onto hem regned in as gret myschef as euyr ded ony men. In þe oþir v bokes he laboureth ageyn þe erroure of hem þat seide good and euel in þis world haue her variauns aftir place and tyme and persones; þat sum place & sum tyme and sum persone schal haue ioye euyr and sum none. In þe oþir xii bokes he spekith of too citees, Ierusalem and Babilonie; Ierusalem, as he seith, longith to God, Babilonie to þe deuele. These too citees spryngin of too loues. The loue of oure selue, þat causeth þe cite of þe deuel, whech growith in heith tyl he comth on þat abusion þat he despiseth God. The loue of God, he makith þe oþir cite, and he may growe so hy to Goddis plesauns, þat he schal for Goddis loue despise alle worldly felicite.

Beside þese werkys he mad many a book, tretys, epistoles, sermones, omelies, þat a man schal not fynde a clerk at þese dayes þat may sey he haue red alle; for þe noumbir of hem ar gessid onto a þousand. Of his werkis spekith a gret clerk in a vers rith þus: *Mentitur quem se te totum legisse fatetur*. Thus it meneth in Englisch, He lyeth þat seith he hath red al þi bokes.

15 þei *preceded by* þai *excised* 21 þoo *interlineated in red above* þat *excised* 36 se *in left margin*; / / *in margin and text*

8 Of þe cyte: *De civitate Dei libri viginti duo*, CCL 47, 48.

10-17 in þis maner...here capitoll] Capgrave expands, including the names of the pagan gods and the blasphemy of comparing Christ unfavourably with Jupiter.

17 capitoll] the temple of Jupiter on the Capitoline Hill in Rome.

21-23 for he schewith...ony men] Capgrave's explanation.

36-37 *Mentitur quem se te totum legisse fatetur*] not in Jordanus, nor in Possidius. The 'gret clerk' is most probably Isidore of Seville. See Arbesmann, *Traditio* 18 (1962) 349-350; Brandt, *Philologus*, 16.

Who Augustyn red ouyr alle his bokes a litil before
43r his deth & corrected hem. / Capitulum xliii

Afftir tyme he had mad alle þese bokes, he ouyr lokid hem ageyn þat þere schul no þing be þerin but trewe. This þing ded he for many causes. On was for he mad many bokes or þe tyme þat he was gretly vsed or exercised in holy scripture. Anoþir cause was for certeyn materis whech he had wrytin þei were dirkly seid; wherfor he declared þoo materes in þis secund writyng. The þird cause was þat he was not aschamed to be aknowe þat he had wrytyn mech þing whech myth a be bettir, & for þis cause he mad þat book whech he clepith his *Retractaciones*. And þat he schuld haue þe more leysere to study and write, specialy for in too councellis alle þe bischoppis of þe lond had reqwyrid him þat he schuld entend onto exposicioun of holy scripture, for þis cause certeyn ȝeres before his deth he prayed ful mekely þe clergy and þe puple þat fyue dayes in þe weke he myth haue pesibily to his study in scripture, and þe oþir too dayes wold he ȝeue attendauns onto here causes to sette rest and pes betwix hem.

But for al þis graunt, oft tyme was his studie interrupt for here causes, to his grete vexacioun but special counfort of his puple. For þis skil he ordeyned anoþir remedye. He say wel þat he felle fast in age, and deth þat no man may escape was ful ny, because he felt himselue so febil. He dred eke þat aftir his deth sum ambicious man schuld be mad bischop whech schuld distroye al þat euyr he had edified. Þerfor laboured he onto þe puple
43v þat þei schuld chese sum good man and iuste, þat / myth occupie þat se aftir his deth; whech man schuld determyn þe causes of þe puple, lest þat þei were grete causes, þo wold he kepe to himself. To his desire þei consented alle, and mad compromisse onto his persone þat whom he wold name, þei schul consent onto him. Vpon þis Augustin named on of his clerkis, þei clepid him Eraclius, a man wel named in þe puple, whom Augustin had enformed in þe weye of Crist in þe best maner. And to þis man comitted Augustin alle þe charge of þat diosise, lest þan þere com ony grete causes, þat he schuld haue þe more leisir to study and wrytyng. Thus er he deyid he ouyr say alle his bokes and mad þese *Retractaciones*. But aftir making of þat werk he mad many oþir bokes whech be not touchid þerin as a man may se in þe redyng.

7 whech] ch *interlineated in red* 9 aschamed] d *interlineated in red* 18 But *preceded by excised long descender* 19 skil *interlineated in red over* cause *excised in red*

10 *Retractaciones*] *Retractationum libri duo,* CCL 47.5-142.

Who his cyte was besegid of dyuers naciones. xliiii

In þis same tyme iii sundry naciones beseged þe cite of Ypone. Þei ar cleped þus: Alani, Gothi and Wandali. These Alani dwelle in a gret cuntre here in þis part of þe world cleped Europe, whech cuntre þei calle Sithia. It is hens northest toward Constantinople. Gothi dwelled fast by hem, for þese cuntres occupied ny fro þe grete flod cleped Danubius unto þat cuntre whech we clepe Denmark, for of þese Gothis cam þese Danes. Wandaly dwelled sumtyme in þe same place where Lumbardes dwelle now, aboute Melan and Pauye. Alle þese puple þus gadered togidyr ded mech harm here in Europe aboute Rome and in Ytale, and þane went
44r þei ouyr þe se into Affrik and þere distroyed þe cuntre; and / at þe last ende of Augustin lyf þei beseged þe cite of Ypone.

Vndir þis tribulacion Augustin had ful heuy dayes and wept both day & nyth for þe myschef þat he say whech þese men ded; for þei spared no cherchis ne prestis ne nunnes ne non ordre. And whan Augustin say sum deye in captiuite, sum in prison, summe of þe swerd; and þat þe seruyse, þe messis, þe ympnis of þe cherch cesed; and many cherchis were brent in þe cuntre and þe clerkis fled, so þat sacramentis were not ȝouen, and þouȝ a man wold haue hem, þere was no man to gyue hem. He seing al þis had ful grete sorow, so þat he felle into greuous seknesse. But ȝet amongis al þis sorow he had þat consolacioun of þe wise man whech saide þus: He hath no grete wisdam þat sorowith whan stones falle, and whan þei deye þat must nedis deye.

In þis tribulacioun he cleped his breþerin togidyr, and þus he saide onto hem: 'Behold now in what mischef we stand in, and I se no remedye. God wil pun[i]sch us in þis wyse for oure synnes. Wherfor I haue prayed my lord þat he schuld delyuere us of þese perelles or elles send us paciens þat we may suffyr hem mekely. Or ellis if he se þat we be worþi for to haue hem lenger, I haue prayed God þat he schal take me oute of þis lyf.' This

2 ar *interlineated in red with red* ^ 3 cleped] d *interlineated* 5 dwelled] *last* d *interlineated with two red //* 6 Danubius *followed by second* us *excised* 19 seing *in right margin;* seying *in text excised* 26 punisch] punsch *MS* 32 he *preceded by* w *excised*

3-12 Alani, Gothi and Wandali...] the horror and panic which attended this invasion are described in Augustine's letter to Honorius (*Epistola* 228, CSEL 57. 484-496) which Possidius used as Chapter 30. The geographic notes on the tribes are Capgrave's.

21-22 He hath no grete wisdam] Plotinus, *Enneads* 14.7. See Courcelle, 'Les dernières paroles s. Augustin', REA 46 (1944) 205-207.

25-29 'Behold now...lyf'] Capgrave expands the quotation from Augustine.

same prayere þat he prayed þei prayed alle, and so on of þese iii peticiones was graunted him, for in þe þird month aftir þei had besegid þe cyte, þe feuerys took him so sore þat he was fayn to kepe his bed.

44v In what maner / Augustyn deyid and what occupacioun he had in his last sekenesse. Capitulum xlv

In þis same seknesse of whech he deyid, þere cam onto hym a certeyn man praying him in þe name of oure lord þat he wold touche him with his hand, for he seide if he wold ley hand upon him, he schuld make him hool of þat seknesse whech he had longe bore. Augustyn answered to hym ageyn and seide he was not wys in his desire, for if he had swech powere to make men hool he wold rather exercise it on himself þane on oþir men. The man replied onto Augustyn in þis maner. He seide þat he had in maner of a goostly consolacioun, in whech he was warned þat he schuld go to Augustyn þe bischop, and with touching of his hand he schuld be mad hool. Augustyn, seing þe grete feith of þis man, leyd his hand upon him & blessed him in þe name of God, and þus was he mad hool.

Thus encresid þe seknesse upon him þat he vndirstood wel he schuld sone deye. And because he had prechid ofte sithe þat þere schuld no Cristen man passe owt of þe world withouten mornyng and compleint for defautes in whech he hath falle, therfor he mad his notari for to write him þe vii psalmes, þoo same whech we rede with þe letanye, in a fayre parchemyn skyn, and þis was sette on þe wal ageyn his beddis hed. These red he with ful grete deuocioun and grete wepyng before his deth. And þat þere schuld no man interrupte him of þis deuocion ten dayes before his deth, he ordeyned þat þere schuld no man com withinne þe chaumbyr where he /
45r lay but his leche and þei þat brout him mete and drynk. And alle þis tyme with ful grete deuocion and mech wepyng he comended his soule to God, and þus þe v kalende of September with hool mynde and alle þe membris of his body not hurt but hool, standyng his breþerin aboute him and comendyng hys soule to God, he ȝald þe goost onto þe fadere of heuene.

Thus hath he left in erde his holy footsteppis. Many men & women of his religioun taute [h]e his doctrine. He hath left eke grete instruccioun to

23 withinne] withimme *MS*; *two minims deleted* 30 he[1]] be *MS*

19 vii psalmes] the seven penetential psalms: 6, 37, 51, 102, 130, and 143. In the 13th century Pope Innocent III recommended them as a suitable Lenten prayer.

þe cherch in tresoure of his bokes, þat þouȝ his body be drawe from vs, ȝet his spirit abideth with us. As þe poete wrot ful wel of alle hem whech leue emolliment of wryting behinde hem, rith þus he wrot in Latin: *Viuere post obitum vatem vis nosce viator, Quod legis ecce loquor vox tua nempe mea est.* Thus mene þei in Englisch, Thou man þat passist by, if þou wilt knowe þat a clerk lyueth aftir his deth, that þou redist I speke, þi voys eke is myn. Augustyn lyued clerk and bischop ny xl ȝere; alle þe dayes of his lyf ar seuenety and sex. Thus endith þe lyf of þis glorious doctoure whom alle Cristen men ar bounde to do worchip, most specialy clerkys and lerned men þat haue grete stuf oute of his bokes to her lernyng.

And as I hope, ȝe gentyl woman, ȝe schuld plese wel þis seint if ȝe wold se his place onys in a ȝere; and þouȝ ȝe left a day in heruest of ȝoure laboure, [ȝ]e coude make retribucioun in oþir party. Thus I comende ȝou to God, and me to ȝoure prayeris; þat we both may com sumtyme where oure fader is, we schal prey both. Amen.

43 ȝe] he *MS*

35-36 Thus mene...eke is myn] The English gloss is Capgrave's.
41-45 And as I hope...Amen] Capgrave adds this admonition.

Jordanus of Saxony

Vita s. Augustine

The Manuscript

Paris, Bibliothèque de l'Arsenal, MS 251

[4rb]

Prologus in vitam sancti Augustini episcopi

Almi patris ac doctoris eximii Augustini Yponensis episcopi ortum procursumque ac finem vite, auxiliante eo qui laudatur in sanctis suis, fideliter descripturus nichil huic operi inserendum censui quod non ipsius propriis dictis aut aliorum autenticis scriptis continetur. Secutus precipue vestigium illius venerandi viri sancti Posidonii Calamensis episcopi eiusdem sancti patris discipuli, et in suo monasterio olim canonici, qui eius gesta prout uiderat et per experienciam didicerat, diffuse conscripsit, ad ea maxime se referens tempora quibus ipse cum eo presentialiter fuerat conuersatus. Neque enim tantus doctor veritatis honorari se gratum duceret laudibus falsitatis. Ipse etenim dicit in primo libro De trinitate: 'Malim,' inquit, 'me reprehendi a reprehensore falsitatis quam ab eius laudatore laudari.' Porro hoc unum obsecro eum qui hec legerit ut si qua hic scripta repererit que vulgatis legendis non habentur, non prius dentem mordacem exerat quam signatarum remissionum loca studiose requirat. Nec temeritati mee quisquam ascribat quod post tam magnorum virorum studia qui legendas eiusdem [4va] sancti doctoris con/scripserunt ausus sum manum ponere, quia profecto sepe spice que maiorum metencium manus effugiunt a paruulis colliguntur.

Incipit tractatus De vita sancti Augustini episcopi

Augustinus doctor egregius ex prouincia Affricana ciuitate Thagathensi honesta prosapia de numero curialium, patre quidem adhuc gentili, Patricio nomine, matre uero dicta Monica christianissima progenitus fuit. Qui diuino nescientes ducti consilio hunc summa eorum cura et diligentia enutritum, litterali inbuendum tradiderunt studio quem prescia futuri diuina clementia tanti ingenii ditauit perspicacia ut non solum coeuorum verum eciam grandeuorum discendi agilitate preuolaret studia. Parentes autem eius tanto profectui congaudentes que illi erant necessaria, magna preparabant diligencia, mirantibus cunctis eorum vicinis cum attenderent quantam illi filio impenderent curam, non considerantes quid expenderent dum pro uoto proficeret. Vna autem dierum puer nimio dolore stomachi vexatus anxius valde laborabat. Hortante igitur matre ut baptizaretur sed renuente [4vb] patre baptisma / dilatatum est. Interim miserante dei gratia dolore quiescente sanatus est, cuius mundacio dilata fuit quasi necesse esset ut adhuc sordidaretur si uiueret quia maius peccatum esset si post baptismum peccaret. Grecas sane litteras quibus docebatur oderat, latinas vero satis diligebat ut ipse hec memoratur in primo libro Confessionum.

Paruo igitur tempore in eo quo natus est municipio et in Madauris ciuitate vicina, quo a parentibus missus fuit, doctus grammaticam, inde reuersus cum decimum sextum etatis sue ageret annum, disposuit longius proficissi doceri rethoricam, sed anno illo cum parentibus demoratus et interposito ocio ex necessitate domestica, interim ab omni scola feriatus, cum ageret annos feruentis adolescencie, per devexa lasciuie vagabundus ruebat, patre quidem adhuc cathecumeno non multum curante, matre uero prout poterat reuocante. At ille matris monita quasi anicularia reputans coeuos et consimiles malebat audire quam matri oboedire, ut ipse in secundo libro Confessionum humiliter confitetur. Tandem valefacto parentibus, Carthaginem profectus ibi in scola cuiusdam rethoris incredibili celeritate doctus est.
55ra Cum igitur decem et nouem esset annorum defuncto iam / patre ante biennium, quem in extremo uite sue mater quoque deo lucrata fuerat, discendi ordine peruenit in librum quendam Cyceronis cui nomen Hortensius qui exhortacionem continet ad phylosophiam. In quo eciam vanitas mundi contempnenda docetur et ex hoc quidem liber ei plurimum placuit; sed hoc solum refrangebat quia nomen Christi non erat ibi. Hoc enim nomen saluatoris in ipso adhuc lacte matris tenerum cor eius biberat, et alte retinebat, et quidquid sine hoc nomine fuisset, quamuis altum, expolitum et veridicum, non eum totum rapiebat, prout ipse tertio libro Confessionum refert. Itaque instituit animum suum intendere in scripturas sanctas, ut videret quales essent. Sed *quia sciencia sine caritate non edificat sed inflat*, ipseque tumens erat inani philosophia, reuerberatus aciem in eas figere non valebat. Diuine ergo ualefaciens scripture in Manicheorum errorem incidit qui dei filium non verum corpus sed fantasticum assumpsisse affirmant et carnis resurrectionem negant; ponunt eciam duo rerum principia, unum bonorum et aliud malorum. Ad has eciam nugas perductus est ut arborem fici plorare crederet cum ab ea ficus uel folium decerperetur, ut ipse in eodem libro tercio Confessionum refert. In predicto autem errore permansit fere
55rb novem an/nis, vt in principio quarti libri Confessionum humiliter confitetur. Mater autem eius pro eo multum flebat, amplius quam flere solent matres corporea funera et ipsum ad unitatem fidei ducere satagebat. Cui pro dolore perdicionis filii pene deficienti data est diuinitus huiusmodi consolacio. Quadam enim vice uidit se stare quasi in quadam regula lignea. Et

67 Mater] = Capgrave vii

ecce iuuenis quidam pulcherrimus cultu splendido vultu hylari adueniens arrisit illi flenti. 'Que,' inquiens, 'tibi causa est doloris et luctus continui?' At illa ait: 'Perdicio filii mei.' Cui iuuenis: 'Esto,' inquit, 'secura quia ubi tu, ibi ille.' Et ecce continuo iuxta se filium suum stare uidit. Quod cum euigilans memoriter retineret, ut prudens et magne fidei mulier, interpretata est veraciter, plane cognoscens et asserens apud se quia quandoque in eadem regula veritatis catholice fidei videret Augustinum in qua videbat et se. Non enim reputabat hoc tamquam sompnium sed tamquam diuinum responsum dicens: 'O mulier magna est fides tua, fiat tibi sicut vis.' Quocirca dum idem visum Augustino recenseret, et ille peruerse interpretari conaretur dicens: 'Falleris mater, non tibi sic dictum est, sed vbi ego ibi tu,' et contra illa
5va dicebat: 'Non, fili, mihi dictum est vbi ille ibi tu, sed vbi tu / ibi ille.'

Accepit illa ad consolacionem sui et aliud diuinitus reponsum per quendam episcopum, virum catholicum et sacris litteris eruditum, ad quem cum supplex veniret plorans et deuote postulans ut Augustinum conueniret eumque ab errore suo revocans ad fidem catholicam inuitaret, ille respondit: 'Filius profecto tuus indocilis adhuc est, superbe tumens nouitate illius heresis, paratus magis questiunculas texere quam docenti acquiescere; sustine igitur paulisper et incessanter ora. Legendo enim reperiet quantum sit secta illa, quam diligit, execranda. Nam et ego ipse, cum essem adolescentulus in eodem errore desipui, et legendo et intelligendo quam fugienda esset, cognoui et fugi.' Que responsio cum illi non sufficeret, sed importunitate feminea cum nimia lacrimarum effusione instaret ut cum filio suo loqui dignaretur et eum ad meliora hortaretur, ille quasi tedio percussus: 'Vade,' inquit, 'secura, impossibile enim est ut filius tantarum pereat lacrimarum.' Quod responsum in tantum sibi placuit ac si de celo ei prophecia sonuisset. Hec ipse in tercio libro Confessionum. Cum autem vicesimum etatis sue annum ageret et magister Carthaginensis decem cathegorias Aristotelis lectitaret et illis uix intelligentibus, iste libellum accepit, et solus
5vb domi legens quidquid in eo / latebat per se intellexit. Omnes denique libros arcium liberalium quoscumque invenit legit, quoscumque legere potuit per se ipsum intellexit, ut ipse fatetur in quarto libro Confessionum. Demum cum iam summus phylosophus et rethor luculentissimus haberetur, prius in sua ciuitate Thagatensi scholas regens, docuit gramaticam et inde regressus Carthaginem pluribus annis inibi docuit rethoricam. Eo tempore scripsit tres libros De pulchro et apto ad Hyerium romane vrbis oratorem, quem non nouerat facie sed amabat hominem ex doctrine fama, ut ipse hec testatur quarto libro Confessionum. Anno autem vndetrigesimo etatis sue

97 Cum] = Capgrave viii

venit Carthaginem quidam Manicheorum episcopus Faustus nomine, magnus laqueus dyaboli, nominatissimus apud eos, quod esset honestarum omnium doctrinarum peritissimus. Qui tante fame et auctoritatis erat apud illos, ut qui eum sequerentur non quemlibet hominem sed spiritum sanctum se sequi arbitrarentur. Ad quem cum Augustinus gratia discendi venisset, expertus est hominem gratum et iocundum verbis sed vere sciencie expertem. Quapropter quia questiones quas super dubiis in lege Manicheorum Augustinus sibi collegerat, per illum talem ac tantum doctorem, auctorem, 56ra ducem / et principem illius secte, ut diu speraverat, enodande solute non fuerunt, nec enim ausus fuit cum Augustino sarcinam disputacionis subire, nec eum puduit confiteri se illa nescire. Augustinus igitur omnem conatum quo proficere in illa secta statuerat, exinde prorsus postposuit, contentus sic interim manere, donec aliud melius eligendum eluceret. Hec ipse libro quinto Confessionum. Demum quibusdam amicis persuadentibus cogitauit pergere Romam ut pocius ibi doceret quod docebat Carthagini, maxime quia audierat quiecius ibi studere adolescentes, et quod Carthagini satis esset inquietudo. Verum hec illius cogitacio dei erat dispensacio. Cum autem inchoasset iter, secuta est eum mater usque ad mare. Sed Augustinus fefellit eam, violenter se tenentem ut aut eum reuocaret, aut cum ipso pergeret. Finxit ergo se nolle eam deserere, donec facto vento nauigaret, et mentitus est matri. Nolente autem matre sine eo redire domum, uix ei persuasit ut in loco, qui proximus naui illorum erat, in memoriam beati Cypriani martiris, ea nocte maneret. Cumque illa paululum diuertisset, ascendens ille nocte nauem clanculo profectus est. Illa autem mansit tota nocte flendo et orando ut impediretur nauigium. Flauit continuo ventus et 56rb impleuit vela nauis et litus subtraxit aspectibus / eorum. Reuersa ergo illa mane ad litus, vbi filium dimiserat, prospiciens rem gestam insaniebat intollerabili dolore et gemitu implebat aures dei et nesciebat quid illi deus gaudiorum facturus erat de absencia eius, et ideo flebat et eiulabat. Post multum vero luctum conuersa rursus ad deprecandum pro eo dominum, abiit ad solita. Ille autem peruenit Romam. Hec ipse libro quinto Confessionum. Cum ergo Rome esset, incurrit egritudinem validam et hoc mater nesciebat, sed pro illo orabat absens, et maiore sollicitudine eum parturiebat spiritu quam carne pepererat, cotidie elemosinam faciens et obsequia sanctis, nullo die pretermittens oblacionem. Bis in die mane et vespere ad ecclesiam sine vlla intermissione veniens, non ad vanas fabulas, sed ut dominum audiret in suis sermonibus, et deus illam in suis oracionibus pro salute filii sui. Recreatus ergo ex illa egritudine cepit sedule agere id propter quod venerat, ut doceret Rome artem rethoricam, et congregabantur ad

122 Demum] = Capgrave ix

hospicium eius multi. Post hec missum est a Mediolano Romam ad Symacum prefectum, ut prouideret magistrum rethorice artis, et Mediolanum dirigeret. Tunc ergo Symacus prefectus misit eis Augustinum probatum magistrum. Et venit Mediolanum ad Ambrosium episcopum in optimis /
56va notum orbi terre et suscepit eum paterne. Cepit autem Augustinus viro dei adherere et eius predicaciones frequenter audire, primo quidem non ut veritatem audiret, quod in ecclesia Christi prorsus desperabat, sed explorans vtrum fame illius facundia conueniret, et delectabatur suauitate sermonis non satagens discere que dicebat. Demum cepit paulatim animum rebus magis quam verbis applicare. Hec ipse quinto Confessionum.

Cum autem quadem die beatus Ambrosius in predicacione de incarnacione domini tractitaret, Augustinus astans in populo nutu dei correptus est, et oblitus sui suarumque omnium cogitacionum, pallens et tremens omnibus qui aderant videntibus obriguit. Finita ergo admonicione quam ad populum beatus Ambrosius ministrabat, Augustinus ad eum peruenit patefaciens ei suam tam subitam mutacionem. Quod audiens beatus Ambrosius cognitoque quod in Manicheorum secta iam fluctuans pene diffideret, et per spiritum sanctum cognoscens, qualiter fidelis et catholicus futurus esset, gauisus ualde placidissime et multum caritatiue eum suscepit. Itaque letabatur beatus Ambrosius super eum sicut in ewangelio de quodam patre legitur qui cadens super collum filii sui quem perdiderat et imponens anulum in digito eius plorans deosculabatur eum. Hec sanctus Dacius Mediolanensis episcopus in Cronica sua. Augustinus autem ex tunc illucescente veritate paulisper sectam Manicheorum quam diu tenuerat reliquendam esse decreuit et tam diu in ecclesia catholica catechumenus esse constituit donec plenius eluceret veritas quam teneret. Vt ipse quinto libro Confessionum humiliter confitetur. Inter hec venit ad eum mater pietate fortis terra marique eum sequens et in periculis omnibus de deo secura. Nam et per maxima discrimina ipsos nautas consolabatur, pollicens eis peruencionem cum salute, quia ei deus hoc per uisum promiserat. Invenit ergo filium qui indicauit ei quod Manicheus iam non esset sed nec catholicus. Tunc illa exiliuit leticia inenarrabili cum audisset eum, licet veritatem nondum adeptum, a falsitate tamen iam ereptum, et pectore pleno fiducie ait: 'Credo in Christo quod priusquam migrem de hac uita uisura sim meum
56vb filium fidelem christianum.' Et fundebat / ad deum preces et lacrimas densiores ut acceleraret adiutorium suum et illuminaret tenebras eius. Diligebat enim et ipsa Ambrosium sicut angelum dei quia per illum cognouerat filium suum ad illam fluctuacionem iam esse perductum. Itaque cum ad

148 Post] = Capgrave x 174 Inter] = Capgrave xi

memorias sanctorum, sicut in Affrica solebat, panem et pultes et merum attulisset, ab hostiario prohibebatur. At ubi hoc episcopum vetuisse cognouit, obedienter amplexa est. Hoc enim egentibus tribuendum ferebat et pro canistro pleno terrenis fructibus, plenum purgacioribus votis pectus ad memoriam martyrum offerre didicerat. Igitur omni die dominico audiebat Augustinus Ambrosium verbum veritatis recte populo disserentem sepiusque in suis sermonibus dicentem: *Littera occidit, spiritus autem viuificat.* Et conferebat Augustinus cum karissimis amicis suis Alipio et Nebridio multas questiones. Quorum alter Alipius scilicet ex eodem quo ipse erat ortus municipio, Nebridius autem relicta patria vicina Carthagini, atque ipsa Carthagine, relicto eciam paterno rure optimo venerat Mediolanum querens Augustinum ut secum uiueret in flagrantissimo studio veritatis. Erant ergo hii tres pariter nutantes in consilio quisnam esset modus uite tenende. Et ecce iam tricenarius erat, ut ipse hec libro sexto Confessionum refert. /

57ra

De eius conversione

Cum autem iam via Christi sibi placeret, sed per ipsam adhuc ire pigeret, misit dominus in mentem eius visumque est ei bonum pergere ad Simplicianum heremitam servum dei. Audierat enim quod a iuuentute sua deuotissime deo seruierat et vere sic erat. Iam vero senuerat et multa expertus multa edoctus erat et beatus Ambrosius vere eum ut patrem diligebat. Cui estus cordis et errorum circuitus manifestans deuote postulauit ut uir sanctus proferret ei quis esset aptus modus viuendi sic affecto ut ipse erat ad ambulandum in via dei. Videbat enim plenam ecclesiam et alius sic ibat alius autem sic. Displicebat quippe ei quidquid agebat in seculo pre dulcedine dei et decore domus eius quam dilexit. Simplicianus autem eum hortari cepit et ad humilitatem Christi precipue inuitauit et inter inuitandum Victorini Romani quondam rethoris conuersionem in medium reuocauit. Rome siquidem multis annis Victorinus ille magister fuerat et ob insigne preclari magisterii statuam in Romano foro habere meruerat; qui tandem conuersus loquacem scolam suam deserens in scola Christi humilis discipulus effectus est. Hoc exemplo commonitus Augustinus ad imitandum exarsit
57rb et soli / deo seruire proposuit. Interea cum quadam die essent Augustinus et Alipius pariter in domo et absens esset Nebridius, venit ad eos Poncianus quidam ciuis Affricanus preclare in palacio militans et consederunt ut colloquerentur. Et videns Poncianus forte super mensam lusoriam que ante eos

201 Cum] = Capgrave xiii 217 Interea] = Capgrave xiiii

erat codicem, tulit et aperuit. Invenitque sane inopinate Paulum apostolum; putaverat enim aliquem esse de libris, quorum professio eos continebat. Tunc arridens Augustinumque intuens, gratulatorie miratus est quod eas et solas pre eius oculis litteras comperisset; Christianus quippe fidelis erat ille. Cui cum indicasset Augustinus illis scripturis se maximam curam impendere, ortus est sermo, ipso narrante Ponciano de Anthonio Egypcio monacho cuius nomen excellenter clarebat apud seruos dei, ipsos autem usque ad illam horam latebat. Inde sermo eius deuolutus est ad monasteriorum greges et incolas deserti heremi spiritu pauperes, qualium est regnum celorum. Et erat monasterium Mediolani plenum fratribus bonis extra urbis menia sub Ambrosio nutritore. Augustinus autem nichil horum nouerat, et ideo intente cuncta tacitus audiebat. Addidit quoque Poncianus quodam die cum ipse apud Treueros cum imperatore fuisset, se et tres alios contuber-
57va nales / exisse deambulatum in ortos muris contiguos, unum secum deorsum, et alios duos seorsum pariter digressos, sed illos alios duos vagabundos irruisse in quamdam casam in qua heremite quidam habitabant, et invenisse ibi codicem in quo scripta erat vita Antonii heremite. Quam legere cepit unus eorum et mirari et accendi. Qui ait ad socium suum: 'Ego iam seruire deo statui in hoc loco et hac ipsa hora aggredior; si te piget imitari noli aduersari.' Respondit ille se uelle adherere socio et sic ambo relictis omnibus secuti sunt dominum. Tunc Poncianus et qui cum eo in alia parte deambulabant, querentes eos deuenerunt in eundem locum et inuenientes monuerunt ut redirent quia declinasset dies. At illi narrauerunt propositum suum. Isti autem illis pie congratulati fleuerunt, seque eorum oracionibus commendantes ad palacium abierunt; illi vero in casa manserunt. Quod audientes sponse eorum, dicauerunt et ipse virginitatem deo. Hiis itaque exemplis Augustinus compunctus rodebatur intus et confundebatur pudore horribili vehementer. Nam exempla seruorum dei quos de nigris lucidos et de mortuis viuos fecerat, congesta in sinum cogitacionis sue urebant et accendebant eum valde. Cumque Poncianus abiisset, Augus-
57vb tinus in illa grandi rixa interioris / domus sue tam vultu quam mente turbatus, inuasit Alipium et exclamauit, 'Quid patimur? Quid audimus? Surgunt indocti et rapiunt celum et nos cum doctrinis nostris ecce vbi volutamur in carne et sanguine. An quia precesserunt pudet sequi?' Et cum hec diceret attendebat in eum Alipius attonitus. Non enim solita sonabat verba, plusque loquebantur anima eius, frons, gene, oculi, color, modus vocis quam verba que promebat. Cum autem tali rixa intrinsecus discerperetur, ortulum hospicio suo contiguum ingressus est; at Alipius pedetentim secutus est eum, sederuntque quantum potuerunt remoti ab edibus. Augustinus itaque fremebat spiritu et erat turbulentissimus et accusabat se ipsum,

247 Hiis] = Capgrave xv

Alipius vero affixus [erat] lateri eius tacitus, eum dolens considerabat. Et inter verba accusantis euerso fundo cordis sui et congesta ante oculos mentis uniuersa massa miseriarum suarum, aborta est procella ingens ferens ingentem ymbrem lacrymarum, ad quam liberius effundendam, relicto Alipio in eo quo consederunt loco, paulo remocius secessit. Solitudo quippe illi ad negocium flendi apcior videbatur. Alipius vero mansit in eo quo consederunt loco, nimium stupens. Augustinus autem doloris incontinens
58ra / sub quadam ficu se proiecit et lamentabiles voces dabat dicens: 'Et tu domine; usquequo? Quamdiu, quamdiu? Cras et cras? Quare non modo? Quare non hac hora finis turpitudinis mee?' Dum hec et hiis similia amarissima contritione cordis sui diceret, iactans voces miserabiles, repente audiuit vocem quasi de vicina dom[o] cum repeticione crebro modulantem: 'Tolle lege, tolle lege.' Statimque mutato vultu intentissimus cogitare cepit utrumnam solerent pueri in aliquo genere ludendi tale aliquid cantitare, nec occurrebat. Intellexit igitur diuinitus se moneri ut accepto codice legeret quod primum capitulum inueniret et quod ab illo doceretur ageret. Itaque repressis lacrimis concitus ad locum ubi sedebat Alipius rediit et arrepto codice apostolico, quem iuxta illum, cum inde surgeret, dimiserat, aperuit et legit in silencio capitulum quo primum coniecti sunt oculi eius, *Non in commessacionibus et ebrietatibus, non in cubilibus et impudiciciis, non in contencione et aemulacione, sed induimini dominum Jesum Christum et carnis curam non feceritis in desideriis*. Nec ultra voluit legere nec opus erat. Statimque cum fine huius sentencie quasi luce securitatis infusa cordi eius omnes dubietatis tenebre diffugerunt. Tunc interiecto digito aut nescio quo
58rb alio signo, co/dicem clausit ac tranquillo iam vultu indicauit Alipio quid legisset. At ille peciit videre et accepto codice vidit, et prospiciens quid ultra quam iste legerat haberetur–ignorabat enim Augustinus quid sequeretur–inuenit ille et legit, *Infirmum autem in fide suscipite*. Quod Alipius ad se retulit et Augustino hylariter aperuit, et mox tali ammonicione proposito bono ei coniunctus est. Inde ad matrem Augustini pariter ingrediuntur indicantes ei ordinem rei ut que pro filio dolebat, cum eo consolacionem acciperet. At illa gaudens gracias egit deo qui ei plus quam petisset concesserat. Videbat enim illum non solum ad amorem fidei, verum eciam ad contemptum seculi omnino accensum. Vnde luctus eius in gaudium, planctus versus est in tripudium, stante iam filio in ea regula fidei in qua ante tot annos ei fuerat reuelatus. Hec ipse octauo libro Confessionum.

Iam liber erat animus eius pulsis anxietatibus curarum et suauitatibus nugarum, quibus carere suaue sibi subito factum est, et quas prius amittere

272 domo] doma *MS* 297 Iam] = Capgrave xvi

metus fuerat, iam dimittere gaudium erat. Et placuit ei non tumultuose, sed leniter se subtrahere a scolarum regimine. Iam enim paucissimi dies supe- 58va rerant ad vindemiales ferias, et statuit tollerare eas ut sollempniter ab/scederet. Euolutis autem diebus viginti qui ei longi et multi videbantur pre amore libertatis ociose, a professione rethorica solutus est. Et quoniam soli deo vacandi, orandi et in lege domini meditandi, toto mentis desiderio estuabat, ut locus proposito conueniret, tumultum ciuitatis deserens in rure Cassiaco prope Mediolanum per honoratum virum Verecundum nomine sibi concesso manere decreuit donec ad baptismum aptaretur. In quo rure ab estu seculi requiescens et diuinis lectionibus vacans cum Alipio et aliis amicis suis eodem desiderio flagrantibus, aliquamdiu commoratus est, matre sua eis semper adherente muliebri habitu, uirili fide, anili securitate, materna caritate, christiana pietate. Ut ipse refert nono libro Confessionum. Ibi eciam plures conscripsit libros adhuc cathecumenus videlicet librum De achademicis, librum De ordine, librum Soliloquiorum, et librum De beata vita. Quem librum ipse occasione tali scripsit, olim enim multi diem natalis sui consueuerunt celebrare et ipse Augustinus ante conuersionem suam hoc consueuit. Accidit autem illis diebus quibus Augustinus erat in rure ut dies natalis sui eueniret. Nolens autem ipse diem illum natalis sui de mortali vita amplius celebrare, per tres dies cum sociis quid esset beata uita, sollici- 58vb te disputauit / et tandem diffinitum est inter eos quod beata uita non nisi in dei cognicione consistit. Et hanc disputacionem continet liber iste, ut hec ipse recitat in libro Retractacionum circa principium. Item scripsit ibidem epistulas ad Nebridium, et nonnulla opuscula alia cum ibi presentibus disputata, ut ipse refert nono libro Confessionum. Cum ergo scripturas diuinas legeret earum valde afficiebatur dulcedine et accendebatur vehementer. Legebat et ardebat et dolebat quod latrasset aduersus litteras de melle celi melleas, et de lumine dei luminosas. Et cum legeret psalmos Dauid, quartum assumens psalmum et eius singulos versus attente legens et attencius relegens, a gemitu cordis sui rugiebat et cum flere non sufficeret, voces dolori congruas proferebat. Perueniens autem ad illum versum, *In pace in idipsum dormiam et requiescam*, ut totus in deuocionem ardebat, pre gaudio exclamabat, 'O in pace, O in idipsum, O qui dixit dormiam et requiescam? Tu es, domine, idipsum valde, qui non mutaris et in te solo requies.' Inter hec et multa alia diuine consolacionis beneficia non defuerunt ei acerbe pocula temptacionis. Contigit enim ut graui dentium dolore vexaretur in tantum ut pre dolore loqui non posset. Recolens itaque fideliter illum versi- 59ra culum, *Dominus / exaudiet me cum clamauero ad eum*, ascendit in cor eius admonere eos qui secum aderant, ut orarent dominum pro eo. Et cum non

323 Cum] = Capgrave xvii

posset loqui, scripsit hec in cera et dedit eis legere. Ut autem suppliciter cum illis ad orandum genua flecteret, dolor ille tam velociter fugit ut ipse admirans expauerit cum nil tale ab ineunte etate in se expertus fuerit. Et tunc insinuati sunt ei in profundo nutus domini, et gaudens in fide laudauit nomen domini. Demum insinuat sancto viro Ambrosio per litteras pristinos errores suos, et presens uotum suum, ut ipse moneret quid de libris sanctis legere deberet, quo percipiende christiane gracie apcior fieret atque paracior. At ille iussit Ysaiam prophetam eo quod pre ceteris ewangelii uocationisque gencium sit prenunciator apercior. Cuius principium cum Augustinus non intelligeret, totumque aliud tale esse arbitrans, distulit ut illud relegeret cum in diuinis scripturis magis exercitatus esset. Unde ubi tempus aduenerit quo nomen eum dare oportebat, relicto rure Mediolanum remeauit. Ut hec ipse commemorat nono libro Confessionum. Reuersus itaque de rure in Mediolanum baptismum percepturus, scripsit ibidem librum De immortalitate anime. Et libros disciplinarum ut ipse ait in primo Retractationum.

De eius baptismo

Baptizatus est igitur Augustinus a beato Ambrosio, anno etatis sue tricesimo secundo tempore paschali, ut ait Possidius, in fontibus, qui Beati Johannis ascribuntur, cunctis fidelibus eiusdem urbis astantibus et videntibus deumque laudantibus. In quibus fontibus Ambrosius et Augustinus prout spiritus sanctus dabat eloqui illis, ymnum 'Te deum laudamus' decantantes cunctis qui aderant audientibus et mirantibus ediderunt. Qui eciam ymnus ab universa ecclesia catholica usque hodie tenetur et religiose decantatur. Ut
59rb hec testatur sanctus Dacius Mediolanensis episcopus / in primo libro capitulo decimo Cronice sue.

Denique in eisdem fontibus simul cum ipso Augustino Alipius et puer Adeodatus de ipso carnaliter natus, spiritualiter renati sunt. Quindecim quippe annorum erat puer ille cum in gracia baptismi factus est beato Augustino coeuus tam velocis et ipse ingenii, ut multos grandeue etatis et magne erudicionis agilitate intelligendi preueniret viros. Mirabatur profecto Augustinus et horrebat ob tale ingenium, cum audiret illum annorum sedecim subtiliter interrogantem, interrogando arguentem ita ut illius magis interrogacioni quam sue intentus esset responsioni. Erat enim puer ille ardentissimus veritatis amator et occultorum diligens inuestigator. Verum cum puer

364 Denique] = Capgrave xviii

ipse flagraret tam desiderio bene viuendi quam studio, cito de medio sublatus est. Ut ipse refert nono libro Confessionum. Accepto igitur baptismi salutaris munere, quasi ditati multis diuiciis et inestimabilibus margaritis, mutuo in deo letantes, cum graciarum actione cibum sumentes, sicut erant magno gaudio gauisi, confortati sunt. Hec sanctus Dacius Mediolanensis episcopus ubi supra. Protinus autem in fide catholica mirabiliter confirmatus, spem omnem quam habebat in seculo, derelinquit. Nec satiabatur / 9va dulcedine mirabili considerare altitudinem consilii diuini super salutem generis humani. Frequentans igitur limina ecclesie et intentus modulacioni ymnorum et melodie psalmorum reficiebatur delectabiliter, flebat hylariter. Hoc quippe genus consolacionis, recens tunc, frequentare inchoauerat Mediolanensis ecclesia, quadam temporis impellente angustia. Cum enim Iustina imperatrix Arrianorum errore seducta beatum Ambrosium atrociter persequeretur, fideles cum episcopo suo mori parati in ecclesia excubabant. Tunc idem antistes aliorum magis quam sue afflictioni compaciens instituit ut, secundum morem orientalium parcium psalmi et ymni in ecclesia cantarentur, ut canticis spiritualibus fideles intenti meroris et tedii presentis obliuiscerentur. Cessante autem persecucione nichilominus consuetudo psallendi in ecclesia remansit et usque in hodiernum diem per totum orbem diffusa est. Hiis itaque psalmorum et ymnorum cantibus Augustinus vehementer affectus illis ymnidicis angelorum choris interesse siciens, ardebat et uberrime flebat. Qui autem in gracia baptismi secum renati fuerant cum eo simul viuebant, consociato eis et Euodio iuuene de eodem municipio 9vb nato et prius se bapti/zato. Simul erant isti, simul habitaturi placito sancto, pariter seruientes domino qui habitare facit unanimes in domo. Hec ipse nono libro Confessionum. Et quoniam exhortacione sancti senis Simpliciani et exemplis heremitarum ad fidem conuersus fuerat, ad quorum eciam imitacionem toto mentis desiderio estuabat, ab ipso sancto Simpliciano sancte conuersacionis habitum formamque viuendi accepit qui postmodum in Affrica exuberans redoleuit. Unde ipse in quodam sermone suo ad presbyteros Yponenses qui incipit, In omnibus operibus vestris, sacerdotes dei dilectissimi karissimi, sic dicit: ‘Cur murmurastis, si in hiis paschalibus diebus presencialiter vobiscum non fui? Placuit enim mihi segregare me a vobis et pergere ad fratres meos in solitudine, quos ut frequenter dixi tales inueni, quales inuenire desideraui. Cur ergo turbamini? Numquid non ipsi vere pauperes? Numquid non obedientes? Numquid non mundum et pompas eius conculcauerunt? Numquid non in forma viuendi vos multo tempore precesserunt? Numquid non vere fratres mei et patres sunt? Numquid non per eorum exempla ad viam veritatis perueni? Numquid non eos sem-

378 Protinus] = Capgrave xix 398 Et] = Capgrave xx

per dilexi et eorum sanctam conuersacionem semper desideraui? Numquid
60ra non eciam per Simplicianum li/guriensem in fide instructus sum? Cur ergo murmurastis? Cur de mea absencia dolorem habere ostenditis? Facite que placita sunt mihi et tunc ubicumque fuero, vobiscum ero usque ad consummacionem seculi.' Hec ipse ibi.

De eius reditu in Affricam

Post hec autem cum instigante eius pia matre de Mediolano recedere et ad Affricam remeare disponeret adiuit sanctum Simplicianum petens ut sibi aliquos de fratribus suis heremitis seruos dei donaret, quos secum in Affricam assumeret et cum eis ibi ordinem plantaret. Cuius piis precibus pius ille pater Simplicianus annuens dedit ei xii fratres viros religiosos cum quibus adiunctis sibi karissimis amicis suis qui diu secum fuerant, Nebridio, Euodio, Alipio et Ponciano cum matre et filio Adeodato, ad Affricam proficiscendi iter arripuit. De hoc ipse in Sermone de tribus generibus monachorum qui incipit, Vt nobis per litteras declarauit sanctus pater Ieronymus loquens de genere et ordine heremitarum, sic ait: 'Isti sunt viri illi perfecti quibus frequenter adhesi tempore errorum meorum, per quos eciam illuminari merui. Quorum eciam sanctitatis fama ad aures meas perueniens baptizari non diu distuli. Et pia matre me instigante apud Mediolanum ut
60rb ad patriam remearem, cupiens eciam eos habere in / visceribus caritatis, et cum eis pariter viuere, ad virum illum Simplicianum qui a iuuentute sua deo deuotissime vixerat, in omni caritate perrexi deprecans cum fletu et gemitu ut mihi quosdam de suis seruos dei donaret. Et donauit eos mihi paterne. Quare donauit eos mihi? Quia sciebat me velle monasterium in Affrica edificare. Et assumptis mecum Anastasio, Fabiano, Seuero, Nicolao, Dorotheo, Ysaac, Nycostrato, Paulo, Cyrillo, Stephano, Iacobo et Vitali pauperculo.' Et infra: 'Hiis mecum assumptis imitari cupiebam cum karissimis meis amicis Euodio, Alipio et Ponciano qui diu mecum fuerant et cum ceteris xii quos nuper assumpseram illos quorum famam eciam sanctus pater Ieronymus mihi descripserat. Et sic perueni in Affricam.' Hec ipse ibi. Predictis autem omnibus fratribus et amicis sancto Augustino consociatis illa pia mater ita curam gessit quasi omnes genuisset, ita seruiuit quasi ab omnibus genita fuisset. Ut ipse dicit nono libro Confessionum. Transiens autem et iter faciens per Thusciam, vbi ut fertur plura erant loca heremitica, vbicumque fratres sui propositi inuenit ipsos caritatiue visitauit et eos suis collationibus salutis pabulo dulciter recreauit. Perueniens autem Romam

413 liguriensem] linguriensem *MS* 418 Post] = Capgrave xxi 441-442 Predictis] = Capgrave xxii

et audiens quod Manichei qui ibi erant multos catholicos decipiebant, ipse 60va eorum / iactanciam tacitus ferre non valens, contra eos ibidem disputauit et duos libros contra eos scripsit quorum unum De moribus ecclesie catholice, alterum De moribus manicheorum intytulauit. Scripsit eciam ibidem librum De quantitate anime, in quo per modum dialogi inter se et filium Adeodatum multa subtilia de anima queruntur ac disseruntur. Scripsit eciam in eadem urbe librum De libero arbitrio, causam sumens ex disputacionibus habitis contra Manicheos, in quo questiones incidentes soluuntur et ostenditur malum non esse exortum nisi ex libero arbitrio. Hec ipse primo libro Retractacionum. Deinde egressi de vrbe, cum essent apud Ostiam Tyberinam post longi itineris laborem instaurantes se nauigacioni, Augustinus et mater stabant soli incumbentes ad quandam fenestram, unde ortus intra domum que eos habebat prospectabatur, remoti a turbis, et colloquebantur soli ualde dulciter de vita eterna sanctorum et inhyabant ore cordis in superna fluenta fontis vite, erigentes se ardenciore affectu in idipsum et gradatim transcendentes cuncta corporalia, attigerunt raptim toto ictu cordis regionem ubertatis indeficientis, fontem vite eterne. Cui suspirantes et ibidem religatas primicias spiritus relinquentes, ad oris collo- 60vb quium redierunt. Vilescebatque eis mundus iste inter / verba cum omnibus delectacionibus suis. Tunc ait illa: 'Fili mi, quantum ad me attinet, nulla re iam delector in hac vita. Quid hic faciam adhuc, et cur hic sim, nescio, iam consumpta spe huius seculi. Unum erat propter quod in hac uita aliquantulum immorari cupiebam ut te Christianum catholicum viderem priusquam morerer. Cumulacius hoc mihi deus meus prestitit ut te eciam contempta felicitate terrena, seruum eius uideam.'

De morte matris

Factum est autem uix infra quinque dies, ut ipsa decumberet febribus, et cum egrotaret quadam die defectum mentis passa, paululum subtracta est a presentibus. Vt autem reddita est sensui, intuens Augustinum et fratrem suum ait: 'Vbi eram?' Illis vero attonitis subiunxit, 'Ponite,' inquit, 'hoc corpus ubicumque, nichil uos eius cura conturbet. Tantum illud vos rogo ut ad domini altare memineritis mei vbicumque fueritis.' Omnem quippe iam reliquerat curam, qua prius estuauerat de sepulchro quod sibi domi iuxta corpus viri sui sumptuose preparauerat. Nam cum paulo ante ipsa cum quibusdam amicis Augustini de contemptu vite huius et de bono mortis loqueretur illisque stupentibus uirtutem femine querentibusque an

457 Deinde] = Capgrave xxiii

61ra non formidaret tam longe a sua ciuitate sepeliri, 'Nichil,' inquit, 'longe / est [a] deo neque timendum est ne ille non cognoscat in fine seculi unde me resuscitet.' Die ergo nono egritudinis sue anima illa religiosa et pia corpore soluta est, anno etatis sue quinquagesimo sexto. Etatis uero Augustini anno tricesimo tercio. Et conuenerunt multi fratres et religiose femine eius exequias de more celebrantes. Hec ipse in libro nono Confessionum.

Quibus peractis Augustinus cum suis in Affricam reversus est

Veniensque Carthaginem a quodam honorato viro Innocentio nomine hospicio receptus est. Qui cum ob grauem corporis infirmitatem a medico incidi deberet, Augustinus suo hospiti pie compaciens sua oracione ipsum curauit, cunctis stupentibus quod ille de tam graui infirmitate sic subito curatus fuit. Hec ipse in libro De ciuitate dei. Inde profectus ad agros proprios propriamque domum, ibi cum amicis et fratribus quos secum de Ytalia assumpserat ac aliis eodem desiderio flagrantibus qui eidem adherebant, ieiuniis et oracionibus vacans, venditis propriis et secundum modum et regulam sanctorum apostolorum pauperibus erogatis, pauper cum pauperibus in ordine adhuc laycali ferme per triennium conuersatus est, in lege domini meditantes die ac nocte et de hiis que sibi deus cogitanti atque oranti intellecta reuelabat et presentes et absentes sermonibus ac libris do-
61rb cebat. Hec in / Legenda Possidonii et in alia Legenda famosa.

Scripsit enim ibi libros duos De genesi contra Manicheos. Item librum De musica, sex libros continentem, quos apud Mediolanum inchoauerat, in quibus presertim in sexto ostendit quomodo a corporalibus et spiritualibus sed mutabilibus numeris ad immutabiles numeros peruenitur, qui iam in ipsa sunt immutabili veritate, et sic invisibilia dei per ea que facta sunt intellecta conspiciuntur; et qui ista nunc conspicere non possunt, et tamen ex fide Christi viuunt, quod post hanc vitam ipsa certitudinaliter atque feliciter aspicient; qui autem ea conspicere possunt, et tamen in fide Christi non viuunt, cum tota sapiencia sua in fine peribunt. Per idem eciam tempus ibidem scripsit librum De magistro continentem dialogum inter se et filium Adeodatum qui eodem anno quo venit in Affricam de medio sublatus est. In quo libro ostendit non esse magistrum alium qui docet hominem nisi deum. Eodem eciam tempore et loco scripsit librum De vera religione in

485 a deo] deo *MS* 492 Veniensque] = Capgrave xxv 505 Scripsit] = Capgrave xxvi 509 que] qua *MS*

quo ostendit quod sola religio christiana et nulla alia religio est vera. Hec ipse in libro Retractacionum. Verum, cum lumen tante sanctitatis et doctrine latere non posset, fama quippe eius ubique diffundebatur et in omnibus libris suis et actibus admirabilis habebatur, apud Yponem Regium erat quidam vir christianus magnarum opum, qui ad eum misit pollicens
61va quod si illum videre et verbum ex ore suo audire mereretur, / iuxta consilium suum relicto seculo totus ad dominum conuerteretur. Quod Augustinus ubi comperit volens deo lucrari animam et nichilominus intendens querere locum aptum ubi constitueret monasterium, in quo secretus cum fratribus suis posset deo seruire, Yponem profectus est et virum predictum ad contemptum mundi et amorem dei quantum deus donabat, exhortatus est. Cuius ille presencia gaudens, exhortacionem eius gratanter accepit, sed tamen quod promiserat occulto dei consilio ad presens implere distulit; inane tamen esse non potuit quod per tale vas mundum diuina sapiencia profudit. Hec in legenda Possidonii.

Quod autem intencione constituendi monasterium Yponem perexerit, expresse ipse idem testatur in sermone primo De communi uita clericorum vbi sic dicit, 'Ego quem deo propicio videtis episcopum vestrum, iuuenis veni ad istam ciuitatem, ut multi vestrum nouerunt. Querebam ubi constituerem monasterium et viuerem cum fratribus meis. Spem quippe seculi omnem reliqueram.' Et infra 'Veni ad istam ciuitatem propter videndum amicum quem putabam me posse lucrari deo ut vobiscum essem in monasterio quasi securus quia locus habebat episcopum.' Hec ipse ibi.

De institucione ordinis heremitarum et edificacione primi monasterii sui in heremo

Itaque apud Yponem in heremo segregato a gentibus locum aptum ad seruiendum deo inueniens cum fauore et subsidio sancti Valerii Yponensis epi-
61vb scopi monasterium ibidem edificauit / et in eo fratres heremitas, quos undique per nemora conquisiuit, una cum amicis et fratribus prius eidem adherentibus collocauit et cum eis viuere cepit secundum regulam sub sanctis apostolis constitutam. Vnde ipse in sermone superallegato ad presbyteros Ypponenses sic dicit, 'Ego, sacerdotes dei altissimi ut multi vestrum viderunt et audire potuerunt, veni ad hanc ciuitatem cum karissimis meis amicis Euodio, Simplicio, Alipio, Nebridio et Anastasio. Securus denique ueni, quia sciebam presulari sanctum senem Valerium. Propterea securus accessi, non

519 Verum] = Capgrave xxvii 540 securus] secretus *MS* 543 Itaque] = Capgrave xxviii

ut haberem in uos potestatem sed ut abiectus essem in domo domini omnibus diebus uite mee, non ut ministrari deberem sed ministrare et pacifice viuere optabam in solitudine nichilque diuiciarum mecum attuli sed dei gracia me coadiuuante fauoratus eciam a sancto sene episcopo Valerio monasterium in heremo a gentibus segregatum multo labore fatigatus edificaui et cum longiori anxietate seruos dei per nemora habitantes in unum congregaui et cum eis pariter viuere cepi secundum modum et regulam sub sanctis apostolis constitutam omnia communiter habentes et possidentes, viuentes in vigiliis et oracionibus ultra id quod explicare possumus.' Hec ipse ibi.

Quod autem sanctus Valerius non solum fauorem sed eciam subsidium ad
62ra structuram monasterii sibi prestiterit testatur ipse / in alio sermone preallegato, Vt nobis per litteras, ubi loquens ad fratres suos in eodem monasterio, sic ait, 'Vos,' inquit, 'vinea mea electa estis in medio ecclesie paradysi plantata. Ad hanc vineam ego solus dei virtute vos congregaui et operarios meos feci ut laborantes in ea usque in finem fructum recipiatis in tempore suo. Ad hanc vineam vos elegi, ad hanc hereditatem vos convocaui licet fauoratus a sancto episcopo Valerio qui de bonis episcopatus, ut monasterium in heremo edificarem, multa mihi donauit. Non enim satis fuit patrimonium meum vendere, nisi eciam ipse me coadiuuisset.' Hec ipse ibi.

In prefato autem monasterio ipse Augustinus copiosum numerum fratrum congregauit quibus et modum viuendi secundum formam vite apostolorum tradidit et sic ordinem heremitarum ipse instituit. Prius enim heremite per diuersa nemora disiuncti singulariter alii sic alii sic viuebant, sed nunc per Augustinum ad communem obseruanciam regule apostolice reducti sub tanto patre in communi viuere inceperunt. De hoc ipse in eodem sermone iam allegato sic dicit; 'Perueni in Affricam pia matre defuncta et edificaui ut videtis monasterium in quo nunc sumus in solitudine a gentibus segregatum. Et placuit deo centenarium numerum fratrum mihi donare illuminans
62rb corda nostra non solum sanctissimos patres / solitarios imitari, sed eciam in hac solitudine more apostolorum omnia communiter possidere[. Haec deus] nos seruare, et postea docere et per me vobis precipere voluit. Sic enim videtis quod ante me multi fuerunt patres quos sequi et imitari debemus, non tamen sicut ego secundum apostolicam vitam alios viuere docuerunt. Caput igitur et principium omnium vestrum me dicere non erubesco.' Hec ipse ibi. Huius itaque ordinis fratrum habitus erat cuculla nigra cincta zona pellicea id est corrigia, ut ipse refert in preallegato sermone ad presbyteros

573 In] = Capgrave xxix 583-584 Haec deus nos] nos *MS*

Yponenses. Ubi comparacionem faciens inter ipsos presbyteros canonicos suos et fratres istos in heremo sic ait, 'Et si vobis graue est et molestum, egredimini foras, pergite ad fratres meos et discite ab eis quia mites sunt et humiles corde pauperes spiritu et filii obedientie. Egredimini foras et quid estis et quid ipsi sunt, considerare uos volo. Numquid enim et uos tales sicut et ipsi sunt? O utinam tales essetis sicut ipsi sunt!' Et infra, 'Vos discursores ciuitatis, et ipsi visus hominum fugiunt. Vos pellibus cuniculorum et variorum ornati iam estis, et ipsi ovino vestitu colore nigerrimo asperrimoque induti sunt. Vos balteis militum mundo apparere desideratis et ipsi zonis camelorum renibus succincti more Helie et Johannis decorati sunt.' Hec ipse ibi.

62vb Porro / hiis fratribus idem pater dedit primo certas tradiciones secundum formam vite apostolice compendiose comprehensas, quas margaritas paradysi appellat in sermone primo ad fratres eosdem, qui incipit, Fratres mei et leticia cordis mei et gaudium meum quod estis. Deinde regulam conscripsit quam ipse speculum appellauit quam et eisdem fratribus tradidit ut habetur ex preallegato sermone Ut nobis per litteras.

Qualiter factus est presbyter

Post hec cum flagitante ecclesiastica necessitate providendum esset ciuitati de presbytero, beatus Valerius Yponensis episcopus comperta Augustini fama eum ad se accersiri fecit. Cumque idem antistes de prouidendo et ordinando presbytero plebem alloqueretur et exhortaretur astantę in populo Augustino securo et ignaro quid futurum esset (solebat enim laycus ab eis tantum ecclesiis, que non haberent episcopos, suam abstinere presenciam), eum ergo tenuerunt et ut in talibus consuetum est, episcopo ordinandum intulerunt, omnibus id uno consensu et desiderio fieri petentibus magnoque studio et clamore flagitantibus. Ubertim eo flente et renitente eo quod multa et magna vite sue pericula de regimine ecclesie prouenire consideraret atque ideo fleuit, nonnullis quidem lacrimas eius superbe interpretantibus et tamquam eum consolantibus et dicentibus, quia locus pres-
62vb byterii licet ipse maiori dignus esset, appropinquaret / tamen episcopatui. Tandem flentem et frustra renitentem beatus Valerius de turba segregauit et licet invitum presbyterum ordinauit. Hec Possidonius.

607 Post] = Capgrave xxx 612 non] non non *MS* 617 lacrimas] lacrimis *MS*

De edificacione secundi monasterii in orto

Reuerso itaque Augustino ad monasterium suum (non enim sine monastica disciplina voluit viuere) placuit sancto seni Valerio ordinatori eius ipsum cum suis fratribus in heremo paterne visitare et eis ad tempus pro deuocione commanere. Et tunc cognito proposito Augustini quod omnino cum fratribus suis nichil habentibus nichil habens optabat viuere, monasterium autem istud in heremo nimium distabat a plebe cuius curam ipse iam presbyter habebat gerere, dedit ei ortum ciuitati propinquum, in quo mox monasterium edificauit et in eo de fratribus prioris monasterii quosdam secum locauit, colligens nichilominus et alios eiusdem propositi fratres clericos seruientes et ibidem deo pariter et in communi viuentes secundum modum et regulam sub sanctis apostolis constitutam, maxime ut nemo quidquam proprium in illa sancta societate haberet sed eis essent omnia communia et distribueretur unicuique sicut opus erat. Quod iam ipse prior fecerat, dum de transmarinis ad sua remeasset, ut ait Possidonius. Et hec que predicta sunt ipsemet in preallegato sermone primo De communi vita clericorum testatur dicens sic: 'Apprehensus presbyter factus sum, et quia hic disponebam esse cum fratribus 63ra / in monasterio, cognito instituto et voluntate mea, bone memorie senex Valerius dedit mihi ortulum illum, in quo nunc est monasterium et cepi boni propositi fratres colligere, compares meos nichil habentes, sicut nichil habebam, et imitantes me ut quomodo ego tenuem paupertatem meam vendidi et pauperibus erogaui, sic facerent et illi qui mecum esse voluissent, ut de communi viueremus.' Hec ipse ibi. Hoc idem expressius dicit in sermone alio ad presbyteros Yponenses qui incipit, In omnibus operibus, ubi loquens de fratribus primi monasterii sic ait: 'Quorum,' inquit, 'fama ad aures sancti Valerii episcopi peruenit et placuit sibi in heremo nos visitare et stetit diebus tredecim donans mihi ortum amenitatibus plenum in planicie positum. Et quia a gentibus erat segregatus, libenter illum suscepi ut edificarem ibi eciam monasterium fratrum, quos tales inueneram, quales inuenire desideraui.' Hec ipse ibi. Hos quoque fratres idem pater in omni disciplina et obseruancia regulari instruxit et nichilominus eos studio sacre scripture erudiuit ut iam non tantum sibi in simplicitate viuerent, sed et aliis prodesse valerent. Sanctus autem Valerius ordinator eius, ut erat vir pius et timens dominum, exultabat uberius et deo gracias agebat suas exauditas a deo fuisse preces, quas se frequentissime fudisse narrabat, ut sibi diuinitus 63rb / homo concederetur talis qui posset verbo dei et doctrina salutari ecclesiam domini edificare. Cui rei se minus utilem preuidebat cum esset natura grecus et in latina lingua et litteris minus

651 Hos] = Capgrave xxxi

doctus. Quocirca Augustino potestatem contulit ut contra morem affricanarum ecclesiarum coram se in ecclesia predicaret. De quo cum multi episcopi ei derogarent, ille sciens illud in orientalibus ecclesiis ex more fieri linguas obtrectancium non curabat, dummodo per eum fieret quod per se fieri non valebat. Unde accensa et ardens leuata super candelabrum lucerna omnibus qui in domo erant lucebat et postmodum, discurrente huiusmodi fama et bono exemplo precedente, nonnulli presbyteri quibus erudita inerat facundia, accepta ab episcopo potestate, ceperunt verbum dei tractare in populo eciam in episcoporum suorum presencia. Hec Possidonius.

Cuius rei gratia Augustinus ordinauit ut fratres sui de secundo monasterio per eum in sacra pagina eruditi quia non tantum distabant a populo ut fratres primi monasterii, verbum dei eciam publice in populo predicarent ac eciam confessiones fidelium audirent et vita pariter et exemplo dei populum salubriter edificarent, prout ipse idem pater testatur in sermone preallegato qui incipit Vt bene nostis, fratres, ubi sic dicit: 'Et licet fratres nostri collocati in orto sancti Valerii episcopi satis distent ab urbe, eorum
63va tamen fama diuinitus diuulgata, or/dinaui ut verbum dei populo salubriter predicarent, animeque fidelium, suam vitam et exempla audiendo et videndo, sponte redirent ad illum qui ex nichilo cuncta creauit. Ecce quomodo terram iudicant, ligant et soluunt que volunt, semper deo fauente.' Hec ipse ibi. Eo tempore in illa Yponensi urbe Manicheorum pestilencia multos tam ciues quam peregrinos infecerat quos precipue illius heresis presbyter nomine Fortunatus loquaci versucia seduxerat. Qui in eadem urbe conuersans magnus apud multos habebatur. Interea multi Yponensium tam Christiani quam Donatiste heretici beatum Augustinum adeunt summopere postulantes ut predictum Fortunatum conueniret et cum eo de lege domini disputaret. Ille vero paratus omni poscenti se reddere rationem de fide et spe que in ipso erat potensque exhortari in doctrina sana et eos qui contradicunt arguere, quod petebatur non renuit. Sed et utrum ille hoc fieri vellet sciscitatus est. At illi statim predictum Fortunatum accedentes petunt instanter ut id non recuset. Ille vero quoniam apud Carthaginem sanctum nouerat Augustinum cum adhuc secum eodem errore detineretur, nisus est vitare congressum, sed cogente verecundia et illorum instancia tandem promisit in commune se esse venturum certamenque disputandi subiturum. Unde
63vb condicto die et loco conuenerunt in unum / concurrentibus quam plurimis studiosis turbisque curiosis. Apertisque tabulis notariorum, ad excipienda verba singulorum, prima die disputacio est cepta et secundo die finita. Erat autem disputacionis illius questio unde sit malum? Augustinus enim tene-

680 Eo] = Capgrave xxxii

bat et dicebat quod malum est exortum in homine ex libero voluntatis arbitrio; Fortunatus autem tenebat quod natura mali deo est coeterna. In qua disputacione doctor ille Manicheus nec catholicam Augustini assercionem potuit infirmare nec Manicheorum sectam adminiculo veritatis potuit probare, sed deficiens responsione et digna affectus confusione, veritati nolens volens cessit. Nec tamen catholicus factus est sed paulo post de ciuitate confusus abscessit. Ac sic per dei seruum Augustinum de omnium cordibus tam presencium quam absencium ad quos illa peruenit disputacio, ille error ablatus est et intimata et confirmata est catholice veritatis religio. Hec Possidonius. Predictam autem disputacionem Augustinus in librum contulit et plures alios libros eodem tempore presbyterii sui contra Manicheos et alios hereticos scripsit. Librum eciam De sermone domini in monte et quamplures alios edidit ut dicit in primo libro Retractacionum.

64ra Predicabat autem Augustinus priuatim et publice loquens verbum / Dei cum omni fiducia omnem hereticum destruens, catholicos instruens infundente ei spiritu sancto ineffabilem graciam, mirantibus cunctis disertam eius facundiam. Cuius famam nominis non solum ecclesia Affricana, verum eciam et transmarina iam nouerat, gaudens quod talem ei deus lucernam contulerat cuius verbo et exemplo illuminari meruerat. Hec Possidonius.

Qualiter factus est episcopus

Cum vero pre ceteris senex ille Valerius exultaret, cepit ut se habet humana fragilitas formidare ne suus ille Augustinus presbyter ab alia quereretur ecclesia et sibi ablatus in episcopum eligeretur. Quod utique aliquando prouenisset, nisi hoc precognito idem episcopus illum fecisset absentari, ne quesitus posset inueniri. Unde ampliore timore concussus presertim cum et corpore esset infirmus et etate defessus, egit secrete apud primatem episcopum Carthaginensem allegans infirmitatem sui corporis etatisque grauitatem et obsecrans ut Augustinus Yponensi ecclesie episcopus ordinaretur, qui sue cathedre non tam succederet quam consacerdos accederet. Cuius ille piis precibus clementer annuens rescripto mediante concessit quod petebat. Demum veniente ad ecclesiam Yponensem tunc primate Numidie cum Megalio Orilamensi episcopo, Valerius antistes episcopis qui forte tunc
64rb ade/rant, et clericis Yponensibus ac uniuerse plebi inopinatam cunctis suam insinuat voluntatem. Omnibus igitur audientibus gratulantibus atque id fieri perficique ingenti desiderio clamantibus in episcopum Augustinus elec-

718 Cum] = Capgrave xxxiii

tus est. Sed cum hoc Augustinus viuente suo episcopo omnimode recusaret, compulsus tamen et coactus tandem subcubuit et episcopalem tam locum quam ordinem cum beato Valerio suscepit. Quod quidem non debere fieri postea dixit et scripsit cum uniuersalis concilii cognouisset decreta que tunc temporis ei erant incognita. Nec quod sibi factum esse doluit, aliis fieri voluit. Factus vero episcopus, quo maiore dignitate refulsit, eo maiore instancia et auctoritate verbum dei predicauit, non in sua tantum ciuitate sed ubicumque eum ecclesastica necessitas inuitauit, uel ad instruendum catholicos, uel ad destruendum hereticos. Hec Possidonius.

De edificacione tercii monasterii in episcopio

Videns autem beatus Augustinus quod necesse erat episcopum assiduam hospitalitatis humanitatem quibuscumque venientibus sive transeuntibus exhibere, quod in monasterio fratrum conuenienter fieri non valebat, voluit in ipsa episcopali domo monasterium secum habere clericorum ut qui presbyter in orto cum fratribus vixerat, in episcopio nichilominus pauper cum pauperibus deo regulariter seruiret. Hec in Legenda famosa. Unde eciam /
4va ipse in sermone primo De communi vita clericorum qui incipit, Propter quod volui, sic ait: 'Placuit deo mihi dicere sursum ascende; usque adeo timebam episcopatum ut quia ceperat iam alicuius momenti inter seruos dei fama mea, in quo loco sciebam non esse episcopum, ne illo accederem cauebam. Sed seruus contradicere domino non debet.' Et infra: 'Perueni ad episcopatum, vidi necesse habere episcopum exhibere humanitatem assiduam quibuscumque venientibus siue transeuntibus, quod si non fecisset episcopus, inhumanus diceretur, si autem illa consuetudo in monasterio permissa esset, indecens esset. Et ideo volui habere in domo ista episcopi mecum monasterium clericorum.' Hec ipse ibi. In alio quoque sermone ad presbyteros Yponenses, qui incipit In omnibus operibus vestris, sic ait: 'Edificato monasterio fratrum in orto placuit ei qui me segregauit ex utero matris mee et vocauit me per graciam suam, mihi dicere Amice surge et ascende superius. Et sic cum molestia et grandi anxietate factus sum episcopus. Et quia cum fratribus meis ut hactenus feceram, semper corpore habitare non poteram, propterea infra domum episcopi vos clericos habere volui et mox vobiscum secundum formam apostolicam viuere cepi.' Hec ipse ibi. Memorata tria monasteria per eundum sanctum patrem constructa et instructa ipse simul commemorat in sermone ad fratres suos in heremo, qui
4rb incipit Vt bene nostis, ubi sic dicit: 'Ut bene / nostis, fratres karissimi, tria

743 Videns] = Capgrave xxxiiii

monasteria apud Yponem dei gracia merui laudabiliter ad honorem sancte trinitatis construere. Quorum primum hoc est in quo iam multis annis modico pabulo contenti alacriter commoramini, bestiis associati, avibus ministrati ciborumque spernentes delicias, visus hominum fugientes, et ideo non solum ego miser, sed vos sepe angelorum estis assueti colloquio. Aliud quoque monasterium in orto edificatum est quem mihi sanctus pater noster Valerius dedit. Et quoniam postquam episcopus factus sum, nec semper hic vobiscum habitare potui nec cum fratribus qui in predicto monasterio in orto sunt propterea intra domum episcopi mecum habere volui monasterium clericorum, et cum eisdem pariter viuere secundum apostolicam tradicionem.' Hec ipse ibi.

Sane propter episcopatus dignitatem se a fratribus priorum monasteriorum suorum minime alienauit sed apud se eorum aliquos semper esse desiderauit vel saltem se eis in pristina vita religionis quantum potuit conformauit. Unde ipse in sermone ad eosdem fratres qui incipit, Ut nobis per litteras, sic ait: 'Et ecce postquam episcopus factus sum Vitalem, Nycolaum, Stephanum, Dorotheum, Paulum, Iacobum, Cyrillum frequenter rogaui ut me solum in episcopatu non dimitterent, quia licet episcopus essem, non credebam tamen paupertatem despicere sed cum Abraham, Ysaac, et Iacob inter diuicias viuere, aut veram paupertatem seruare optabam, ut de medio eorum essem, de quibus dicit apostolus, *Tamquam nichil habentes et omnia*
65ra *possidentes*. Eos igitur frequenter rogaui ut venirent / non ut essent rebelles heremi, sed solitarie eciam in ciuitate viuentes, habitare possemus in placito sancto. Sed ecce noluerunt venire tamquam de se ipsis timentes, ne a seculo caperentur. Noluerunt venire. Quare noluerunt? Non quia non digni, sed quia non solum pauperes esse voluerunt sed eciam supra id quod in speculo nostro edidimus, facere voluerunt. De quo nunc summum gaudium habere debemus, quia facere voluerunt que deo et mihi promiserunt. Et quia solus stare non poteram episcopus, ideo rogaui sanctum senem Valerium qui mihi iam potestatem predicandi in populo dederat, ut intra domum episcopi monasterium clericorum constituerem; et placuit sancto episcopo mihi condescendere, et sic cum eisdem in omni paupertate viuere cepi. Non manducamus carnes, nisi dum hospites veniunt, sed tantum olera et legumina absque oleo et butyro, sicut ante vobiscum cum gaudio consueueram. Igitur fratres mei, licet me in cathedra episcopali videatis, paupertatem mihi caram sponsam tenere congratulor, quia ipsa est eciam Christi sponsa, sanctorum possessio, beatorum vita, fidelium securitas, clericorum ornamentum, monachorum vita, nobilium pulchritudo, diuitum magnificencia. Hec est illa sancta paupertas, quam qui tenet et amat, nulla indigencia laborare potest. Nec mirum, fratres, quod sibi datur omnium domi-
65rb nium possidere. Ipsa est enim speran/tibus in se thesaurus in paupertate,

solacium in sollitudine, gloria in abiectione, honor in contemptu, umbraculum in omni protectione.' Hec ipse ibi. Sepe eciam ipse strepitum secularium negociorum fugere volens, ad alterum monasterium fratrum in heremo declinabat et cum illis aliquibus diebus pro sua devocione et fratrum exhortacione manebat, ita ut de hoc eciam nonnumquam sui canonici murmurarent. Unde ipse in sermone ad presbyteros Yponenses preallegato sic ait loquens canonicis: 'Cur,' inquit, 'murmurastis si in hiis paschalibus diebus presencialiter vobiscum non fui? Placuit enim mihi segregare me a uobis et pergere ad fratres meos in solitudine quos ut dixi tales inueni quales inuenire desideraui. Cur ergo turbamini?' Et infra, 'Cur de mea absencia dolorem habere ostenditis? Facite que placita sunt mihi, et tunc ubicumque fuero, vobiscum ero usque ad consummacionem seculi. Decreueram enim cum eisdem rusticanis meis in caritate humiliter habitare usque ad festum sancte Ascensionis domini nec ad vos redire optabam quousque vos emendatos esse cognouero. Sed quoniam Fortunatum aduersarium ad partes occulte velud lupum peruenisse iam sencio, ideo compulsus reuersus sum ad uos, cupiens illum videre et cum eo pariter disputare, et illum con-
55va culcare, domino auxiliante, qui totis visceribus dissi/pare conatur et iugulare filios quos peperi in visceribus caritatis.' Hec ipse ibi. Fratres autem predicti sicut de presencia patris tanti potissime consolabantur, ita de eius recessu quam plurimum turbabantur. Unde ipse in sermone De prudencia ad eosdem fratres sic dicit: 'Supplico vobis, fratres, ut non turbemini de meo recessu. Decreueram enim diu inter vos consolari et vobiscum habitare usque ad festum Ascensionis dominice, sed quia aduersarius noster Fortunatus ad partes peruenerit, ideo redire Yponem omnino compellor, cupiens illum videre et cum illo pariter disputare.' Hec ipse ibi.

Consolabantur nimirum memorati fratres sepius ab ipso patre non solum sua dulci presenciali conuersacione et sermonum suorum suaui refeccione, sed eciam caritatiua temporalium prouisione. Unde ipse in sermone ad eosdem fratres sic ait: 'Non tedeat vos orare quia non familiam regere, sed tantum deo placere debemus. Et ut bene psallere et orare possitis absque magno corporis impedimento, de bonis episcopatus ecclesie Yponensis centum et quadraginta vestimenta cum calciamentis vobis dilectis fratribus meis deportari precepi, ut tempore frigoris quantum necesse fuerit unusquisque recipiat, reponentes ea et custodientes in communi vestiario cum omni dili-
55vb gencia et caritate, scientes quod vera caritas *non querit / que sua sunt sed que dei*.' Hec ipse ibi.

812 monasterium] monasteriorum *MS* 836 Consolabantur] = Capgrave xxxv

Proficiente igitur sancti viri sana et sancta doctrina, multi diuino afflati spiritu valefacientes seculo, ad monasteria sua confluxerunt ibique relicta seculari proprietate et propria voluntate, sub tali ac tanto patre et doctore deo deuote seruierunt. Quorum sancta continencia, paupertas voluntaria, humilis obediencia longe lateque suauem odorem effudit. Unde nonnulli episcopi tante sanctitatis emulatores effecti, multos ex eisdem monasteriis fratres sibi donari pecierunt, sub quorum cura multas ecclesias ad serviendum deo commiserunt. Ex quibus eciam fere decem in episcopos sunt sublimati. Illi vero propositi sui non immemores, et doctrinam salutarem quam a sancto viro Augustino acceperant redolentes, monasteria eciam collectis fratribus instituerunt. E quibus postmodum multos, proficiente eorum religione et fidelium deuocione, ad instruenda alia monasteria emancipauerunt; et sic non solum in Affrica sed eciam in transmarinis partibus huius sancte religionis propositum dilatatum est. Denique vir iste sanctus in cultu, gestu et habitu, in sermonibus et moribus talem se exhibuit omnibus, ut ad utilitatem omnium omnia fieret omnibus. Religiosis quippe honeste maturus, secularibus vero mature iocundus aderat ut illos in sanctitate cepta ex-
66ra emplo / sui confirmaret et istos ad sanctitatem congrua hylaritate inuitaret. In disciplinaciones quoque et trangressiones suorum, regula recta et honesta, arguebat et tollerabat quantum decebat et oportebat, in talibus precipue docens ne cuiusquam cor declinaret *in verba maligna ad excusandas excusaciones in peccatis*. Indumenta eius et calciamenta et lectualia ex moderato et competenti habitu erant, nec nitida nimium nec abiecta plurimum. Plerumque enim sicut nimia vestium pulchritudo, sic arguitur earum turpitudo. At ipse medium tenebat, volens eciam seipsis dare aliis formam viuendi non materiam detrahendi. Hec Possidonius. Unde ipse in sermone De communi uita clericorum qui incipit Caritati vestre sic ait: 'Nolo quia talia offerat sanctitas vestra quibus ego quasi decencius utar; verbi gracia, offeratur mihi byrrum preciosum: forte deceret episcopum sed non decet Augustinum hominem pauperem de pauperibus natum. Ne forte dicturi sint homines quod inueni preciosas vestes quas non possem in domo patris mei habere. Talem debeo habere qualem si non habuerit, fratri meo possim dare. Si quis in elemosinam dederit, vendo ut quando vestis non potest esse communis, precium vestis possit esse commune. Si hoc eum delectat ut habeam ego, det talem, de quo non erubescam. Fateor ego vobis quod de pre-
66rb ciosa veste eru/besco. Quia non decet hanc ammonicionem, non decet hanc professionem, non decet hec membra, non decet hos canos.' Hec ipse ibi. Mensa frugali et parca semper usus est; et inter olera et legumina, propter infirmos et hospites plerumque carnes habebat. Semper autem vinum habebat quo sobrie utebatur iuxta consilium apostoli Ad Thymotheum scri-

860 Denique] = Capgrave xxxvi 884 Mensa] = Capgrave xxxvii

bentis: *Noli adhuc aquam bibere sed modico vino utere propter stomachum tuum et frequentes tuas infirmitates.* Pauper quippe sibi et parcus, aliis diues et largus habebatur, sibi ieiunans aliis epulabatur. Hostium eius viatori patuit, mensa eius hospitibus seruiuit. In ipsa autem mensa magis lectionem uel disputacionem quam epulaciones diligebat. Et contra pestem detractionis hos versus scriptos habebat: *Quisquis amat dictis absentem rodere vitam; Hanc mensam indignam nouerit esse sibi.* Nam et aliquando cum sibi quidam familiarissimi coepiscopi ad detraccionem linguam laxassent, adeo dure eos redarguit ut diceret quod, nisi desisterent, aut versus ipsos deleret aut de mensa recederet. Quod profecto aliquando contigit ut surgens cubiculum suum ingrederetur, cum in mensa aliquis plus iusto loqueretur. Quadam vice cum quosdam suos familiares ad prandium inuitasset, unus eorum curi-
6va osior ceteris coquinam ingressus est. Cumque / omnia frigida reperisset reuersus ad Augustinum interrogauit, quid ciborum pransuris pater familias ipse preparasset. Cui Augustinus talium epularum nequaquam curiosus respondit 'Et ego vobiscum nescio.' Vasa domus eius uel marmorea uel lignea erant uel testea, non inopia necessitatis sed proposito voluntatis, coclearibus tantum argenteis utens. Conpauperum semper memor erat eisque ex hiis que habere poterat erogabat. Nam et de vasis dominicis propter pauperes et captiuos aliquando iubebat frangi et conflari et indigentibus dispensari. Cum autem ecclesie pecunia deficeret, hoc ipsum in populo christiano denunciabat se non habere quod indigentibus erogaret. Consanguineis sic benefecit, non ut diuicias haberent sed ut aut non aut minus egerent. Hec Possidonius. Unde ipse in sermone Ad fratres in heremo Yponensi qui incipit Ut nobis per litteras sic ait: 'Non debemus habere temporalia ad possidendum, nec ego qui episcopus sum habere debeo nisi tantum ad dispensandum quia bona ecclesiarum patrimonium pauperum sunt. Unde ego qui episcopus sum summe cavere debeo, ne res pauperum quas Yponensis ecclesia conseruare videtur, diuicibus largiantur. Quod bene feci huc usque, nam consanguineos habeo et nobiles se dicere non erubescunt; ad me episcopum veniunt et aliquando cum minis aliquando
6vb cum blandimentis dicentes, Da nobis aliquid / pater, caro enim tua sumus. Et tamen dei gracia et vestris oracionibus mediantibus, aliquem consanguineum me preditasse non recolo. Cariores eos mihi reputo pauperes quam diuites, quia *habentes victum et vestimentum fideles omnes contenti* esse debent, maxime nos clerici in cuius signum capita tonsa et rasa habere debemus ne diuiciarum capilli occupent mentem seruorum dei.' Hec ipse ibi. Pupillos et viduas in tribulacione constitutos et egrotantes postulatus visitabat eisque sup[p]licibus manus imponens facta oracione infirmitates eorum sanabat. Acceperat enim donum curacionis ab eo qui dixit *Super*

924 Pupillos] = Capgrave xxxviii

egenos manus imponent et bene habebunt. Quadam eciam vice rogatus ut pro quibusdam energumenis pacientibus oraret, ipse eis compaciens et lacrimas fundens deum pro eis orauit et demones ab illis hominibus fugauit. Hec Possidonius. Ipse eciam in libro vicesimo secundo De ciuitate dei duo miracula de se tamquam de quodam alio refert dicens: 'Yponi quamdam virginem scio quam, cum oleo se perunxisset cu[i] pro illa orans presbyter lacrimas suas stillauit, mox a demone fuisse sanatam.' In eodem eciam libro sic ait: 'Scio eciam episcopum semel pro adolescente, quem non vidit, orasse illumque a demonio curauisse.' Nullum autem dubium videtur quin
67ra de se loquatur sed humilitatis causa / seipsum non vult nominare. Senibus quoque etate defessis ualde compaciens erat, quos eciam cum quadam veneracione pie subportabat. Unde ipse in sermone ad fratres in heremo Yponensi De ociositate fugienda, qui incipit Apostolus Petrus fratres karissimi, sic ait: 'Et si aliqui sunt ex vobis qui per annos octoginta et amplius sunt sanctissime in heremo conuersati iugo sancte obediencie, paupertatis et castitatis decorati, iam gaudeant *exspectantes beatam spem et aduentum domini*: isti enim ut videmus qui amplius ieiuniis et oracionibus et operibus monasterii insistere non possunt, fecerunt enim dum potuerunt. Propterea filioli mei, si modo non faciunt ea que facere consueverant, non sit vobis molestum, si quiescunt, non miremini, si venerantur a me ut patres, non tristemini, quia ipsi digni sunt. Non enim dolere debetis quia *caritas non cogitat malum, gaudet autem de bono*. Ideo volumus et in Christi nomine ordinamus ut et ipsi qui centum annorum sunt et amplius, Pater noster sedendo in lectulo dicant, et diligenter eis sine murmure serviatur, ut et ipsi pro nobis intercedant in celis, quorum habitacio iam ibi est.' Hec ipse ibi. Denique in hiis que ecclesia possidebat, implicatus amore non erat. Domum uel agrum numquam emere volebat, multas eciam hereditates sibi dimissas respuebat eo quod mortuorum filiis [et] propinquis pocius ipsa deberi dice-
67rb bat. / Domus curam omnemque substanciam, ad vices valencioribus clericis delegabat, a quibus de perceptis et expensis completo anno rationem audiebat, numquam clauem huiusmodi distribucionum in manu habens nec se talibus occupacionibus implicans, sed in superioribus et spiritualibus suspensus ad disponenda temporalia aliquando descendebat, non propria ductus voluntate, sed fratrum coactus necessitate. Hiis uero pro tempore dispositis, tamquam a spinis et tribulis euocans animum, ad superiora et interiora reuocabat mentis intuitum, *in lege domini meditans die ac nocte*. Nouarum quoque fabricarum studium numquam habere volebat, deuitans in eis implicaciones sui animi quem semper liberum habere volebat ab omni molestia corporali, ut libere vacare posset continue meditacioni et assidue leccioni. Non tamen illa edificare volentes prohibebat, nisi forte immo-

932 cui] cum *MS*

derate fieri conspexisset. Feminarum nullam umquam intra domum suam passus est conuersari, nec eciam germanam sororem aut fratris sui filias, que deo pariter seruiebant. Dicebat enim quod etsi de sorore uel neptibus nulla mali possit oriri suspicio, tamen quia tales persone non possunt sine aliis sibi necessariis esse, et ad eas eciam alie aduenirent, et viri sancti sine aliis clericis et laycis non sint, ex illis possent infirmiores aut humanis temptacionibus commoueri, aut certe malis hominum suspicionibus infa
7va mari. Nec umquam / cum muliere solus loqui volebat eciamsi secretum aliquid interesset. Eapropter si forte aliqua earum, ut ei loqui dignaretur, petebat, numquam sine fratribus aut clericis testibus eam accedere permittebat. Docti ergo viri cautela magna debet nobis esse instructio. Hec Possidonius. Ipse enim dixisse legitur in libro De cohabitacione clericorum et mulierum: 'Experto crede, [expertus] loquor, coram deum non mentior, cedros libani, duces gregum, sub hac peste cecidisse repperi, de quorum casu non magis suspicabar quam Ambrosii vel Hieronymi impudica turpitudine.' Quocirca familiaritatem feminarum sicut venenum fugiendam docuit, nec minus, ut dicebat, eo timende sunt, 'quia religiose videntur; quia quanto religiosiores uidentur, tanto cicius alliciunt et sub pretextu pietatis latet viscus libidinis.' Hec ipse ibi. Feminarum eciam monasteria nonnisi vrgentibus necessitatibus visitabat.

Tria retulit se a beato Ambrosio didicisse. Primum quod vxorem cuiquam numquam peteret; secundum, quod militare volentem ad hoc non commendaret; tercium, quod ad conuiuia inuitatus non iret. Causa primi est ne si illi inter se non conueniant, sibi maledicant et utique satis videtur incongruum ut vir religiosus professus continenciam, aliquos carnalem inuitet ad copulam. Causa secundi est, ne si militantes calumpniam exerceant, in eum
7vb alii culpam refundant. Cau/sa tercii est, ne temperancie modum perdat.

Omnia iuramenta eciam que a nonnullis religiosis frequentantur, et a quibusdam simplicioribus iuramenta non putantur, videlicet, deus testis est, deus scit, et cetera huiusmodi, summa cura summaque vigilancia tamquam pestem exhorruit. Et si quis commensalium suorum in aliquod huiusmodi iuramentum laberetur statutum fuit ut unam de statutis perderet pocionem; erat enim suis secum commorantibus et conuiuantibus numerus poculorum prefixus. Asserebat enim summopere tenendum esse illud ewangelicum, *Sit sermo vester: est, est, non, non*, ne consuetudine iurandi quis laqueum incidat periurandi.

979 expertus] episcopus *MS* 987 Tria] = Capgrave xxxix

Laudabat vir sanctus plurimum illos quibus moriendi desiderium inerat, et super hoc exempla trium episcoporum sepius recitabat. Beatus enim Ambrosius cum in extremis esset et rogaretur, ut prelongacionem vite sibi precibus optineret, respondit: 'Non sic vixi, ut pudeat me inter vos viuere, nec mori timeo, quoniam bonum habemus dominum.' Quod responsum Augustinus mirabiliter extollebat. De quodam eciam alio episcopo retulit quod cum ei diceretur eum ecclesie multum fore necessarium et ideo eum adhuc dominus liberaret ait: 'Numquam, bene; si aliquando, quare non modo?' De alio quoque episcopo aiebat Cyprianum referre, quod cum in infirmitate graui laboraret, adhuc sibi sanitatem restitui exorabat. Cui iuue-
68ra nis / speciosus apparens, cum indignacione infremuit et ait: 'Pati timetis, exire non wltis. Quid faciam vobis?' Raro pro aliquo litteris uel verbis intercedere volebat, recolens quemdam philosophum contemplacione sue fame, amicis multa non prestitisse, addens quoniam plerumque potestas que petit, premit. Cum autem id faciebat, sic stilum temperabat, ut onerosus non esset, sed mereretur urbanitate dictaminis exaudiri. Volebat pocius inter ignotos quam inter amicos causas audire, dicens quia inter illos libere poterat cognoscere iniquum, et unum ex hiis esset amicum facturus, pro quo scilicet iusticia mediante sentenciam daret; ex amicis vero esset unum perditurus scilicet contra quem proferret sentenciam. Hereticos vir iste sanctus validissime confutabat, ita ut ipsi inter se publice predicarent, peccatum non esse interficere Augustinum quem tamquam lupum occidendum esse dicebant et occisoribus omnia peccata sua a deo dimitti indubitanter asserebant. Multas ab eis insidias mortis pertulit, sed dei prouidencia ita pugilem suum preseruauit, quod nec vi nec dolo sibi nocere potuerunt. Nam aliquando cum armati in insidiis laterent, et illum de more ad visitandas, instruendas uel exhortandas catholicas plebes euntem occidere disponerent, contigit ut diuina dispensacione sed ducatoris hominis errore recto itinere ammisso, uel dimisso, per aliam viam vir sanctus quo tenderat,
68rb perueniret et sic presidio erroris / manus illorum euaderet. Quo postea cognito, deo gracias egit, qui quomodo wult liberat quos saluare disponit. Verumptamen a predicacione verbi dei timore incussus non destitit sed semper et vbique cum tempus et locus exigeret, illorum errorem pressit et oppressit, et pro eis nonnumquam dampnatis apud principes seculi intercessit. Eodem siquidem tempore multe et quasi infinite hereses in Affrica pullulabant. Donatiste namque velut sub professione continencium ambulantes, erant in ingenti numero per omnes fere affricanas regiones constituti, qui Circumcelliones dicebantur, superba audacia homines eciam violenter et cum armis ad suam sectam trahentes. Manichei nichilominus versuta calliditate multos seducebant; Pelagianiste similiter nouas hereses publice et per domos disseminare callide conabantur. Felix eciam hereticus, Maxenci-

1022 Hereticos] = Capgrave xl

us, Pascencius, Felicianus, Faustus, Secundinus, Petilianus et multi alii heretici quos enumerare longum et superfluum esset, doctrinas varias et prophanas in cordibus infirmorum seminabant. Contra quos omnes preclarissimus magister ecclesie et veritatis velut fortissimus adhleta, pro fidei sinceritate scriptis et dictis continue dimicauit et eos publica disputacione confutauit. Quorum multi diuina inspiracione et Augustini disputacione et predicacione ad fidem catholicam sunt conuersi. Plerumque eciam ei prae- 8va dicanti accidit, ut digressionem a materia faceret, et tunc / dicebat hoc deum ad profectum salutis alicuius ordinasse, sicut in quodam Manicheorum negociatore patuit, qui in quadam predicacione Augustini, ubi ipse digressionem faciens contra hunc errorem predicaverat, conuersus fuit. Concilia eciam episcoporum et synodos sacerdotum, colloquia principum, ab eis invitatus frequentauit a quibus, *non que sua sunt, sed que Jesu Christi sunt* quesiuit, ut scilicet quod iustum erat confirmaretur, et quod iniustum discrete corrigeretur. Hec Possidonius.

Eodem preterea tempore scilicet episcopatus sui multos conscripsit libros ad edificationem fidelium, et roboracionem fidei orthodoxe. Primo quidem scripsit librum Ad Simplicianum. Cum autem Augustinus erudicione Simpliciani ut supra dictum est conuersus fuisset, et ipse Augustinus ad Affricam remeasset, ipse Simplicianus Mediolanensis episcopus factus, beato Ambrosio succedens, audiuit famam celeberrimam de Augustini sapiencia et eius admirabili doctrina eumque episcopum esse factum. Propter quod sibi misit quasdam questiones subtiles de sacra scriptura soluendas. Ac Augustinus suis questionibus respondens hunc librum, duos libros continentem, transmisit sibi. Item scripsit librum Confessionum, tredecim libros continentem, in quibus de malis suis propriis confitetur, et de bonis deum laudat iustum et bonum. Quos quidem libros fecit ut exercitaret suum intellectum et inflammaret ad deum suum affectum. In tantum namque ipsum excitabant et 8vb inflammabant, quod non est aliquis ita durus et indeuotus / qui non excitetur ad deuocionem et inflammetur ad amorem, si ipsos libros cum attencione legerit. Omnia enim verba in ipsis libris posita sunt ad dei amorem inflammancia, melle diuine dulcedinis condita et deuocione suauissima plena. Item scripsit librum De opere monachorum. Cum enim in Affrica cepissent esse multa monasteria monachorum, inter eos magna questio est exorta. Quidam enim dicebant quod propriis manibus operari oportebat iuxta verbum apostoli dicentis: *Qui non laborat nec manducet,* et iterum *Nocte et die laborantes fuimus, ne vestrum aliquem graueremus*; alii vero econtrario dicebant quod ipsi nichil debebant propriis manibus operari, adducentes pro se verbum ewangelii dicentis: *Respicite volatilia celi etc.*, et

1059 Eodem] = Capgrave xli

iterum, *Respicite lilia agri*, et in tantum augebatur ista contencio, ut ex hoc fere tota ecclesia turbaretur, aliis defendentibus istos, aliis illos. Propter quod Aurelius Carthaginensis episcopus rogauit Augustinum ut super hoc aliquid scriberet et doceret, et dirigeret tam ipsos monachos quam alios. Augustinus ergo de hoc librum composuit, in quo ostendit quod certis horis et temporibus oracioni est insistendum; ostendit eciam ibi quante necessitatis et utilitatis sit propriis manibus laborare. Scripsit preterea librum De trinitate, quem iuuenis incepit et senex edidit, libros quindecim continentem. Item scripsit De ciuitate dei, continentem viginti duos libros; cum
69ra enim Ghoti Romam cepissent, pagani / et infideles insultabant Christianis et deum verum blasphemauerunt dicentes quod postquam Roma a cultura deorum recesserat et Christum coluerat semper ab hostibus victa fuit. Vnde Augustinus zelo domus dei plurimum exardescens hunc librum scripsit. In primis quinque libris repellens errorem illorum, qui dicunt quod omnia bona et omnia prospera illis accidunt qui diuersos deos colunt; in aliis quinque refellitur error illorum qui dicunt quod in hac vita bona et mala numquam defuerunt nec umquam deficient sed variantur diuersimode secundum loca, tempora, et personas. In duodecim vero aliis libris sequentibus aduersa predictorum redarguit, ostendens iustos in hac vita premi et impios florere debere. Vbi de duplici ciuitate scilicet Ierusalem et Babylonia, et eorum regibus ait: Quia rex Ierusalem Christus, rex Babylonis dyabolus. Quas duas ciuitates, ut ibidem dicit, duo amores sibi fabricant; quia ciuitatem diaboli constituit amor sui crescens usque ad contemptum dei, ciuitatem vero dei amor dei constituit, crescens usque ad contemptum sui. Hec ipse in secundo libro Retractacionum. Preter hos plures alios et pene innumerabiles scripsit libros, tractatus, epistolas ad diuersas personas, omelyas et sermones in tanta copia, ut vix aliquis possit sufficere ad legendum, cum Augustinus sufficeret ad scribendum. Multos quidem scripsit /
69rb adhuc laycus, multos religiosus et presbyter factus, plurimosque episcopus dictauit. Hec Possidonius. Cum autem ipse predictos libros et tractatus fecisset, voluit relegere omnes et diligenter examinare, ut si qua essent in eis non sane dicta, ea prouide retractaret; si qua dubia, explanaret; et si qua obscura, elucidaret; maxime ea et circa ea que scripsit dum adhuc cathecuminus et secularis esset secularis sciencie consuetudine adhuc inflatus, sicut ipse in prologo libri Retractacionum refert. Vt autem ad faciendum hoc magis ocium haberet, maxime quod in duobus conciliis episcoporum ab omnibus coepiscopis ipsi Augustino cura de scripturis esset imposita, per aliquot annos ante suum obitum peciit humiliter a clero et populo ut per quinque dies in ebdomada liceret sibi assidue vacare ocio, ymmo pocius litterali inseruire negocio et in reliquos dies exteriorum ne-

1089 Scripsit] = Capgrave xlii 1112 Cum] = Capgrave xliii

gociorum tumultus differre. Quod quidem ei concessum exstitit, sed cogente necessitate frequencius irruptum fuit. Quapropter ut adhuc liberius posset vacare studio, attendensque etate se grandeuum et eum, qui ordine nature preteriri non potest, terminum non longe abesse et timens ne post decessum suum aliquis ambiciosus vel minus ydoneus cathedram episcopalem acciperet, vel forte in eleccionis negocio scisma in ecclesia fieret,
9va consuluit et consulendo peciit, ut eo viuente religiosum eligerent / episcopum, qui eo decedente absque dissensione episcopatum susciperet, eo quia viuente ille negocia ecclesie et populi pro eo disponeret et maiora, cum oportunum esset suum consilium, ad ipsum referret. Sicque factum est ut compromisso in Augustinum facto, ipse quendam virum religiosum, Eraclium nomine, ad succedendum sibi eligeret. Quem ipse Augustinus in scola Christi erudierat et tam sanctitate quam sciencia inbuerat adprime; cuius eleccione tam clerus quam populus consensu unanimi acclamauit. In quem eciam Augustinus de omnium consensu suarum occupacionum sarcinam refudit; ipse vero studio vacauit. Tunc igitur omnes libros suos reuidit, relegit et examinauit atque ad unguem correxit et sic librum Retractacionum fecit. Et nichilominus plures libros postmodum conscripsit. Hec in Legenda famosa. Verum aliquanto post tempore, cum Wandali adiunctis sibi Alanis et Ghotis, totam Affrice prouinciam occupassent, vastantes omnia, nec parcentes sexui, ordini vel etati, demum ad Yponensem ciuitatem venerunt, et ipsam manu valida obsederunt. Sub hac tribulacione Augustinus pre ceteris sue senectutis amarissimam et lugubrem duxit vitam. Fueruntque sibi *lacrime sue panes die ac nocte*, cum videret alios hostili nece extinctos, alios effugatos, ecclesias sacerdotibus et ministris destitutas, virginesque sacras
9vb et quosque continentes / vbique dissipatos. Et in hiis alios tormentis defecisse, alios in captiuitate, perdita animi et corporis integritate ac fide malo more et duro hostibus deseruire; ymnos et laudes dei de ecclesiis deperisse, edificia ecclesiarum pluribus locis ignibus concremata, solempnia diuinorum desisse, sacramenta divina vel non queri vel querenti qui tradat non facile reperiri. Ipsosque ecclesiarum prepositos et clericos, qui forte necem euaserant, rebus omnibus spoliatos atque nudatos, egentissimos mendicare, si tamen essent qui eis subuenirent. Inter omnia tamen hec et multa alia mala, cuiusdam sapientis sentencia se consolabatur dicentis: Non est magnus magnum putans quod cadunt lapides et moriuntur mortales. Conuocatis autem fratribus dixit eis: 'Ecce rogaui dominum ut aut nos ab istis periculis eruat, aut patienciam tribuat, aut me de hac vita suscipiat.' Et hoc ipsum coepiscopi et alii qui aderant, per eum exhortati, a domino petiuerunt. Et ecce tercium quod petiuit optinuit et tercio obsidionis mense febri-

1141 Verum] = Capgrave xliiii   1157 moriuntur] molimur *MS*

bus laborans lecto decubuit. Quo egrotante quidam eger ad ipsum venit et ut sibi manum imponeret, et ab infirmitate curaret ipsum instanter rogauit. Cui Augustinus respondit: 'Quid est hoc, fili, quod loqueris? Putas si tale quid facere possem, mihi hoc ipsum non conferrem?' Ille autem instabat,
70ra asserens sibi in visione doctum esse: 'Vade ad Augustinum episcopum / vt tibi manum imponat et saluus eris.' Videns autem Augustinus fidem eius, facta oracione manum egroto imponens, infirmus infirmo sanitatem restituit. Intelligens autem vir dei dissolucionem sui corporis imminere, quia frequenter predicauerat non debere presbyterum et quemlibet quantumcumque laudatum christianum, de hac vita sine luctu et penitencia egredi, hoc ipse adimplere voluit. Et septem psalmos penitenciales, quos sibi scribi fecerat in lectulo suo, contra parietem habebat eosque legebat et relegebat et inter legendum ubertim flebat. Et ut deo vacaret liberius ac eius intencio a nullo distraheretur ante decem dies sui obitus, nullum ad se ingredi precepit, nisi vel medicus ingrederetur vel cibus et quodlibet aliud necessarium inferretur. Et per illud tempus assidue incubuit oracioni et deuocioni ac ploracioni. Ad extremam autem horam veniens scilicet quinto Kalendas Septembris, membris omnibus sui corporis incolumis, integro aspectu atque auditu, fratrum conuentu astante et exitum eius cum oracionibus domino commendante, senex et plenus dierum obdormuit in pace.

Testamentum nullum fecit quia unde faceret, pauper Christi non habuit. Clerum sufficientissimum et monasteria tam virorum quam feminarum plena continentibus reliquit, instructa moribus et ornata libris quos ipse dictauit. In quibus nobis adhuc viuit quamuis carne obierit; viuit quippe
70rb deo, viuit et / nobis quia et perfecte inheret deo et per scripta sua loquitur nobis, prout quidam poeta eleganter designauit, qui suis quos moriens relinquebat in tumulo suo hos versiculos scribere mandauit: Viuere post obitum vatem vis nosse viator? Quod legis, ecce loquor, vox tua nempe mea est. Vixit autem in clericatu vel episcopatu annis ferme xl, etatis vero illius anni[s] lxxvi. Hec Possidonius. Talem igitur virum, et tantum patrem ac doctorem omnes venerentur catholici et precipue religiosi et clerici cum et illius doctrina omnium sit instructio catholicorum et illius vita sit forma et norma omnium religiosorum et clericorum. Ipse quippe est decus et forma huius nostre professionis, ipse speculum et regula nostre religionis. Nulli dubium quin ipse iam receptus in consorcium angelorum ubi videt principium *in splendoribus sanctorum*; non immemor est fratrum suorum, sed quantum spero et presumo de eo, nos sibi subditos reconciliabit deo qui viuit et regnat in secula seculorum. Amen. Hec Possidonius et in Legenda famosa.

1162 Quo] = Capgrave xlv

[Nota] Et sciendum quod Legenda famosa appellatur hic Legenda quedam sollempnis et antiqua stilo venusto, more veterum compilata a quodam qui Philippum se nominat. Circa finem eiusdem Legende sic dicens, Eligant alii quod sua cuique suggerit ambicio. Sed si Philippo daretur opcio, mallet sanctam paupertatem qua deus pontificem ditauit Augustinum quam regnum et diuicias quibus regem extulit Alexandrum. Et habetur illa Legenda in multis antiquis monasteriis Canonicorum Regularium et Premonstratensium.

Bibliography

A. Extant Works of John Capgrave

Life of St. Norbert (before 1422)
San Marino, California, Henry E. Huntington Library, MS HM 55.
Ed. Cyril Lawrence Smetana. Toronto, 1977.

Commentarius in Genesim (1437-1438)
Oxford, Bodleian Library, MS Oriel 32.

Commentarius in Exodum (1439-1440)
Oxford, Bodleian Library, MS Duke Humfrey b.1.

Life of St. Katharine (before 1445)
London, British Library, MS Arundel 20 no. 1.
London, British Library, MS Arundel 168 no. 9.
London, British Library, MS Arundel 396 no. 1.
Oxford, Bodleian Library MS Rawlinson Poet. 118.
Ed. Carl Horstmann. Early English Text Society, O.S. 100. London, 1893.

De illustribus Henricis (c. 1447)
Cambridge, Corpus Christi College, MS 408.
London, British Library, MS Cotton Tiberius A VIII.
Ed. Francis C. Hingeston. Rolls Series 7. London, 1858.

Life of St. Augustine (c.1451)
London, British Library, Add. MS 36704 no.1.
Ed. J. J. Munro. Early English Text Society, O.S. 140. London, 1910.

Life of St. Gilbert of Sempringham (1451)
London, British Library, Add. MS 36704 no. 2.
Ed. J.J. Munro. Early English Text Society, O.S. 140. London, 1910.
The Book of St. Gilbert. Ed. Raymonde Foreville and Gillian Keir. Oxford, 1987.

Tretis of tho Orderes that be undyr þe Reule of oure Fader Seynt Augustin (1451)
London, British Library, Add. MS 36704 no. 3.
Ed. J.J. Munro. Early English Text Society, O.S. 140. London, 1910.

The Solace of Pilgrimes (c. 1451)
Oxford, All Souls College, MS 17 (fragment).
Oxford, Balliol College, MS 190 (fragment).
Oxford, Bodleian Library, MS 423 no. 5.
Ed. C.A. Mills. British and American Archaeological Society of Rome. London, 1911.

Super actus apostolorum (c. 1457)
Oxford, All Souls College, MS 17.
Oxford, Balliol College, MS 189.

Abbreuiacion of Cronicles (1462)
Cambridge, Corpus Christi College, MS 167.
Cambridge, University Library, MS Gg. 4.12.
The Chronicle of England. Ed. F.C. Hingeston. Rolls Series 1. London, 1858.
Ed. P. J. Lucas. Early English Text Society, 285. London, 1983.

De fidei symbolis (c. 1462)
Oxford, All Souls College, MS 17.
Oxford, Balliol College, MS 190.

B. Select Bibliography

Altaner, B. "Augustinus und die griechische Patristik." *Revue Bénédictine* 62 (1952) 201-215.

——. "Augustinus und die griechische Sprache." In *Pisciculi Studien zur Religion und Kultur des Altertums*, pp. 19-40. Münster, 1939.

Arbesmann, R. "The Edition of the *Vita s. Augustini* in Boston Public Library MS 1483." *Revue des études Augustiniennes* 11 (1965) 43-54.

——. "Henry of Friemar's Treatise on the Origin and Development of the Hermit Friars and its True and Real Title." *Augustiniana* 6 (1956) 37-145.

——. "Jordan of Saxony's *Vita s. Augustini* the Source of John Capgrave's *Life of St. Augustine*." *Traditio* 1 (1943) 341-353.

——. "The 'Malleus' Metaphor in Medieval Characterization." *Traditio* 3 (1945) 389-391.

——. "The Question of the *Regula s. Augustini*." *Augustinian Studies* 1 (1970) 237-261.

——. "The *Vita Aurelii Augustini Hipponensis episcopi* in Cod. Laurent. Pluto 90 sup. 48." *Traditio* 18 (1962) 319-355.

Athanasius. St. *Vita Antonii*. PL 73.125-170 (Evagrius' translation).

Bokenham, Osbern. *Legendys of Hooly Wummen*. Ed. M.S. Sergeantson. Early English Text Society, O.S. 206. Oxford, 1938.

Bonner, Gerald. *St. Augustine of Hippo, Life and Controversies*. Revised ed. Norwich, 1986.

Brandt, S. "Versus Hieronimi ad Augustinum." *Philologus Zeitschrift für klassische Altertums*, NF 16 (1903) 623-633.

Brown, Peter. *Augustine of Hippo, a Biography*. London, 1967.

——. *Religion and Society in the Age of Augustine*. London, 1972.

Catalogue of Additions to the Manuscripts in the British Museum. London, 1907.

Colledge, Edmund. "The Capgrave Autographs." *Transactions of the Cambridge Bibliographical Society* 6 (1974) 137-148.

——. "John Capgrave's Literary Vocation." *Analecta Augustiniana* 40 (1977) 185-195.

Colledge, Edmund and Cyril Smetana. 'Capgrave's *Life of St. Norbert*: Diction, Dialect and Spelling." *Mediaeval Studies* 34 (1972), 422-34.

Courcelle, P. "Les dernières paroles s. Augustin." *Revue des études anciennes* 46 (1944) 205-207.

Coyle, John Kevin. *Augustine's De moribus ecclesiae catholicae*. Paradosis 25. Fribourg, 1978.

de Meijer, Alberic. "John Capgrave OESA (1393-1464)." *Augustiniana* 5 (1955) 400-440; 7 (1957) 118-148, 531-575.

Decret, F. *Afrique Manicheenne (ive-ve siècles). Étude historique et doctrinale*. Études augustiniennes. Paris, 1978.

Delehaye, Hippolyte. *The Legends of the Saints*. Tr. Donald Attwater. New York, 1962.

Dibelius, W. "Capgrave und die englische Schriftsprache." *Anglia* 23 (1901) 153-194, 323-375, 427-472; 24 (1901) 211-263, 269-308.

Dickinson, John Compton. *The Origins of the Austin Canons and their Introduction into England*. London, 1950.

Emden, Alfred Brotherston. *A Biographical Register of the University of Cambridge to 1500*. Cambridge, 1963.

Fredeman, Jane. "John Capgrave's *Life of St. Augustine*." *Augustiniana* 28 (1978) 288-309.

——. "The Life of John Capgrave." *Augustiniana* 29 (1979) 197-237.

Frend, W.H.C. *The Donatist Church, a Movement of Protest in Roman North Africa*. Oxford, 1971.

——. "The Gnostic-Manichaean Tradition in North Africa." *Journal of Ecclesiastical History* 4 (1953) 13-53.

——. "A note on the Berber Background in the Life of Augustine." *Journal of Theological Studies* 43 (1942) 188-191.

Gregory the Great. *Gregorii magni dialogi libri quatuor*. Ed. Umberto Moricca. Rome, 1924. Also PL 77.127-432.

Gwynn, Aubrey O. *Austin Friars in the Time of Wyclif*. Oxford, 1940.

Hefele, Karl Joseph. *History of the Councils of the Church*. New York, 1972.

Hugo of St. Victor. *De sacramentis christianae fidei*. PL 176.183-618.

Isidore of Seville. *Isidori Hispalensis episcopi etymologiorum sive originem, libri XX*. Ed. W. M. Lindsay. Oxford, 1911.

Jones, J. W. "Observations on the Division of Man's Life," *Archaeologia* 35 (1853) 167-189.

Jordanus de Saxonia. *Liber vitasfratrum*. Ed. R. Arbesmann and W. Hümpfner. New York, 1943.

——. *Vita s. Augustini*. *Supplementum Patrum*. Ed. J. Hommey. Paris, 1686. 569-625.

Kaehler, E. *Studium zum Te Deum and zur Geschichte des 24 Psalms in der alte Kirche*. Göttingen, 1958.

Landulphus Senior. *Mediolanensis historia libri quatuor*. Ed. Alessandro Cutolo. Rerum Italicarum scriptorum 4.2. Bologna, 1942.

Lawless, George. *Augustine of Hippo and His Monastic Rule*. Oxford, 1987.

——. "Augustine's First Monastery: Thagaste or Hippo?" In *Miscellanea di Studi Agostiniani in onore di P. Agostino Trapè = Augustinianum*, 25 (1985) 65-78.

Lucas, Peter J. "An Author as Copyist of His Own Work: John Capgrave OSA (1393-1464)." In Richard Beadle, et al., *New Sciences out of Old Books...*, pp. 227-248. Aldershot, 1995.

——. "Consistency and Correctness in the Orthographic Usage of John Capgrave's *Chronicle*." *Studia Neophilologica* 45 (1973) 323-355.

——. "The Date of John Capgrave's *Life of St. Norbert*." *The Library*, Sixth series 3 (1981) 328-330.

——. "A Fifteenth-Century Copyist at Work under Authorial Scrutiny: An Incident from John Capgrave's Scriptorium." *Studies in Bibliography* 34 (1981) 66-95.

——. *From Author to Audience: John Capgrave and Medieval Publication*. Dublin, 1997.

——. "The Growth and Development of English Literary Patronage in the Later Middle Ages and Early Renaissance." *The Library*, Sixth series 4 (1982) 219-248.

——. "John Capgrave and the Nova Legenda Anglie, a Survey." *The Library*, Fifth series 25 (1970) 1-10.

——. "John Capgrave O.S.A. (1393-1464) Scribe and 'Publisher'." *Transactions of the Cambridge Bibliographical Society* 5 (1969) 1-35.

——. "Robert Kemp and the Holograph Manuscript Containing Capgrave's *Life of St. Gilbert* and *Tretis*." *British Museum Quarterly* 36 (1971) 80-83.

——. "Sense Units and Use of Punctuation-Markers in Capgrave's *Chronicle*." *Archivum Linguisticum*, New series 2 (1971) 1-24.

Mansi, G. D., ed. *Sacrorum conciliorum nova et amplissima collectio*. Venice, 1759-1798.

McIntosh, Angus, M.L. Samuels and Michael Benskin. *A Linguistic Atlas of Late Medieval English*. 4 vols. Aberdeen, 1985.

Meech, S. B. and H. E. Allen, eds. *The Book of Margery Kempe*. Early English Text Society 212. Oxford, 1940.

Minio-Paluello, Lorenzo. "The Genuine Text of Boethius' Translation of Aristotle's Categories." In *Opuscula: The Latin Aristotle*, pp. 1-27. Amsterdam, 1972.

Mirabella Roberti, Mario. "Il Battistero di Ambrogio." In *Il Battistero Ambrosiano di San Giovanni alle Fonti*, ed. Mario Mirabella Roberti and Angelo Paredi, pp. 9-33. Milano, 1974.

Munier, C., ed. *Concilia Africae a. 345-a. 525*. CCL 259. 1974.

O'Meara, John J., tr. *St. Augustine Against the Academics*. Ancient Christian Writers No.12. Westminster, Maryland, 1950.

Paredi, Angelo. "Dove fu Battezzato S. Agostino." In *Il Battistero Ambrosiano di San Giovanni alle Fonte*, ed. Mario Mirabella Roberti and Angelo Paredi, pp. 67-81. Milano, 1974.

Perler, Othmar. *Les voyages de saint Augustin*. Études augustiniennes. Paris, 1969.

Phillipus de Harveng. *Vita beati Augustini Hipponensis episcopi*. PL 203: 1206-1234.

Possidius. *Sancti Augustini vita scripta a s. Possidio episcopo*. Ed. T. Weiskotten. Princeton, 1919. Also PL 32.33-66.

Sanderlin, George. "John Capgrave Speaks Up for the Hermits." *Speculum* 18 (1943) 358-362.

Seymour, M.C. "John Capgrave." In N.F. Blake, et al., *William Caxton....*, pp. 200-256. Authors of the Middle Ages, 3, nos. 7-11: English Writers of the Late Middle Ages. Aldershot, Hants, 1996.

——. "The Manuscripts of John Capgrave's English Works." *Scriptorium* 40 (1986), 248-255.

Tanner, Thomas. *Bibliotheca britannico-hibernica: sive De scriptoribus qui in Anglia, Scotia et Hibernia ad saeculi XVII initium floruerunt*. London, 1748.

Taylor, Hammond. "Augustine and the Hortensius of Cicero." *Studies in Philology* 60 (1963) 487-498.

Testard, Maurice. *Saint Augustin et Ciceron*. Études augustiniennes. Paris, 1958.

Trapp, Damasus A. "Dreistufiger Editionsprozess und dreiartige Zitationsweise bei den Augustiner-Theologen des 14. Jahrhundert." *Augustiniana* 25 (1975) 282-292.

van Bavel, T.J. "Augustine's View on Women." *Augustiniana* 39 (1989) 5-53.

Verheijen, Luc. *La règle de saint Augustin: I. Tradition manuscrite; II. Recherches historiques*. Études augustiniennes. Paris, 1967.

Victorinus, Marius. *Opera exegetica*. CSEL 83, I (1971).

——. *Opera theologica*. CSEL 83, II (1981).

Walpole, A. *Early Latin Hymns*. Cambridge, 1922.

Warnock, R. G. and A. Zumkeller. *Der Traktat Heinrichs von Friemar über die Unterscheidung der Geister, Lateinisch-mittelhochdeutsche Textausgabe mit Untersuchungen*. Cassiciacum 32. Würzburg, 1977.

Winstead, Karen A. "John Capgrave and the Chaucer Tradition." *Chaucer Review* 30 (1996) 389-400.

Wolpers, T. *Die Englische Heiligenlegende des Mittelalters*. Tübingen, 1964.

Workman, S. K. *Fifteenth Century Translation as an Influence on English Prose*. Princeton, 1940.

Zumkeller, Adolar. *Augustine's Ideal of the Religious Life*. Tr. Edmund Colledge. New York, 1986.

Capgrave's Debt to Jordanus

CAPITULUM	JORDANUS, *VITA*	CAPITULUM	JORDANUS, *VITA*
[v]-vi	37-66	xxvi	505-518
vii	67-97	xxvii	519-540
viii	97-121	xxviii	543-572
ix	122-148	xxix	573-605
x	148-173	xxx	607-644
xi	174-199	xxxi	651-679
xii	[*Conf.* 6.9]	xxxii	680-709
xiii	201-217	xxxiii	718-741
xiv	217-246	xxxiv	743-765
xv	247-296	xxxv	836-860
xvi	297-320	xxxvi	860-883
xvii	323-361	xxxvii	884-923
xviii	364-377	xxxviii	924-986
xix	378-397	xxxix	987-1022
xx	398-416	xl	1022-1058
xxi	418-441	xli	1059-1089
xxii	441-456	xlii	1089-1112
xxiii	457-489	xliii	1112-1140
xxiv	[*Conf.* 9.13]	xliv	1141-1162
xxv	492-504	xlv	1162-1194

Glossary

Words and forms that may prove difficult for a modern reader because of unfamiliarity of meaning or spelling have been included. Generally only the first instance is recorded, although significant nuances of meaning are noted. A computer concordance, generated from the text of Capgrave's *Life of St. Augustine*, was used to assist in the preparation of the Glossary.

For purposes of alphabetization, 'þ' is treated as 'th'; 'v' as a vowel as 'u' (e.g., 'vndirstand'); 'y' as a vowel as 'i' (e.g., 'tyme'). Entries with initial 'ȝ' follow 'g'.

Note: References are to *capitulum* (chapter) and line number of the text.

ABBREVIATIONS

adj.	adjective	*pl.*	plural
adv.	adverb	*pp.*	past participle
comp.	comparative	Pr	Prologue
conj.	conjunction	*pr.p.*	present participle
fig.	figurative	*prep.*	preposition
imp.	imperative	*pron.*	pronoun
impers.	impersonal	*reflex.*	reflexive
inf.	infinitive	*rel.*	relative
inter.	interrogative	*sg.*	singular
n.	noun	*subj.*	subjunctive
num.	numeral	*v.*	verb
poss.	possessive	*vbl.n.*	verbal noun
p.t.	past tense		

a *v. inf.* have 5/11 (*see* **haue**)
abide(yde) *v. inf.* wait 3/10, 11/53, stay 9/17, live 23/19; **abiden** *p.t.* remained 10/16; **abideth** *3 sg.* remains 45/32; **abo(o)d** *p.t.* kept 6/6, remained 6/43, 19/30, lived 16/18, awaited 23/7
able *adj.* fitting 8/18, mature 11/53, capable 17/31
abusion *n.* perversion 42/30
acord *n.* peace 39/41
acorde *v. 3 pl.* ~ **not weel** are not compatible 39/7 **acorded** *p.t.* harmonized 10/12; *pp.* **were** ~ agreed 11/46; **acordith** *3 sg.* harmonizes Pr/30
aferd *adj.* afraid 11/6, 23/35
af(f)tir, aftyr *prep.* according to Pr/8
aga(e)yn *adv.* again 3/42
aga(e)yn *prep.* contrary to 3/43, 31/16, against 8/24, 16/25, opposite 45/20
aknow(e) *v. pp.* **is** ~ acknowledged 8/7, 10/15; **am** ~ admit 36/32; **be** ~ admit 43/9
al *adv.* completely 7/8
alle *adj.* whole 1/5
allegaunce *n.* objection 33/22
allegge(i)d *v. pp.* mentioned 11/48, cited 30/35, quoted 31/29
allegging *v. pr.p.* pleading 30/15
amende *v. inf.* correct 10/11
amys *adv.* wrongly 7/21
anachorites *n. pl.* solitaries 29/10
annexid *v. pp.* joined 15/19
anon *adv.* immediately 8/35, as soon as 21/35
answere *n.* explanation 39/24; **answeres** *n. pl.* responses 8/25, solutions 35/17
answere *v. inf.* give an explanation 32/8
appechid *v. pp.* charged 12/2
approximat *adj.* **more** ~ **onto** more related to 1/26
aqweyntauns *n.* **in** ~ **with** got acquainted with 28/3; **not gretly of his** ~ not too well known 39/41
aray *n.* clothing 36/18
arayed *v. pp.* dressed 29/25; **araying** *vbl.n.* preparation 37/22
areste *v. 3 pl.* apprehend 12/18
arsmetrik *n.* arithmetic 8/8
articules *n. pl.* doctrines 6/16
asined *v. p.t.* directed 13/11
aspie *v. inf.* find out 7/36, notice 10/23; **aspied** *p.t.* recognized 7/40, detected 8/28, saw 34/29; *pp.* perceived 40/24
assigned *v. p.t.* directed 41/8; *pp.* designated 39/16
astates *n. pl.* governors 39/38
astoyned *v. pp.* astonished 17/26, amazed 23/26
attached *v. pp.* seized 12/32
attendauns *n.* attention 43/16
aucter(e) *n.* altar 23/29; **aucteris** *pl.* altars 11/27; **auter** altar 9/31
aucto(u)res(is) *pl.* authors Pr/25
auctorite *n.* authority 32/32
avise *n.* reason 10/5
avised *v. pp.* considered 3/11, qualified 38/37
avoideth *v. 3 sg.* empties 6/41
avow *n.* resolve 14/37

barbare *adj.* barbaric 1/22
bare *see* **bere**
barres *n. pl.* stripes (of gold or silver) 20/10
batayle *n.* **held** ~ made war 6/3
be *prep.* by Pr/2, in 3/35, through 7/7, according to 16/28

be *v. 1 sg. subj.* am Pr/9; *3 pl.* are Pr/10; *pp.* been 19/13
be *conj.* but 31/18
befor(e) *prep.* previous to 6/5; fer ~ far ahead 20/22
beleue/byleue *n.* belief 7/25, faith 40/12
ber(e) *v. inf.* take 30/5; *p.t.* hold 38/21; **bare** *p.t.* bore 3/45; **bore** *pp.* born 1/1, spread about 31/32, suffered 45/6
berk(e) *v. 3 pl.* ~ **ageyn** denounce 40/17; *inf.* ~ **ageyn** speak against 17/7
besi, besinesse *see* **bisi, bisinesse**
beside *prep.* near by 5/13
bete *v. pp.* whipped 5/9
bettir *adj.* greater Pr/19
by *adv.* fast ~ next to 6/20, near 13/8
bye *v. inf.* purchase 38/34
byleue *see* **beleue**
billis *n. pl.* letters 8/41
byrying *vbl.n.* burial 23/31
bisi(y)/besi *adj.* assiduous 3/33, eager 5/17, devoted 7/5
bisily *adv.* anxiously 15/13, eagerly 17/1
bisi(y)nesse/besinesse *n.* insistence 9/16, diligence 11/19, work 11/48, preoccupation 13/12, care 18/15, worry 18/16
bitith *v. 3 sg.* slanders 37/14
blame *n.* censure 37/15; **put in no** ~ not censured 3/33
blaspheme *n.* blasphemy 42/15
blessed(id), blissed *adj.* happy 16/36, holy 38/1
blow *v. pp.* blown 22/18
bodely *adj.* material 26/8
bokes(is,ys) *n. pl.* (*fig.*) writings Pr/58
bond *v. p.t.* fused 24/18
bord *n.* table 14/8
bore *see* **bere**
boundes *n. pl.* bonds 21/21
boundyn *v. pp.* vowed 39/9
boystously *adv.* harshly 36/13
brennyng *v. pr.p.* burning Pr/43; **brent** *v. p.t.* burned 15/6; *pp.* burned 44/17
brynk *n.* shore 9/23
brith *adj.* **make** ~ enlighten 11/20
broke *v. pp.* broken 3/27
brovt *v. pp.* brought 13/29
but *conj.* except 6/32
buxum *adj.* obedient 20/21

capit(u)le *n.* chapter Pr/3, 17/49
capitoll *n.* temple (of Jupiter) 42/17
capteyn *n.* leader 32/4
carde *v. 3 pl.* process (wool) 41/53
case *n.* **sette** ~ propose the situation 36/24
cast *v. p.t.* ~**in his hert** determined 10/30
caue *n.* cave 14/26
cause *n.* reason Pr/14, 5/18; **causes** *pl.* suits 34/4, affairs 40/50, legal cases 43/16
cause *v. inf.* bring 9/25; **caused** *p.t.* brought about 12/27, got 18/20; **causeth** *3 sg.* gives rise to 42 /29
caute *v. p.t.* contracted 33/4
cautele *n.* caution 38/55
cenobites *n. pl.* monks 29/10
cessacion *n.* ending 16/10
chanones *n. pl.* canons 2/33
charge *n.* responsibility 38/21
chase/chese *v. inf.* choose 11/47; *p.t.* chose 30/13
chaungable *adj.* variable 26/9
cher(e) *n.* expression 7/9, disposition 11/13, countenance 23/22, character 36/10; merie

~ cheerful expression 11/17
chere *v. inf.* entertain 34/29
cherch *n.* church Pr/17
cherischid *v. p.t.* treated fondly 10/9
childhold *n.* childhood 2/13
childirn(yr, yrn) *n. pl.* children 2/14
choi(y)s *n.* **free** ~ free will 22/25
clateryng *adj.* babbling 3/31
clene *adj.* pure 18/24
clene *adv.* completely 16/5
clennesse *n.* purity 5/3
clepe *v. 1 pl.* call 14/12; *inf.* call 9/15; **cleped(id)** *p.t.* called Pr/4; *pp.* called Pr/28; **clepyng** *pr.p.* calling 24/12
clerk *n.* cleric Pr/46, scholar 42/34, writer 45/36; **clerkis(ys)** *pl.* clergy 13/11, scholars 30/32
cloth *n.* clothing 37/49
coeterne *adj.* coeternal 22/28
col(l)ege *n.* community 21/11
comaundment *n.* request 21/18, direction 31/5
com(m)unicacio(u)n *n.* debate 8/36, conversation 23/15, discussion 35/17
comoun *adj.* general 21/46, communal 27/28; **go in** ~ live in common 28/20; **al ... ~ onto hem** they have all things in common 29/16
comoun *v. inf.* discuss 7/30; **comound** *p.t.* discussed 7/17; *pp.* communicated 8/40; **comuned** *p.t.* communicated 27/5
comounly *adv.* generally 4/4
compelled *v. p.t.* forced 40/26
complei(y)nt *n.* lament 3/39, grief 45/17; **compleintis** *pl.* grievances 9/24
compowned(yd) *v. pp.* composed Pr/53
comprehendid *v. pp.* summed up 29/29
compromisse *n.* **mad** ~ agreed 43/27
compunccion *n.* contrition 15/20
compunct *v. pp.* moved 14/29
conceytes *n. pl.* thoughts 24/24
concluded *v. pp.* hemmed in 8/30
condicioun *n.* **hasti** ~ volatile disposition 3/7, characteristic 38/32; **condiciones(is)** *pl.* circumstances 2/13, characteristics 3/1, principles 38/1, attitudes 39/1
confermed *v. pp.* strengthened 19/3
confirmacio(u)n *n.* strengthening 40/40
conflict(e) *n.* dispute 32/27
congregacion *n.* community 28/8
consciens *n.* scruples 5/6
consecrat(e) *v. pp.* dedicated 9/17, consecrated 33/24
consent *n.* harmony (mus.) 19/12
consolacio(u)n *n.* solace Pr/22
constituciones *n. pl.* directives 41/61
constreyned *v. pp.* forced 19/22
contencio(u)n(e) *n.* dispute 41/54
conteyne(y)th *v. 3 sg.* takes up 1/10
conuenient *adj.* suitable 27/31, proper 33/22, fitting 38/35
conuersacio(u)n *n.* way of life 20/7
conuersaunt *adj.* familiar 8/33
conuicte *v. p.t.* proved guilty 32/2
conyng *n.* intelligence 18/12
cope *n.* tunic 29/19
corage *n.* inclination 2/7, interest 7/38
costful *adj.* expensive 36/17
costis *n.* cost 13/9

costly *adv.* ful ~ at great expense 23/32
cosynes *n. pl.* cousins 2/26
couchid *v. pp.* laid 6/30
couchis *n. pl.* beds 15/43
coueti(y)se *n.* greed 37/51
councel(l) *n.* advice 7/34, deliberation 11/44, design 19/6, council of the church 33/28, matter of privacy 38/53
councell *v. inf.* advise 39/5; **councelled** *p.t.* advised 9/16
counfort *n.* be of good ~ be comforted 7/12, courage 7/15, encouragement 13/4, satisfaction 43/19
coynoures(is) *n. pl.* minters 12/9, *pl. poss.* 12/12
cristend(h)am *n.* Christianity 14/15
crying *vbl.n.* pleading 37/45
cumpany *n.* group 11/36; part ~ leave 14/33; **cumpanyes** *pl.* groups 14/18
cunnyng *n.* intelligence 6/34, wisdom 27/10, learning 31/8
cuntre *n.* country 1/1, land 11/26
cure *n.* administration 33/24
cured *v. pp.* covered 12/12
custom *n.* practice 19/29
custumablely *adv.* usually 2/20, regularly 31/28

daliauns *n.* conversation 11/10
damesellis *n. pl.* girls 3/31
debate *n.* dissension 3/30
declare *v. inf.* state 16/41; **declared** *p.t.* clarified 43/8; **declareth** *3 sg.* explains 41/16
ded(e) *v. p.t.* did 3/28
dede *n.* deed 12/18, proposition 32/11
dedly *adj.* mortal 4/5
defaute *n.* wrong 6/11, transgression 12/24; **defautes** *n. pl.* sins 5/5, misdeeds 6/10
defouled *v. pp.* tainted 24/8
degre *n.* level 34/26
delectabily *adv.* sweetly 19/12
delectable *adj.* pleasant 16/19, delightful 19/8, enjoyable 41/17
delectacio(u)n *n.* pleasure 23/17; **delectacionis** *pl.* pleasures 13/16
delyuered *v. pp.* freed 12/32
denouns *v. inf.* announce 37/31
denye *v. inf.* refuse 32/12
departed *v. pp.* divided 1/5, distributed 37/29
desert *n.* wilderness 13/5
desire *n.* wish Pr/24, longing, yearning 7/41, request 17/24, prayer, request 21/5
desired *v. p.t.* requested Pr/15, asked 17/29, wished 21/3, yearned for 21/5; **desiri(y)ng** *pr.p.* requesting 3/35
desolat *adj.* abandoned 16/7
despect *adj.* ordinary, humble 2/2
desperat *adj.* unrelated 40/44
despised *v. p.t.* scorned 23/21, looked down on 38/45
determyn *v. inf.* settle 43/25; **determineth** *p.t.* concludes 22/27
detraccio(u)n *n.* vilification 36/22
dettis *n. pl.* debts Pr/12
dettoure *n.* debtor Pr/8
deuly *adv.* continually 9/26
deuoci(y)o(u)n *n.* piety Pr/45, dedication 17/18
deuoute *adj.* sincere 11/31, spiritual 36/12
deuout(e)ly *adv.* earnestly 11/32
dew *adj.* proper 3/24
dewid *v. pp.* rained 17/8
deye *v. inf.* die 2/11; **deye(i)d** *p.t.* died 2/12

deynte *n.* **be more in** ~ are more highly regarded 8/20; **no** ~ **in** no esteem for 8/45
differre *v. inf.* put off 15/28
direccion *n.* instruction 31/22
dirkly *adv.* obscurely 43/7
disceptacioun *n.* debate 32/18
discrecioun *n.* **of grete** ~ with great prudence 30/24
disdeyned *v. p.t.* scorned 10/19
dysmittid *v. pp.* relieved 16/12
disparplied *v. pp.* scattered 28/19
dispensacio(u)n *n.* providence 9/8; **in** ~ for distribution 37/45
disport *n.* relaxation 14/24
dispose *v. inf.* arrange 9/10; **disposed** *v. p.t.* ~ **him** decided 9/11
disputacioun *n.* debate 32/23
dispute *v. inf.* debate 8/43; **disputeth** *3 sg.* discusses 16/36
disseyued *v. p.t.* deceived 9/12
dissolue *v. inf.* answer 41/14
dissoluere *n.* resolver 41/12
distauns *n.* dissension 11/50
dyuers *adj.* various 1/23
dyuersite *n.* singularity 11/36
dyuynes *n. pl.* theologians 42/4
diuinite, dyui(y)nyte *n.* theology 31/5
do(o) *v. inf.* do 3/24, act 36/8; ~ **aftir** act according 11/38; *pp.* done 3/12, committed 4/10, performed 41/61; **had be** ~ would have been done 33/6; **doyngis** *vbl.n.* carrying out of 40/8
doctouris *n. pl.* doctors (of the church) Pr/36
doctri(y)ne *n.* learning 15/11
dome *n.* ~ **place** court 12/14
doutes(is)/dowte *n.* uncertainty 13/13; *pl.* doubts 8/40, uncertainties 41/14
doutir *n.* daughter 3/34
draw(e) *v. 1 sg.* ~ **me** keep myself away 34/27; *inf.* follow 13/14; *pp.* brought 30/30; taken 33/31
dred *v. p.t.* feared 43/21
drenchid *v. pp.* drowned 15/12
durst *v. p.t.* dared 8/43

edificacion *n.* building 28/31
edifie *v. inf.* build 21/25; **edified** *p.t.* built 28/1; *pp.* built up 43/23; **edifiyng** *vbl.n.* building 28/24
eyne *n. pl.* eyes 15/16
eyr *n.* air 6/40
eke *adv. conj.* also Pr/19, moreover Pr/41
eld(e) *adj.* ancient 6/15, former 17/29
elementis *n. pl.* fundamentals 5/12
elmesse *n.* alms 9/31
emolliment *n.* treasure 45/33
encres *n.* growth 19/31
encrese *v. inf.* grow 17/5; **encresed(id)** *p.t.* grew 17/19
ende *n.* stage 44/12; **last** ~ latter part 24/3
endewid *v. pp.* initiated Pr/9
endewred *v. p.t.* persevered 38/20
endyti(y)ng *vbl.n.* writing 8/24
enformed *v. pp.* trained 43/30
enforsed *v. p.t.* based 41/50; **enforsyng** *vbl.n.* strengthening 40/40
engrosed *v. p.t.* extended Pr/33
ensaumple *n.* example 31/23; **ensaumples** examples 31/34
entend *v. inf.* direct efforts 43/13
entent *n.* purpose 1/30, outlook 11/23, resolve 14/38, mind 19/37, heart 38/42, reason 41/45

entre *n.* hold 41/63
epistil *n.* letter (scriptural) Pr/37
er *adv.* before 43/33
erde *n.* world 18/19
erdly *adj.* earthly 23/13
erroures *n. pl.* sins 10/11
erudicioun *n.* instruction 33/11
ese *n.* **wel at** ~ very comfortable 37/42
esy *adj.* light Pr/13
ethimi(o)logie *n.* etymology Pr/28
euene *adv.* fully 22/7
euerlasting, euerlestyn *adj.* eternal 23/10
euerych *pron.* everyone 29/9
euyr *adv.* always Pr/7
ex(e) *n.* axe 12/11
excedid *v. p.t.* went to excess 3/10
excersised, exercised *v. pp.* practiced 7/28, experienced 43/6
exerc(s)ise *n.* practice (of teaching) 8/14
excite *v. inf.* stir up 39/9
exequies *n.* funeral 23/40
exposicio(u)n *n.* explanation 32/30

fadere(i)s *n. pl.* founders 29/14
fayn *adj.* forced 8/43; pleased 16/25, obliged 44/32
faire(yre) *adj.* handsome 7/8[2], beautiful 7/8[1], fine 8/24, considerable 11/42, pleasant 23/5, gentle 36/14, flattering 37/43, clean 45/19; ~ **spok** *adj.* eloquent 8/39
falle *v. inf.* happen 39/45; *pp.* passed 16/5; *p.t.* dropped 32/26, declined 43/20
fame *n.* estimation 2/4, reputation 9/38, rumour 13/7
familiare *adj.* sociable 36/9
fantastical *adj.* phantom 6/39
fast *adv.* quickly 9/38; ~ **by** next to 6/20, close to 13/8; ~ **be** near 11/42
fedyng *vbl.n.* nourishment 16/34
fel(le) *v. see* **falle**
felau(w)chip *n.* companionship 6/7, group 8/36, company 9/5, community 11/39, companions 18/23
felaw *n.* comrade 14/24; **felawe(i)s** *n. pl.* companions 14/21
feld *n.* country 16/15
fele *v. inf.* grasp 26/15
felicite *n.* joy 14/17, happiness 23/22
fer(re) *adj.* far, remote 1/32, far 10/25
ferd *v. p.t.* fared 31/21
fere *n.* **all in** ~ together 23/1
fere *n.* fear 10/21
ferforth *adv.* **as** ~ as far 41/42
ferme *adj.* well-founded 33/14
feste *n.* feast day Pr/21
festfull *adj.* festive 2/17
feuerys *n.* fever 44/32
feyned *v. p.t.* pretended 9/13
feynt *adj.* weak 15/52
filt *v. p.t.* filled 9/23
fyred *v. pp.* aflame Pr/27
flesch *n.* body 3/23, flesh 10/20
fleschly *adj.* bodily 16/34
flete *v. inf.* overcome 24/16
flod *n.* river 44/6
folow *v. inf.* pursue 6/26
fond *v. p.t.* found 6/29
foot *n.* ~ **be** ~ step by step 15/20
for(e) *conj.* because Pr/32, since 1/29; *prep.* because 3/26, for the sake of 5/9
forbode *v. pp.* forbidden 11/28; **forbodyn** *pp.* forbidden 37/15
forgete(y)n *v. pp.* forgotten 23/12
forȝoue *v. pp.* forgiven 40/8

forme *n.* method 16/28, design 20/6, model 20/22, manner 27/19, principle 28/20; **aftir ... ~** according to the sequence 3/40
forso(o)k *v. p.t.* refused 32/10
foule *adv.* bitterly 32/25
found(e) *v. pp.* provided for 2/7, laid down 8/13, established 35/1
fre *adj.* free 16/2; **~ of hert** generous 3/5; **~ hertet** generous 28/5
frendly *adj.* helpful 22/4
freschly *adv.* elegantly 41/54
fro *prep.* from 1/32, without 34/9
frutes *n. pl.* crops Pr/42
ful *adj.* full 11/31
ful *adv.* very Pr/15, completely 7/22, extremely 37/40
fully *adv.* completely 6/29, definitely 9/11

gadered *v. p.t.* assembled 33/18
gaf *see* **ȝeue**
gat *v. p.t.* received 8/5; **goten** *pp.* brought 31/21
geaunt *n.* giant 40/39
gelosie *n.* uneasiness 33/5
gendres *n. pl.* kinds 21/15
gentil(l), gentyl *adj.* noble Pr/15
gessid *v. pp.* estimated 42/35
gestis *n. pl.* guests 37/21
girdil *n.* belt 20/10
gyuyst *see* **ȝeue**
go(o) *v.* **~ fro** depart 40/46; *inf.* **~ from** leave 16/9; **~ in comoun** become common property 28/20; *pp.* gone 3/10
go(o)d *n.* support 28/24, store 37/33; **godes(is)** *n. pl.* property 25/19, goods 35/11
goost *n.* spirit 8/34
go(o)stly *adj.* spiritual 9/35
gouernauns *n.* control 3/7, behaviour 6/9, charge 30/16
graunt *n.* agreement 43/18
graunt *v. inf.* grant 21/7; **graunted** *p.t.* granted 15/56, permitted 16/17, entrusted 21/1, given 23/20
grete *adj.* powerful 8/22, dear 11/40, admirable 13/16, important 13/18, numerous 30/16
gretly *adv.* highly Pr/4, very 4/16, deeply 8/39
grettir *adj. comp.* higher 6/1
greuauns *n.* grievance 5/19
greue *v. 3 pl.* hurt 4/12; *inf.* burden 41/49; **greued** *p.t.* pained 3/45
greu(v)ous *adj.* grave 9/27, serious 25/10
groundes *n. pl.* bases 6/44
grucch *v. 2 pl.* complain 20/17; *inf.* complain 38/47; *imp.* find fault 14/32; **grucchid** *v. p.t.* complained 31/18; **grucching** *pr.p.* complaining 38/28, murmuring 10/17; *vbl.n.* complaining 31/19

ȝald *v. p.t.* yielded 45/28
ȝaue *see* **ȝeue**
ȝere *n.* year Pr/43
ȝet *adv.* even though 38/49
ȝeue *v. inf.* give 11/30; **gyuyst** *2 sg.* give back 21/48; **ȝeueth** *3 sg.* gives 18/22; **ȝeuyng** *pr.p.* giving 15/36; **gaf/ȝaue** *p.t.* gave 9/31, 12/28; **ȝoue(n)** *pp.* given Pr/31, 18/9, devoted 14/17
ȝong *adj.* young 18/31
ȝoue(n) *see* **ȝeue**

habite *n.* comportment 36/1
had *see* **haue**

hald *v. inf.* live 11/45; *pp.* considered 34/30
halowid *v. pp.* dedicated 17/43
hambyr *n.* hammer 40/3
hand *n.* **eld** ~ ancient script 1/30; **with** ~ manually 41/62
happe(i)d *v. p.t.* happened 3/12, chanced 6/24
hardnesse *n.* difficulty 13/3
hast *n.* haste 12/16
hast *v. inf.* hasten 11/20; **hasted** *p.t.* hurried 14/36
hasti(y) *adj.* volatile 3/18
haue *v. 1 sg.* ~ **in possessioun** possess Pr/13; **a/had** have 5/11, extant 26/7
he *pron.* he Pr/3; **her/he** it 23/9, 42/30; **himself/himselue** himself 1/28, itself 27/6; **his(e)** *poss. adj.* his Pr/18, its 2/37
hed *n.* notice 12/19
heed *n.* head 10/16
heyly *adv.* earnestly 10/27, exceedingly 33/21
heith *n.* height 42/30
held *v. p.t.* led 27/4
helth *n.* welfare 9/35, healing 17/27
hem *see* **þei**
hepes *n. pl.* masses 15/23
her *n.* hair 37/50
herborowid *v. p.t.* lodged 25/9
her(e) *adv.* there Pr/6, here 2/25
her(e) *see* he, þei
here *v. 2 pl.* hear 9/32; *imp.* hear 24/12; **heryng** *pr.p.* hearing 41/13
heri(y)tage *n.* inheritance 25/19
hert *n.* heart Pr/27; **hertis** *pl.* hearts Pr/50
hertly *adv.* genuinely 7/3, devotedly 35/10
heruest *n.* harvest 16/8
heuy *adj.* sad 7/10, sorrowful 20/26
heuynesse *n.* grievousness 19/27
hy *adj.* profound 42/31
hire *see* sche
hith *v. p.t.* was named 2/12, entitled 22/14
ho(o)l *adj.* **not be** ~ not be healed 25/11; **was** ~ was sound 25/14; **were made** ~ were healed 38/6; **were** ~ were cured 38/7
hold *n.* **cacch no** ~ find no reason 3/9
hold *v. inf.* join 8/47, maintain 34/5; *pp.* held 12/7
holpe *v. pp.* helped 28/34
hoot *adj.* strong 37/9
hope *v. 1 sg.* think 45/41
hopped *v. p.t.* leapt 11/13
horribil *adj.* uncontrollable 15/2
hosyn *n. pl.* stockings 35/12
hote *adj.* hot, burning Pr/49
hothous *n.* bath house 2/18
housyng *n.* roofing 12/9
husbondry *n.* farming 25/20
huscher *n.* instructor 21/33

ydilnesse *n.* idleness 38/17
ydiotis *n. pl.* laymen Pr/5
ydoles *n. pl.* idols 42/21
ymaginacioun *n.* fancy 42/15
implicat *v. pp.* involved 38/44
ympne *n.* hymn 17/46; **ympnis(ys)** *pl.* hymns 19/2
imprended *v. p.t.* engraved 7/45
in *n.* inn 9/14
incli(y)nacioun *n.* setting 14/35
infect(e) *v. pp.* tainted 19/15
inow *adv.* sufficiently 26/16
insolens *n.* arrogance 6/8, rash deeds 6/19
instauns *n.* urging Pr/15, insinuation 19/20, persistence 32/12, prompting 39/32

instruccioun *n.* teaching 45/30
interogaciones *n. pl.* **makith ~** asks questions 18/22
intit(u)led *v.* entitled 8/17
intollerablely *adv.* excessively 9/23
inuectiones *n. pl.* objections 8/42
iocunde *adj.* pleasant 8/39
iocundnesse *n.* good humour 36/12
ioye *n.* delight 6/28, joy 7/19, happiness 9/24, bliss 18/23, glory 41/54
iqwenchid *v. pp.* blinded 6/35
ire *n.* anger 3/10
irous *adj.* irascible 3/18
ispoke *pp.* expressed 6/31
it *pron.* it Pr/19; **his** *poss. adj.* its 2/37
iteration *n.* repetition 13/24
iuuent *n.* youth 10/4

kalende *n.* calends 45/26
kepand *v. pr.p.* keeping 21/45
kynrod *n.* family 2/1, relations 27/18
kirk *n.* church 13/22
knowlech *n.* knowledge 1/27, acquaintance 3/13; **felle in ~** became acquainted with 10/7
knyth *n.* soldier 40/10
kunning(yng) *n.* intelligence 12/23, learning 26/17

laboure *n.* effort Pr/13; **~ with hand** manual labour 41/62
labour(e) *v. inf.* endeavour Pr/46, work 30/6; **labourand** *pr.p.* being preoccupied 38/42; **laboured** *p.t.* endeavoured 18/17, influenced 43/23; **laboureth** *3 sg.* **~ ageyn** belabours 42/24
lakkyn *v. 1 pl.* fault 36/18
lamentable *adj.* mournful 15/26
largely *adv.* intemperately 37/16, generously 37/27; **more ~** at greater length 3/40
laschid *v. pp.* beaten 5/10
last *adj.* **at þe ~** finally 13/25
lec(c)heri(y)e *n.* lust 5/4
lech *n.* physician 25/11
lede *v. inf.* lead 13/33
left(e) *v. 2 sg.* took off 45/42; *p.t.* abandoned 6/37; *inf.* raise up 38/5; *pp.* passed 24/19, left (unsaid) 39/13
lei(y)sir(yre) *n.* freedom 15/25, leisure 43/11, free time 43/32; **haue at ~** have at (his) disposal 8/9
lendes *n. pl.* loins 29/27
lenger/longir *adv. comp.* longer 39/22
lenyng *v. pr.p.* leaning 23/8
lerne *v. inf.* study 1/23, teach 10/1; **lerned** *p.t.* learned 5/11, taught 31/1; *pp.* learned 5/11, instructed 20/26
lernyng *n.* study 2/7, education 5/12, lesson 38/56; **to her ~** for their instruction 45/40
lesingis *n. pl.* lies 24/9
lesse *conj.* **~ þan** except when 38/46
lesson *n.* reading 38/45
lest *prep.* **~þat** unless 43/25
lestith *v. 3 sg.* lasts 5/2
lettered(yd) *v. pp.* educated 2/28
letteres(is, ys) *n. pl.* letters, literature 1/24
lettid(yd) *v. pp.* hindered 9/5; **letting** *vbl.n.* ceasing 7/35
lettirure *n.* letters Pr/9, learning 34/7
leuand *v. pr.p.* living 41/13
leue *n.* permission 31/16; **had take his ~** left 15/8
leue *v. imp.* believe 38/57

leue/lyue *v. inf.* live 14/34; **leued** *p.t.* lived 3/27; **lyuyng** *pr.p.* **him** ~ while he was alive 35/19; **leue** *v. inf.* stop 37 /18
lewid *adj.* uneducated 30/31
leyd *v. p.t.* placed 15/46, put 17/36
liberte *n.* freedom 9/6
licorous *adj.* gluttonous 37/21
likid/lyked *v. 3 sg.* **it** ~ **him bettir** he preferred 11/43
lykyng *n.* **fleschly** ~ physical attraction 39/9
liknesse *n.* image 13/18
list *v. 2 sg.* wish 14/31; *p.t.* wished 30/29
lite/lith *n.* brilliance 6/36, light 15/47, 21/17, candle 22/18; **more** ~ easier 19/25
lit(h)ly *adv.* easily 37/7, readily 37/18
litigious *adv.* disputable 12/6
litil *adv.* little 6/6, shortly 43/1
long *adj.* extensive 7/39
long(e) *adv.* for a long time 8/14
long(e) *v. 3 pl.* pertain 22/23; *inf.* belong 12/31; **longid** *p.t.* belonged 23/9; **longing** *pr.p.* pertaining 3/42, belonging 16/16; **longi(e)th** *3 sg.* pertains Pr/28; *3 pl.* belongs Pr/5
lordchip *n.* dominion Pr/33, honour 24/9
losed *v. pp.* released 23/38
loth *adj.* reluctant 13/3
low *v. p.t.* laughed 6/10

magre *prep.* in spite of 10/16
mayde *n.* virgin 40/29
maydenhed *n.* virginity 14/41
maystires *n. pl.* teachers 8/3
make *v. 3 pl.* cause 3/30; **mad** *p.t.* wrote 1/28, effected 2/23, established 2/35, affected 6/27, gave 8/25, raised 8/43, indulged in 15/1, caused 15/24, expressed 17/6, composed 19/10; ~ **a game** laughed 5/10; ~ **hem redy** prepared 21/12; ~ **an ende** finished 26/6; *pp.* ~ **comendable** praised Pr/25; ~ **cristen** christened 2/11; written 22/21; **do** ~ have had made 35/12; **maki(y)ng** *vbl.n.* writing 17/41
maker *n.* author 6/25
mal *adj.* male 18/9
malencolie *n.* anger 3/6
maner(e) *n.* fashion 10/10, kind of 11/45, custom 14/7; **in þis** ~ in this way 9/13; **be** ~ **of** by way of 13/23, in the form of 22/22; **in** ~ considerably 15/16, specifically 22/26, as it were 23/12; **swech** ~ some--such 23/16; **in no** ~ in any sort of 23/17
maneres(is) *n. pl.* morals 22/15, customs 36/1
margarites *n. pl.* pearls 29/29
markette *n.* forum 13/19
mater(e) *n.* topic 3/3, affair 9/29, matter 12/25, subject 26/14, basis 36/21; **skole** ~ scholastic field 42/5; **matere(i)s** *pl.* things 19/8
matrones *n. pl.* women 3/13
mech *adj.* much Pr/53; ~ **of a** great number of 19/23
mech *adv.* passionately 19/21
medeled *v. pp.* mixed 37/8
mel *n.* mealtime 37/11
mene *adj.* compromise 30/26, poor 36/28
menes *n. pl.* means 10/29
mene *v. 3 pl.* mean 40/29; **meneth** *3 sg.* means 42/37
meny *n.* community 22/1, group

40/25
merciable *adj.* merciful 13/4
meritory *adj.* meritorious 40/7
merk *n.* sign 3/17; **merkys** *pl.* marks 3/13
meruayl(e), meruei(y)l(e) *n.* **haue** ~ be surprised 3/21, surprise 12/24, wonder 18/13
merue(y)ling(yng) *v. pr.p.* astonishing 8/12, wondering 15/20
mery *adj.* jovial 8/38, joyous 19/31, cheerful 36/9
mesurable *adj.* moderate 36/17
mesurablely *adv.* moderately 37/8
mete *n.* food 11/30
mete *v. inf.* meet 12/22
meued(yd) *v. p.t.* moved Pr/14; *pp.* moved 3/6, raised 34/17, led 41/47
meyre *n.* prefect 10/3
mynd(e) *n.* attitude 8/46; **haue** ~ **of** recall 3/20; **had...** ~ recalled 4/13; **gadered...** ~ recalled 15/24; **have...** ~ remember 23/31; **be had in** ~ commemorated 24/20; **makith** ~ mentions 35/6
minstres *n. pl.* helpers 9/10
myrth *n.* joy 36/12
myth *v. p.t.* could 2/8, 3/37
mischef *n.* misfortune 7/5, trouble 44/25
mo(o) *adj. comp.* more 1/13
molten *v. pp.* melted down 37/29
morer *n.* enlarger Pr/33
mornyng *vbl.n.* mourning 45/17
moti(y)ues *n. pl.* propositions 8/32

named *adj.* renowned 25/6
named *v. p.t.* nominated 43/28
namely *adv.* in particular 3/30, especially 28/5
narratyf *adj.* factual 22/24
nede *n.* **for** ~ out of necessity 6/19, need 36/31
nedful *adj.* necessary 4/16
nedis *n.* **must** ~ of necessity 44/23
nedith *v. 3 sg.* **me** ~ I need 22/19; **him** ~ he requires 35/14
neu(w)ly *adv.* recently Pr/48, again 40/23; ~ **ageyn** anew 3/42
ny *adj.* near 43/21
ny *adv.* nearly 40/21
ny *prep.* near 9/18; **more** ~ nearer 34/21; **nyher** *comp.* nearer 34/16
nyth *n.* night 7/5
norcher *n.* promoter 36/3
norchid *v. pp.* reared 2/13; **norching** *vbl.n.* rearing 3/42
noryce *n.* promoter 38/15
notable *adj.* noteworthy 8/25, important 22/24
notaries *n. pl.* secretaries 32/15
noþing *adv.* not at all 23/36
notwithstand(ing) *conj.* although 3/18
noueltes *n. pl.* novelties 7/38
noumbres *n. pl.* symbols 26/9
nowt *adv.* not 1/21, not at all 4/4
noyse *n.* uproar 22/11

o(n) *adj. num.* one Pr/26, 3/23
o(n) *see* **on**
occupacioun *n.* administration 30/22, occupation 38/41, preoccupation 45/2; **occupaciones** *pl.* exercises 38/41
of(f) *prep.* from Pr/12, of Pr/15, about, concerning Pr/34, in regard to 9/2, by 25/12, among 25/14; **oute** ~ from Pr/16
on *prep.* on 2/19, in 21/43, at 23/25
ongentil *adj.* discourteous 34/30

ongilty *adj.* innocent 12/25
onlerned *v. pp.* uneducated 15/10
onstabilnesse *n.* instability 16/19
onto *prep.* for Pr/41, against 3/45; **more** ~ more towards 1/20
onweting *v. pr.p.* unaware 40/15
onwise *adj.* uneducated Pr/5
ope *v. inf.* open 15/37
openly *adv.* publicly 37/31
opinion(e), opynyoun *n.* regard 8/32, belief 32/20, view 32/24
or *conj.* otherwise 4/5
or *adv.* before 2/23
order(re) *n.* (religious) order 29/5; **ord(e)res** *pl.* sacred orders 25/22; **gaf him his** ~ ordained him 30/19
ordeyn *v. 1 pl.* direct 38/26; *inf.* ordain (to ministry) 30/4; **ded** ~ provided 19/25; **ordeyned** *v. p.t.* devised 11/51, proposed 30/24, directed 31/32 , found 43/20; *pp.* determined 9/9, prepared 23/11, appointed 35/8
ordinauns *n.* rule 27/20
oriso(u)n *n.* prayer 3/39; **orisones** *pl.* prayers 41/60
oþ(th)ir *pron.* other Pr/11; *pl.* others 4/7
oþir *adj.* different 33/31
othis *n. pl.* oaths 39/14
ouyr *adv.* too 30/22, especially 36/17; ~ **sone** too soon 12/35; ~ **lokid** re-read 43/3; ~ **say** looked over 43/33
ouyr *prep.* above 12/12, across 22/20
owt *n.* aught 12/30

pay(e) *v. inf.* repay Pr/8
paynem *n.* pagan 2/20
paleys *n.* palace 14/5, bishop's residence 34/2
parchemyn *n.* parchment 45/19
parfite, parfith *adj.* holy 21/16, religious 37/48, complete 39/29
parfithly *adv.* totally 11/12, thoroughly 30/7
part, party, partie(ye) *n.* part 1/7, share 15/55, division 41/54; **in** ~ somewhat 5/10; **for þe moost** ~ usually 22/8; **in oþir** ~ in another way 45/43; **parties** *pl.* parts 1/3
pase *n.* Easter 17/42
passyng *adv.* very 17/35
passyng *prep.* exceeding 36/26
peyne *n.* hardship 16/5, pain 17/22, punishment 24/11
peyre *n.* pair 17/23
peysed *v. p.t.* stressed 40/50
perauenture *adv.* perhaps 39/43
perfithnesse *n.* holiness 21/10
pertinent *adj.* proper 36/33
peruerted *v. p.t.* ~... **fro** turned from 32/5
pes *n.* peace 3/25
pesibily *adv.* without disturbance 28/14
pestilens *n.* plague 38/60
plant *v. inf.* ~ **in** insert 34/37
plente *n.* measure 37/33
plenteuous *adj.* abundant 35/5
plenteuously *adv.* profusely 15/24, abundantly 32/9
plesauns *n.* enjoyment Pr/22, kindness 3/34, honour 3/43, favour 10/26
plesaunt *adj.* pleasing 2/14
plete(n) *v. inf.* plead 12/5
pleynly *adv.* clearly Pr/37
plith *n.* condition 11/25
possessio(u)n *n.* store Pr/13, property 2/5, wealth 27/13, resources 35/1
potage *n.* porridge 11/27

practik *n.* practice, policy 32/16
pra(e)y *v. inf.* pray 16/14; **prayed** *p.t.* begged 39/21; **praying** *pr.p.* requesting 10/3
prayer *n.* request 22/13; **praieres** *pl.* prayers 11/19
prechid *v. p.t.* preached 19/21
pre(e)s *n.* crowd 23/10
preest *n.* priest 2/35
prys(e) *n.* cost 24/18; **set no ~** set no store 31/19
priuy *adj.* secret 33/8
pryuyly *adv.* secretly 22/12
processe *n.* story 12/3, arrangement 30/34, drift, tenor 41/26
proferen *v. 3 pl.* attempt 4/13; **profered** *p.t.* offered 21/39
profession *n.* order Pr/18
profitable *adj.* beneficial 5/9
progenitoures(is) *n. pl.* parents 2/1
proporcioned *adj.* corresponding 7/19
proporcioun *n.* ratio 39/18
proposicion *n.* statement 21/47
proued *adj.* recognized 10/5, select 21/10
prouision *n.* providence 42/12
puple *n.* people Pr/44
purpose *n.* resolve 14/37
purpos(e) *v. 1 sg.* propose 14/30; *inf.* propose 7/33, resolve 15/58; **purposed** *p.t.* intended 6/33, decided 10/31
purueyid *v. pp.* conveyed 27/26

quiete *n.* peace 9/7
quod *v. p.t.* said 7/20
qwech *see* **whech**

ran *v. 3 sg.* **~ it in his mynde** occured to him 17/20
rase *v. inf.* erase 37/17
rawt *v. pp.* snatched 4/7
receuye *v. inf.* accept 7/34
receytis *n. pl.* income 38/39
receyuour *n.* recipient 6/14
redde *v. p.t.* taught 8/4
red(e) *v. 1 pl.* read 1/23; *pp.* read Pr/37
redinesse *n.* preparation 8/13
redy *adj.* quick 3/5, prompt 3/33, prepared 17/32, fluent 33/11
refeccioun *n.* meal 34/6
refelle *v. inf.* refute 32/7
refresch *v. inf.* renew 14/9; **refreschid** *pp.* strengthened 19/7, renewed 22/10
regned *v. p.t.* prevailed 33/34, ruled 42/23
reherse *v. inf.* recall 3/11; state 8/40, recount 24/24, repeat 39/20; **rehersed(id)** *p.t.* uttered 39/15; *pp.* recounted 4/8, repeated 6/43
reise *v. inf.* resurrect 23/37
religio(u)n(e) *n.* faith 32/33, (religious) order 45/30
religious *adj.* belonging to a religious order 36/6
renne *inf.* run 12/26; **~ in veyn** come to nothing 27/25
renneres *n. pl.* **~ aboute** gadabouts 29/24
rennyth *v. 3 sg.* empties 23/6
report(e) *v. inf.* record 10/14
repreuyth *v. 3 sg.* disproves 42/19
requyred, reqwired, reqwyred(id) *v. p.t.* requested 32/6, asked 32/12; *pp.* needed 23/3
rered *v. pp.* recovered 9/35, erected 13/18
reson *n.* conclusion Pr/56, thought 15/46; **resones** *pl.* arguments 6/44
resorted *v. p.t.* **~ ageyn** returned 8/15
rest *n.* peace 43/16

retribucioun *n.* compensation 45/43; **retribuciones** *n. pl.* gifts Pr/23
reuel *n.* merry-making 9/5
reuerens *n.* reverence 30/18, respect 38/16
reuers *adj.* opposite 4/5
reule *n.* principle Pr/2, straightedge 7/8, rule 29/31, administration 30/2; **reules** *n. pl.* directives 29/28
rydily *adv.* readily 15/46
ryp *adj.* **ful ~** full-blown 17/10
rith *adj.* right Pr/58, true 20/23
rith *adv.* just 7/8, precisely 12/29
rithful *adj.* just 41/21
rithfully *adv.* **not ~** illicitly 33/31
rood *v. p.t.* travelled 6/6
rore *n.* **o ~** in an uproar 41/55
rowt *v. p.t.* **~ not** took no account 31/18
rubrich *n.* heading 2/30

saciat *adj.* sated 19/5
sad *adj.* mature 5/9, serious 6/11, grave 36/7, wise 36/10
sadnesse *n.* seriousness 14/9, serenity 36/5
sauely *adv.* safely Pr/11
sauo(u)red *v. p.t.* relished Pr/8, preferred 35/24
say *see* **sey**
schal *v. 3 sg.* **~ to** should take 11/24; **schuld(e)** *v. 3 pl.* would 6/17
schamful *adj.* disgraceful 15/43
schape *v. pp.* shaped 20/9
sche *pron.* she Pr/17; **hir(e)** it Pr/16[2]; **onto ~** for her Pr/16[1]; *reflex.* herself 38/10
schewid *v. p.t.* bestowed upon 7/7, pointed out 15/50; *pp.* shown 1/21, revealed 25/25
schippe *v. inf.* take ship 21/13
schon *n. pl.* shoes 35/13
schryuyth *v. 3 sg.* **~ him** confesses 6/18
schuld(e) see **schal**
sciens *n.* learning 13/18; *pl.* knowledge Pr/10, arts (i.e., liberal arts) 8/9, disciplines 8/11
scrowes *n. pl.* notices 21/36
se *n.* sea 11/2
se *v. inf.* find out 14/6
secte *n.* religion 11/45, school 16/25
see *n.* diocese 33/2
sey/say *v. p.t.* saw 3/44; **sene** *pp.* seen 3/30; **seying** *pr.p.* perceiving 31/8
sey(e) *inf.* say Pr/11; **seid(e)** *p.t.* said Pr/6; *pp.* expressed 43/7; **~ ... ageyn** deprecate 38/46; **be seyn** have said 4/5; **seying** *pr.p.* telling 11/29
sek(e)nesse *n.* illness 5/16
seld *v. p.t.* sold 25/20
semeth(yth) *v. impers.* it seems 2/15, it is proper 36/27; **me ~** it seems to me 34/21
semly *adj.* fitting 39/8
sentens *n.* sense 10/15, meaning 15/42
sere *n.* sir 12/31; **seres** *pl.* sirs 11/8
serueth *v. 3 sg.* **~ not mech** is not of much value 16/25
seruyse *n.* worship 15/28, utensils 37/1, serving 39/16, ministry 44/16; **do ... ~** serve 3/24
seruyseable *adj.* attentive 22/5
sette *v. 3 sg.* put down 11/37; *p.t.* placed 18/19, established 30/32; **~ hem down** got down 17/24; **~ up** posted 21/36; *inf.* establish 43/16; **set(te)** *pp.* laid down Pr/2, destined 1/8, fixed 11/52, resolved 13/31,

rooted 16/3, intent 22/7, planted 28/26, situated 28/28; ~ in certeyn is certain 16/24
sewid *v.* followed 18/6
signes *n. pl.* ~ **owtward** appearances 12/35
sikir *adj.* sure 18/19, secure 27/33
sikirly *adv.* certainly 9/12
siki(y)rnesse *n.* assurance 7/43; **maner of a** ~ sense of security 28/10
simple(il) *adj.* ordinary Pr/5
singuler *adj.* special 36/26
sith(e) *adv.* since 10/25; **often** ~ oft times 31/9
sith *n.* sight 15/22
skape *v. inf.* escape 5/7
skil *n.* aptitude 31/14, reason 43/19
skole *n.* school 2/6, group, following 11/11, community 36/21
skoleres *n. pl.* scholars 9/7, students 16/7
slaunder(ir) *n.* vilification 11/36
slauth *n.* tardiness 15/22
slitte *v. pp.* lanced 25/12
sluttynesse *n.* slovenliness 36/19
sly *adj.* wily 40/31
smal(e) *adj.* basic 5/12, little 10/15
snybbe *v. inf.* reprimand 3/36
sobbyng *vbl.n.* grief 17/12
sobir *adj.* grave 15/9, serene 23/22
sobirly *adv.* serenely 23/10
solemply *adv.* formally 16/9
solempne *adj.* solemn Pr/21, important 42/8
solitari(e) *adj.* eremetical 14/34, secluded 16/11, alone 41/33
solitarily *adv.* in retirement 16/14
sone *adv.* soon 3/6
sones *n. pl.* sons 1/4
songen *v. pp.* sung 19/2
sonnere *adv.* sooner 38/30
sophisticacioun *n.* sophistry 7/25
sore *adv.* bitterly 15/7, greatly 17/5, intensely 44/32
sore *n.* wound 25/11
sory *adj.* poor 6/9
sotil(l) *adj.* subtle 6/36, penetrating 8/42, ingenious 18/12, abstruse 18/17, fine 37/20
souered *p.t.* suffered 24/14
souereyn *adj.* excellent 40/38
sounde *v. 3 pl.* evoke 41/28; **soundeth(ith)** *3 sg.* signifies Pr/32, means 16/22; **soundyng** *pr.p.* singing 15/33
sou(w)t(e) *v. p.t.* sought 2/16, 11/1
special *adv.* **in** ~ in particular 6/19
specialte *adv.* exclusively 36/24; **of** ~ especially 23/29
sped(e) *v. p.t.* succeeded 23/3; *inf.* succeed 27/22
speke *v. 3 pl.* speak 1/31; *inf.* ~ **ageyn** contradict 3/14; **spak** *p.t.* spoke Pr/6
sperd *v. p.t.* closed 15/45
spirith *n.* animation 11/17
springe *v. inf.* rise 9/38
stabil, stable *adj.* immovable 7/24, sound 33/14
stale *v. p.t.* stole 9/20
stand(e) *v. 1 pl.* stand 44/25; *3 sg.* stands 11/24; *inf.* standing 7/13; **stant** *3 sg.* stands 28/17; *3 pl.* are situated 1/11
statua *n.* statue 13/18
statute *n.* rule 39/15
stedfast *adj.* firm 14/16, constant 36/10
stere *v. inf.* move 41/24; **stered** *p.t.* moved 15/58; *pp.* inclined 3/27, moved 27/8
sterres *n. pl.* stars Pr/36
stert, stirt *v. p.t.* ran 15/18, hurried 37/21

stewe *n.* garden house 2/19; **stewis** *pl.* brothels 6/9
streit *adv.* directly 25/4
strete *n.* street 12/27
streytly *adv.* strictly 34/15
stroki(y)s *n. pl.* blows 3/17
studious *adj.* thoughtful 41/17
study(e) *n.* **stand in** ~ hesitates 11/24
stuf *n.* material 45/40
subieccioun *n.* submission 3/24
substauns *n.* considerable amount 2/9, essence 6/41
sufficiens *n.* sufficient amount 37/32
suffi(y)r *v. 1 sg.* bear with 3/22; *1 pl.* wait for 15/10; *inf.* endure 3/26, permit 5/17; **suffered** *p.t.* permitted 11/52
sundry *adj.* diverse 13/32
supposed *v. p.t.* expected Pr/18
suspecious *adj.* suspect 6/12
suspense *adj.* apprehensive 8/46
swech *adj.* such Pr/12
swem *n.* sorrow 21/22
swete *adj.* pleasing Pr/44, mild 36/14

tables *n. pl.* **reporting** ~ casebooks 12/7, (wax) tablets 17/23
take *v. pp.* ~ **cristendam** become a Christian 14/15
talkyng *n.* conversation 2/22, speech 36/9
tarying *vbl.n.* **mad a grete** ~ made a long stay 17/11
tempered *v. p.t.* moderated 39/39
temporal *adj.* seasonal 19/10
tete *n.* breast 6/30
tewnys *n. pl.* tunes 19/13
þai *see* **þei**
þan/þan(n)e/than *adv.* then Pr/21, 1/24
þan/þan(n)e *conj.* than Pr/11, Pr/20; **for** ~ because 2/11
þankyng *vbl.n.* thanksgiving 14/14
þei/thei *pron.* they Pr/50, 1/5; **hem** them Pr/8, those Pr/10; **her(e)** *adj.* their 2/15
þing *n.* thing Pr/17; **þing(g)is** *pl.* things 11/14
þinking *v. pr.p.* considering 10/29
þirknesse *n.* darkness 11/21
þo(o)/tho(o) *pron.* those 8/20; *adj.* those 6/28
tho(o) *adv.* then 6/37
þongis *n. pl.* strips 29/26
þorw *prep.* through 7/39
þout(ȝ) *v. p.t.* considered 7/7
þretis *n. pl.* threats 37/43
þrew *v. p.t.* cast 15/26
tydyngis *n.* information 9/32
tyme *n.* season 28/29
to *prep.* for Pr/2. among 1/5, toward 11/24
tokne *n.* sign 15/50; **toknes** *pl.* identification marks 21/37, signals 30/9
tong(e) *n.* speech Pr/58, language 1/14; **tongis** *pl.* languages 1/27
too *n. num.* two 3/18
too *adj.* two 1/11
touched(id) *v. pp.* treated 2/37; **touchith** *3 sg.* treats 3/41
touching *prep.* regarding Pr/29
translate *v. pp.* translated 1/28
trauayle *v. inf.* work 28/28; **trauayled** was in labour 3/42
tremel *v.* tremble 10/22
treso(u)re *n.* resources Pr/12, treasury 45/31
trespas *v. inf.* ~ **onto** sin against 3/44
treuly *adv.* faithfully Pr/16, indeed 11/8
treuth *n.* honesty 21/39

trouble *n.* contention 8/37
trowe *v. 1 sg.* believe 37/6
tuycioun *n.* protection 19/24

vndir *prep.* under 2/35, according to 39/18, during 44/13
vndyrstanding *n.* knowledge 6/36
vndirtake *v. inf.* guarantee 40/8
vnsperd *v. p.t.* opened 14/11
uphap/vphap *adv.* perhaps 14/27, 36/26
vsage *n.* practice 11/35
vse *n.* custom 11/32, habit 37/6
vse *v. 3 pl.* practice 6/9, play 15/35; *inf.* attend 19/7; **used/ vsed** *p.t.* frequented 6/8, accustomed 7/14, practiced 14/11
vttir *v. 3 sg.* expresses 33/19; **vttyr** *inf.* utter 23/14; **vttered** *p.t.* communicated 25/25; **uttirryng** *pr.p.* speaking 15/32

vani(y)te(e)s *n. pl.* worthless concerns 16/3
variauns *n.* divergence 42/25
veyn *adj.* useless 5/12, vain 27/25
venemhous *adj.* poisonous 19/15
veniauns *n.* **in maner of** ~ a kind of vengeance 4/13
very *adj.* true 6/39
vikere *n.* vicar, representative 31/10
vis *n.* vice 37/12
voyd *adj.* free 37/51
voyde *v. inf.* dismiss 7/42

wayte *n.* ambush 40/9
wakyng *vbl.n.* keeping vigil 38/20
wanted *v. p.t.* lacked 11/6
war *adj.* careful 37/40
warned *v. pp.* refused 37/9, advised 45/10
warnyng *n.* directive 15/37
wast *n.* waste 37/20
wauntown *adj.* reckless 6/8
wecch *n.* vigilance 19/25, vigil 28/22
we(e)l *adv.* greatly 1/24, highly 10/4, clearly 34/3
weggis *n. pl.* materials 37/29
welfare *n.* well-being 14/7
wenyng *v. pr.p.* suggesting 33/7
were *v. inf.* wear 36/24; **wered** *p.t.* wore 36/28
werk *n.* deed 24/15
wey(e) *n.* course 7/32
weyk *adj.* weak 25/12
whan(ne) *conj.* when 1/23, 41/10
what *prep.* ~ **for** due to 6/7
whech/qwech *adj.* which 1/25, such 42/15; *rel.* which 8/25
whech *pron.* who Pr/7
who *pron., rel.* who 1/30; *inter.* who 2/36[2]
who *adv.* how 2/36[1]
wil *v. 1 pl.* wish 38/26; **willed** *pp.* endowed Pr/23
wil(l) *n.* **with þe bettir** ~ more willingly Pr/19, desire 39/37
wildyrnesse *n.* solitary region 14/19
wilful *adj.* voluntary 21/27
wise/wys *adj.* erudite 6/31, prudent 45/7
wise/wyse *n.* manner 8/16, way 44/26
wit(te) *n.* intellect 18/11; **wittis** *pl.* senses 23/24, intellects 26/16
wite *v. inf.* blame 39/11
witnesseth(ith) *3 sg.* declares 17/48
wodis *n.* woods 14/24
wold *v. p.t.* would Pr/19, wished 11/48, chose 32/21
wone *adj.* accustomed 15/14, wont 16/8
worchip *n.* honour Pr/22, recogni-

tion 38/26; do ~ respect 45/39

worchipful *adj.* distinguished 16/16

worchipfully *adv.* repectfully 27/22

worchip(p)id *v. p.t.* venerated 13/10; *pp.* honoured 38/24

wortes *n. pl.* vegetables 37/5

worthi(y) *adj.* distinguished 13/17

wot(e) *v. 1 sg.* know 1/30; **wist** *p.t.* knew 9/24

wrecched *adj.* mean 36/17

writi(y)n *v. pp.* recorded 2/31

wrong *n.* **haue** ~ suffer injustice 3/22

wrongfully *adv.* unjustly 12/32

wroth *adj.* angry 3/15

wroute *v. 3 pl.* worked 12/10